# The Unfinished Quest for Unity

# THE UNFINISHED QUEST FOR UNITY

## Africa and the OAU

Zdenek Červenka

AFRICANA PUBLISHING COMPANY
NEW YORK

A division of Holmes & Meier Publishers, Inc.

First published in the United States of America 1977 by
Africana Publishing Company
101 Fifth Avenue
New York, NY 10003

Library of Congress Cataloging in Publication Data

Červenka, Zdenek, 1928-
    The unfinished quest for unity.

    1. Organization of African Unity. 2. Africa—
Politics and government—1960-      I. Title.
DT1.C47    1977      341.24'9      77-16103
ISBN 0-8419-0353-0

PRINTED IN GREAT BRITAIN

# CONTENTS

# PREFACE

The purpose of this book is to help fill one of the widest gaps in understanding African affairs: although the Organization of African Unity is one of the largest international organizations in the world, less is known about it than almost any other.

Writing books on Africa has always been a hazardous enterprise. This is not only because of the rapid changes on the continent, which can outdate a manuscript overnight; more intimidating is the growing mistrust in Africa of books written by non-Africans. Given that Africa has for decades been the object of European and American research and experiments, based often on false premises and foregone conclusions, this hostility is understandable. The findings of the various research projects, which have been lavish and arrogant in dispensing advice to Africa on how to cure its ills, have seriously weakened confidence in the value and integrity of such investigations — particularly when the governments and trans-national foundations financing the research have often been largely responsible for those ills in the first place. On the other hand, some outsiders have gone out of their way to push 'the African point of view', ending up more pro-African than the Africans themselves — which pleases neither side.

What is needed is a new approach. The author firmly believes that the future of Africa lies in co-operation with Europe and the outside world; indeed that such co-operation is going to be vital for both sides. The efforts to create a new relationship in the economic field are known as the search for a 'New International Economic Order'; but its equivalent in the political, social and cultural spheres has yet to be defined.

Much of the present conflict between Africa and the outside world arises from the lack of international understanding of the African scene. There has been great reluctance to face the facts for fear they might be different from the assumptions upon which policies have been based. This has been particularly true of the OAU, which to this day has not been credited as it deserves for its important role in shaping the destiny of the continent.

This book reflects the experiences and opinions of a wide circle of people, both African and European. I am greatly indebted to my friends at *Africa* magazine, in particular Raph Uwechue, Peter Enahoro and Godwin Matatu, who have given me an invaluable insight into African thought on international relations and African affairs in general. I am also grateful to Colin Legum for his co-operation in writing jointly the annual survey of OAU activities for his *Africa Contemporary*

*Record,* and for his guidance in understanding Western policies towards Africa. I would also like to thank Diether Habicht-Benthin and his colleagues at *3 Welt Magazın* in Bonn, for their assistance and material towards the chapter on Afro-Arab co-operation; Peter Onu, for his help in supplying me with OAU documents and reading parts of my manuscript; George Magombe and Mohamed Sidky, for their help with the chapter on the OAU Liberation Committee; the Swedish diplomatic corps in Africa and at the Swedish Foreign Ministry, for their help both in Sweden and during my visits in Africa; Stanley Moody, who helped me edit the manuscript and encouraged me when it needed sweeping revision; and Christopher Hurst, Liz Clemens and my editor, for their editorial suggestions.

Finally, I owe a great deal to the Dag Hammarskjöld Library for help with UN documents, and to the Scandinavian Institute of African Studies for the great support I have enjoyed throughout the long process of producing this book.

Uppsala, 1977                                                    Zdenek Červenka

# INTRODUCTION

## The OAU — Time for a change

The Organization of African Unity was founded at a time when African leaders were experiencing their first taste of independence and were anxious to consolidate their leadership. Across the continent they saw the danger posed by the divisions of language, culture and religion, by the economic inequalities, by the controversies over boundaries arbitrarily drawn by the colonial powers. It quickly became clear that a high degree of co-operation was necessary among the fledging African States, if the continent was to survive as a viable economic and political entity. It was to achieve this co-operation that the OAU was established.

Understandably, there were considerable differences of opinion as to how African unity could best be attained. The signing of the Charter establishing the OAU was quite an achievement at a time when Africa was sharply split into three rival blocs — the Casablanca group, the Monrovia group and the Brazzaville Twelve. Indeed, it is not sufficiently realized that, because of these deep divisions the OAU represents a largely negative agreement — not to move too much to the left nor too far to the right. As a result of this stagnating consensus, the OAU has in the past fourteen years moved hardly at all. Kwame Nkrumah's call for continental unity was brushed aside, and the African leaders settled for a superficial unity which brought together African Heads of States but not African peoples. This in no way affected the sovereignty of each independent State, and they were left free to pursue policies in which continental priorities were sacrificed to narrow national interests.

This arrangement suited the so-called 'moderate' conservative governments in countries such as Ethiopa (as it was then under Emperor Haile Selassie), Nigeria under Prime Minister Tafawa Balewa, Liberia under President Tubman, and Libya under King Idris; they had commanded a majority in the Organization, and made sure that none of the OAU decisions would conflict with their interests. The willingness, on the other hand, of the 'radicals' — such as Kwame Nkrumah of Ghana, Ben Bella of Algeria, Modibo Keita of Mali, Sekou Toure of Guinea, Julius Nyerere of Tanzania and Milton Obote of Uganda — to join the OAU was based on a hope that they would gradually would be able to convince the others to come their way and shift the

Organization to a unity of greater depth and closer co-operation than that offered by the loose provisions of its Charter. The radical stand on decolonization and apartheid adopted early on by all OAU members, irrespective of their domestic policies and international outlook, seemed at first to justify their expectations. Indeed they succeeded, for example, in turning the OAU Liberation Committee, an *ad hoc* organ, into the Organization's most important institution second only to the Assembly of Heads of State and Government and on a par with the Council of Ministers.

This was not a development without serious difficulties (see Chapter IV); but it produced good results, as manifested by the April 1975 Dar-es-Salaam Declaration on Southern Africa which clearly defined the tasks of the OAU in the decolonization of Zimbabwe and Namibia. The Declaration also put an end to the confusion between 'dialogue' and 'détente', and thwarted South Africa's attempts to use its contacts with the governments of Botswana, Mozambique, Tanzania and Zambia for dressing up its apartheid windows. The talks between the Presidents of these four countries and South Africa were restricted exclusively to the questions of a peaceful transfer of power to the black majority in Zimbabwe and the bringing about of independence in Namibia.

In an overall assessment of the OAU's achievements, it must be said that the Organization, in spite of its many glaring weaknesses, deserves some credit. For the past fourteen years it has provided a forum for airing the views of Africa on international issues affecting Africans. On the continent itself, it has sometimes provided a basis for the peaceful settlement of disputes among its members. The unity which it has managed to preserve has given the Organization, as far as African affairs are concerned, a moral standing which no single African country or limited group of countries can possibly match. A decade ago, for example, during the Nigerian Civil War, it was the OAU's unequivocal stand for 'a solution that preserved the integrity of Nigeria' which made it impossible for any big power to side effectively with Biafra. More recently in Angola, it was the declared stand of a majority of the OAU members in favour of Agostinho Neto's MPLA, which similarly kept away interested Western powers from giving sustained or overt support to either the FNLA or UNITA. The international rejection of the Transkei's 'Independence' stems as well from the OAU's stand on the issue.

Unfortunately, the list of the OAU's achievements is much shorter than that of its failings. Perhaps most lamentable has been its performance in the economic field, where the absence of co-ordinated planning has left yawning gaps in the development of the continent's great potential. Almost every African State today is in economic difficulties. A rich country like Zambia, for example, suddenly finds itself in serious financial straits because of a sharp fall in the price of copper, a commodity to which the country's economy has been geared both before and since independence. The heavy dependence on outside markets means that the life of a number of African countries hangs on the whims of outsiders. With the single exception of oil, African export commodities have their prices determined by non-African buyers rather than by African producers. This is, of course, a simplification of a complex problem, but it illustrates the economic difficulties of the continent which, despite its wealth in oil, diamonds, gold and other precious metals and minerals, and, indeed its potential for a 'green revolution' in agriculture, has not yet evolved a mechanism capable of dove-tailing the economic needs and activities of the various countries in a way that would benefit Africa as a whole.

One reason why in the past fourteen years economic matters have been overshadowed in the OAU by political issues is that political events are usually more compelling and spectacular, while economic difficulties develop insidiously and are seldom so specific or dramatic. When we talk of the OAU's inability to achieve a satisfactory degree of economic co-operation among African countries, and of Africa's continued dependence on non-African powers, we console ourselves by blaming the colonial past — and do very little about it. When there is a Pan-African political crisis or war, everybody talks about it and the OAU is asked to resolve the problem. Nobody demands that it should tackle with equal vigour and collective spirit the continent's transport, agricultural or economic problems, which are in reality no less a danger to Africa's survival.

Another important problem area in which the OAU has been relatively ineffectual is the resolution of inter-state conflicts in Africa. One year after its inception, the OAU established a Commission on Mediation, Conciliation and Arbitration whose mandate was to mediate between disputing States. In part this was an acknowledgement of the ominous threat posed to African unity by intra-African quarrels. Regrettably, the Commission has not made much headway. Today there are volatile fratricidal conflicts in every sub-region of the continent, some as old as the OAU itself. The upshot of this situation is that some African countries have diverted their scarce resources to the purchase of armaments for mutual destruction, instead of strengthening unity and focusing attention on the priority areas of social and economic development.

Let us hope that in this regard a corrective step may have been taken with the establishment recently of an *ad-hoc* committee of ten member nations to replace the moribund Commission. In principle, this committee has more power to deal with intra-African crisis situations than the Commission had. Its small composition is designed to facilitate meeting at the shortest possible notice to help defuse situations which could spark off armed conflict between member-States. The extent to which this new body succeeds will be a test of the OAU's maturity in its second decade.

Nowhere else perhaps is the OAU's weakness more clearly exposed than in matters involving Africa's collective security. The Angolan crisis brought this out vividly. The programme for Angola's independence was known well in advance. Yet the OAU, admittedly in part frustrated by the short-sighted rivalry among the Angolan leaders themselves, did too little to fill the political and military vacuum which, in the prevailing circumstances, Portugal's chaotic withdrawal was bound to create. Predictably that vacuum sucked in ever-ready interlopers with the inherent danger of turning Africa into a battleground for super-power rivalry. To date the course of the liberation struggle in southern Africa generally, and in Zimbabwe in particular, continues to underline the irresolute attitude of OAU member *vis-à-vis* their responsibilities in the armed confrontation between independent Africa and the continent's racist minority régimes.

There are now many Africans who think that the OAU should not remain riveted to a Charter drafted fourteen years ago under circumstances profoundly different from those of today. It is felt that African States, despite the difficulties encountered since independence, have developed considerably, and that the OAU has not grown along with them. The revolutionary forces on the continent are beginning to lose patience with the *status quo* which the OAU tries to maintain. There are already indications that these radical forces might try, on their own, to achieve a faster pace in African development. It is thus increasingly obvious that if the OAU is to survive as a truly continental organization, it has to accommodate the concept of a politico-economic union somewhat along the lines advocated by Kwame Nkrumah. The arguments as to whether this is to be achieved through a merger of regional unions or by creating central institutions such as the African High Command, the African Monetary Union, the African Common Market, and similar bodies with executive powers, will no doubt continue. What is important, however, is that whichever approach is chosen, it must lead to a political arrangement capable of containing both the political and the economic pressures in the continent. In short, the time has come to give the OAU 'teeth' and to make it a positive instrument that can shape the destinies of the African peoples.

In this regard, there has recently appeared a ray of hope in the recommendations of the Turkson Committee, whose 'Report on the Structural Reform of the OAU General Secretariat' is currently under consideration by the Member-States. Its terms of reference include strengthening the role of the chief executive of the OAU, the

Administrative Secretary General, *vis-à-vis* the Member-States and his own staff; a complete overhaul of the internal structure of the OAU Secretariat; and the establishment of a Supreme Organ of the OAU to deal with the economic problems of Africa. A step in the right direction for the future is possible, but only if a thorough analysis and assessment is made of the past. Zdenek Červenka's book critically but sympathetically examines the fourteen years of the OAU. It provides a detailed analysis of the world's largest continental organization, and contributes to a better understanding of the problems it is facing.

London

July 1977

Raph Uwechue

# AUTHOR'S NOTE

## The 14th OAU Summit in Libreville, Gabon (2-5 July 1977)

Since the main part of this book was completed the flow of dramatic events shaping the fate of the continent of Africa has inevitably overtaken many of the developments recorded here. And, sad to say, it is dissent rather than unity that has characterized African affairs during the last few months.

In his address to the Assembly of Heads of State and Government of the OAU at Libreville on 2 July 1977 President Anwar Sadat said:

'The centre of international conflict has moved to our continent in the past months, with all that this means in the sowing of seeds of dissention, division and disruption among the sons of the continent and involving them in conflicts from which they reap no benefit and which permit interference in the internal affairs of the African states. Suddenly, these states have found themselves in a conflict that is designed to subjugate and make them follow a course conflicting with the concept of the destined solidarity of Africa.'[1]

President Sadat was referring to the situation in the Horn of Africa where the conflict between Ethiopia and her neighbours, Sudan and Somalia, had been made more serious by the supply of Soviet arms to Ethiopia (formerly the major recipient of US military aid in Africa). This had led the United States and Britain to pledge arms supplies to Somalia, whose armed forces had been built up with Soviet help and equipped with Soviet arms. Paradoxically, barely three weeks after the OAU Summit President Sadat's own country was embroiled in a major armed clash with Libya.

Vivid accounts were heard at Libreville of numerous conflicts in various parts of Africa. The limited space available for this postscript does not allow for detailed examination of these developments;[2] suffice it to say that, despite the attendance at the Summit of as many as twenty-three Heads of State and Government, the meeting showed few signs of 'African Unity'.

The Libreville Summit will, however, be remembered not so much for the fratricidal war of words between its members as for the following three significant events:

- the admission of the Territory of the Afars and the Issas as 49th member of the OAU;
- the recognition of the Patriotic Front as sole leader of the armed struggle in Zimbabwe; and
- the emergence of Nigeria as a great new pan-African force.

The magazine *Afrique-Asie* dubbed the Libreville meeting 'le sommet du sauvetage'.[3] This was a reference to President Bongo's invitation to the Conference in his opening speech as host: 'Let us indulge in African "palaver" . . . let us wash our dirty linen . . .', which is precisely what most of those present did.

The other label attached by the mass media to the Libreville Summit — 'a victory for the moderates' — was certainly less accurate. The 'moderates' have always commanded a comfortable majority at OAU sessions, but they have not always been able to make use of it. On several occasions in the past (such as in the 1971 debate on 'dialogue' with South Africa or the 1973 debate on support for the Arab cause) they have been compelled to bow to the pressure of the much smaller group of 'progressives': the progressive states have made a concerted effort to present their case with clarity and conviction, through the diplomatic skill of Presidents Nyerere and Boumedienne, and almost invariably with African public opinion behind them. Not quite so at Libreville in 1977. There President Kenneth Kaunda of Zambia, the sole representative of the five front-line Presidents at the Summit, was hard put to it to secure recognition of the Patriotic Front of Zimbabwe (an alliance between Joshua Nkomo and Robert Mugabe to which the front-line Presidents had already accorded exclusive recognition in January 1977). He succeeded only when the Nigerian Head of State, General Obasanjo, lent his support. However, the OAU recognition was not 'exclusive'. The Patriotic Front was recognized only as sole leader of the armed struggle in Zimbabwe — a formulation leaving entirely open the question of political representation of Zimbabwe.

The following are the main points of the OAU resolution on Zimbabwe:

- commendation of the successful continuation of the armed struggle in Zimbabwe, as carried out by the Zimbabwe People's Army under the leadership of the Patriotic Front;
- a call on all Zimbabweans devoted to the struggle for the liberation of their country to do so within the Patriotic Front;
- a call on Member-States to increase their financial, material and political support to the people of Zimbabwe in their fight to regain their rights to self-determination and independence. The resolution also urged OAU Members to refrain from supporting individuals (an obvious reference to Bishop Muzorewa and Sithole), which was

'running the risk of creating more than one army for the liberation and defence of an independent Zimbabwe'.

It became apparent that the five front-line Presidents no longer enjoy the kind of support for their policies on Southern Africa that they had in 1975, when the 'Dar-es-Salaam Declaration' became a recognized OAU political guideline. A sample of African opinion was published in the influential Kenyan *Weekly Review*, of 27 June, which quoted a commentary on the OAU meeting by Kenya Radio sharply criticizing the front-line states as follows:

'...Unanimity in the condemnation of the racist and apartheid regimes in Southern Africa is expected as has always been the case. But member states should demand a full report of the Zimbabwe and Namibia liberation struggles from the front-line states which have so far monopolized the struggle with little effect. All they have succeeded in doing so far is to divide the struggling masses in Zimbabwe. They have succeeded in dividing the Zimbabweans into what they call nationalists and imperialist stooges, yet have failed completely in putting into power in Rhodesia the leadership that they think suits the people of Zimbabwe.'

The Nigerian *Daily Times* also warned against what it called 'rigid postures' in an editorial entitled 'After a free Zimbabwe':[4]

'The OAU had to take the painful decision of giving its support to the Patriotic Front. There was hardly any other viable option open to it, given the fact that, since 1965, rebel Ian Smith had made it clear that only armed struggle by the African nationalists could make him budge from his white supremacist standpoint. And the fact that Ian Smith is even thinking of stage-managing an election for cosmetic effects is due largely to the heroic efforts of African freedom fighters, a majority of whom are behind the political leadership of the Patriotic Front. While Africans should treat rebel Ian Smith's election plans with contempt, the time is now ripe for African leaders, and particularly those in Zimbabwe, to start thinking seriously about the country's internal political structure and evolution when an African government emerges. The human realities in Zimbabwe are such that neither the OAU, the frontline presidents, nor the Patriotic Front can afford to maintain rigid postures in a dynamic and fluid political situation which Zimbabwe is going to present in the foreseeable future.'

The unanimity on Zimbabwe and the display of solidarity with Mozambique (at that very moment pleading its case before a meeting of the UN Security Council in New York convened to consider Rhodesian aggression)[5] was offset by the reversal of the OAU policy on Western Sahara. The representatives of POLISARIO (a liberation movement recognized by the OAU) were not given visas to enter Gabon, whereas President Bongo spared no efforts to secure the return of Morocco to the OAU (Morocco had left the Council of Ministers' meeting in February at Lomé in protest against POLISARIO's presence). The retiring OAU Chairman Sir Seewoosagur Ramgoolam, Prime Minister of Mauritius, explained that the Extraordinary OAU Summit on Western Sahara decided upon at Port Louis last year had not taken place 'because a quorum had not been achieved and no country had expressed a desire to act as the venue for such a Summit'. At Libreville a new date was agreed upon, October 1977; the venue, Lusaka.


REFORM OF THE OAU

Several 'reforms of the OAU' were given prominent publicity in the OAU press releases on the conference (the only source of news on the OAU meetings for the assembled journalists). The first was the introduction (to replace the inert OAU Defence Commission) of a new ten-member *ad hoc* Defence Committee composed of Togo, Algeria, Guinea-Bissau, Chad, Cameroon, Uganda, Lesotho, Liberia, Tanzania and Egypt to provide aid 'in all forms' to Mozambique, Botswana and Zambia against future attacks from Rhodesia. The proposal put forward by the OAU Administrative Secretary-General William Eteki Mboumona, to set up an OAU combined defence force which could intervene against aggression from white–ruled southern African and put some body into the new committee, was, however, rejected. None of the obstacles to Kwame Nkrumah's 'African High Command' (an idea raised several times on the OAU Agenda under various names) had really been moved. In order to take such a step a much more solid unity is required than the one offered by the OAU in its present shape.

The second reform exchanged an equally sluggish OAU body — the Commission of Mediation, Conciliation and Arbitration — for a Standing Committee, with Gabon, Togo, Tunisia, Madagascar, Zaire, Zambia and Nigeria as its members. But not a word was uttered publicly about the 'Report of an *ad hoc* committee on the structural reform of the OAU', known in OAU circles as 'the Turkson Report' (after its Chairman, one of Ghana's most able diplomats, Ambassador Yaw Turkson).

The Turkson report goes far beyond the scope suggested by its title and contains not only proposals for profound structural changes in the OAU Secretariat but also a recommendation to establish an Assembly for Development Co-operation — that is, an Economic Summit of the OAU.[6] The committee of nine countries (Algeria, Cameroon, Ghana, Guinea, Egypt, Nigeria, Senegal, Tanzania and Zaire) spent two years considering various proposals for amending the OAU Charter. 'Moments occur in the life of all human institutions', states the report, 'when a combination of factors not only brings into sharp focus the strength and weakness of that institution but pointedly makes the need for reappraisal and reform of that institution an urgent necessity, if that institution is to continue to serve the dynamic objectives for which it was established by its founding fathers.'

Needless to say the decision on the report was postponed until the next Summit, which is how all previous proposals for OAU reform have failed.

With the little attention it paid to the economic problems of Africa the Libreville Summit could easily have been dismissed as yet another non-productive Summit had it not been for the performance of Nigeria which gave the meeting a truly pan-African imprint. During the past year Nigeria has emerged as the most vigorous advocate of African unity. Its foreign policy, amply demonstrated at Libreville, has represented a rare blend of militancy and economic pragmatism, free of any ideological bias which would allow us to call Nigeria either pro-East or pro-West. Nigeria is, above all, pro-African. She carries considerable weight with the 'moderates', who are attracted by and feel solidarity with her wealth and capitalist prosperity. But Nigeria's pan-African strength lies in her close alliance with the five front-line states, through which she occupies a place in the forefront of Africa's confrontation with South Africa. 'Africa is wasting too much valuable time and resources trying to stock-pile arms and ammunitions for threatening our own brothers instead of helping the liberation movements in southern Africa', said the Nigerian Head of State, Obasanjo, in his speech to the OAU Summit on 4 July:

'. . . A sound beginning in this direction is a decisive action by all member states to ensure, even before we leave Libreville, that we shall discharge our financial obligations to the OAU and its liberation committee. Let us ensure that at least in this regard our actions conform to our slogans. "Armed struggle is the only solution to the South African problem." . . . For it is not enough to shout slogans and dream that the louder we proclaim our opposition to apartheid the more likely it would disappear.'

The volume of material and military aid to ZIPA in Zimbabwe and SWAPO in Namibia is reported to have been very substantial. Nigeria's goal is to make African liberation movements independent of non-African sources of arms and military assistance: she has made it clear on several occasions that the great powers' intereference in African affairs should be brought to an end. That is all very well for Nigeria who, at least within the African framework, is a great power herself. It would not be difficult for her to meet all the military requirements of southern African liberation movements. 'But this should not be a task of one power, no matter how strong, but for the OAU as a whole' is the argument of the Nigerian diplomats.

The near future will show whether Nigeria's efforts to 'keep Africa one' will be as successful as her efforts to sustain the Nigerian Federation. It is that Federation which may well become the model for the Union Government of Africa proposed by the late Dr Kwame Nkrumah of Ghana fifteen years ago.

Zdenek Červenka

Uppsala, August 1977.

1. Summary of World Broadcasts, BBC London, 5 July 1977 (ME/5554/B/11).
2. For a more detailed account of the 14th OAU Summit, see author's essay 'OAU in 1977' in *Africa Contemporary Record 1977-78*, edited by Colin Legum (London: Rex Collings, 1978).
3. Article 'Les dexu Afriques', by Fode Amadou in *Afrique-Asie*, No. 140, pp 31-32.
4. *Daily Times*, Lagos, 27 July 1977, p. 3.
5. The white minority régime of Rhodesia, which has made more than 140 armed incursions into the territories of neighbouring African States during the last 15 months, had mounted on 29 May 1977 a major military operation penetrating deep into Mozambique territory. The Rhodesian armed forces commanded by Lt-General Walls, under the cover of heavy bombardment by the Rhodesian Air Force, had seized the town of Mapai. Mozambique took the case to the UN Security Council. Concurrently with the session of the Council of Ministers a meeting of the UN Security Council was opened on 29 June in New York to consider Mozambique's complaint about Rhodesian aggression. The Council of Ministers sent to New York an OAU delegation of Foreign Ministers from Algeria, Gabon, Lesotho, Nigeria and Tanzania to present the OAU point of view. Brigardier Josef Garba, Nigeria's Commissioner for foreign affairs, told the Security Council: 'Mr Smith is steeped in African blood and his allies in South Africa and the West share responsibility for the present situation. Nigerian armed forces have been alerted to the unfolding situation in southern Africa and Nigeria could not remain uninvolved if a racial conflagration were to engulf the region.'
6. The content of the Turkson Report was revealed by *Africa* magazine (London), No. 71, July 1977, pp. 66-67.

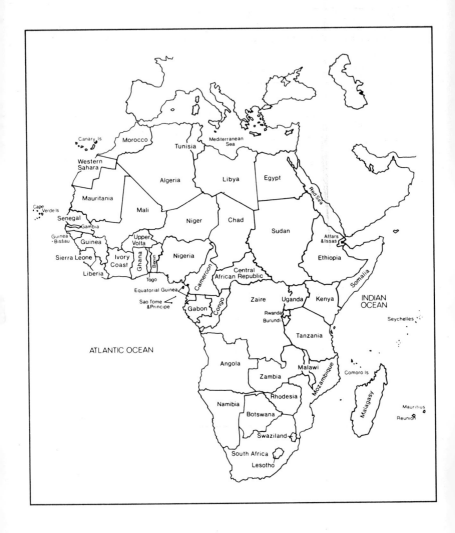

# Chapter I

# THE ESTABLISHMENT OF THE ORGANIZATION OF AFRICAN UNITY

## 1. AFRICA BEFORE THE OAU

At the beginning of 1963 the African States were divided into three main political groups: the Casablanca group[1], the Monrovia group[2], and the Brazzaville Twelve[3]. There were several reasons for the division. One of them was the disagreement of the Casablanca States with the United Nations policy in the Congo (Zaire), a policy supported by the States of the Monrovia group as well as the Brazzaville group. Another was the support of the Casablanca States for the Algerian independence struggle, and their recognition of the Algerian Provisional Government which was accorded full membership of the group. This was strongly opposed by the Brazzaville States who, because of their close links with France, regarded the Algerian conflict as a problem to be solved by France alone. The relationship between the Casablanca group and the Monrovia and Brazzaville States was further aggravated by the support that the Casablanca States gave to Morocco, contesting the legitimacy of the independent existence of Mauritania, a member of the Monrovia group. On the issue of African unity the Casablanca group was convinced that political unity was a prerequisite for the subsequent integration of African economies, while the Monrovia and Brazzaville groups maintained that African unity should be approached through economic co-operation only.

However, there was a similarity in the fundamental aims of the three groups — particularly those concerning decolonization, racial discrimination, maintenance of world peace, and the urgent need for economic co-operation between African States — which is apparent in the instruments establishing the respective organizations. Thus, despite the divisions, there was a sustained desire to unite all the independent African States, and each of the three groups made frequent attempts to end the division — through diplomatic channels, in the lobbies of the UN, and at various international gatherings attended by delegations from African States. Because governmental policies in Africa are largely determined by personalities, the compromise agreement was reached by direct talks between Heads of State during their mutual visits, which, since 1962, have been mainly preoccupied with African Unity.

President Sekou Touré of Guinea and Emperor Haile Selassie of Ethiopia were leading figures in the process of reconciliation, and at the meeting of these two statesmen in Asmara, Ethiopia, on 28 June 1962, a summit conference of all the independent African States was proposed.

After a difficult period in January 1963, when the Togo *coup d'état*[4] threatened to thwart the agreed terms of the rapprochement, preparations for the summit conference gathered momentum and during March 1963 the date for the Conference of Heads of State and Government of Independent African States at Addis Ababa was fixed for 23 May 1963. A secretariat was set up in Addis Ababa to carry out the detailed preparations. It was agreed that the Conference of Heads of State and Government was to be preceded by a meeting of the Foreign Ministers to prepare the agenda for the main event.

On the eve of the Foreign Ministers' meeting, four different attitudes to African unity emerged. First there was the view that all that was needed was a single African Charter, to supercede the existing Charter of the Casablanca group, the Lagos Charter of the Monrovia group and the UAM Charter of the Brazzaville Twelve. This Charter would lay down broad principles to which all African States could subscribe. It would be comparable to the Bandung Declaration of the non-aligned nations of Asia and Africa[5], or the Atlantic Charter promulgated during the Second World War[6]. This was the view held by States such as Libya and the Sudan, which believed in the necessity of a united Africa but assumed that each African State would conduct its business at home and abroad very much as before.

The second view was that, in addition to a 'Declaration of Principles', a loose association of African States should be formed within the framework of an all-African organization. The model for this organization was the Organization of American States, regarded by some African statesmen — among them President William Tubman of Liberia — as the most suitable type for African conditions.

The proponents of the third view claimed that it was premature to consider organic African unity and that the situation merely required increased economic co-operation among African States. The main arguments advanced in support of this view were the vastness of the African continent, the poor state of inter-continental transport and communications and the need to achieve something immediately which was practical and economically viable. The advocates of this approach were from such widely separated regions as East Africa and West Africa (Ethiopia and Nigeria), and included practically all members of the Brazzaville Twelve. There were demands for improved telecommunications, roads and air links, for increased trade, and for a Pan-African university. Since such measures would suffer from the limitations

2

imposed by the geography of the continent, it was argued that regionalism must be an intermediate step towards African unity.

The fourth view was that the Addis Ababa Conference should bring about political unity in Africa on a truly continental scale. This view was advanced by Ghana and it was shared by some members of the Casablanca group. Ghana demanded the setting up of a Union Government of Africa with all the machinery needed to make it work, an African civil service, an African High Command, a Court of Justice, and other all-African institutions. The view was based on the belief that political unity should precede economic co-operation and that only a Continental Union modelled on the constitutions of the USA and the USSR could be an effective instrument against colonialism and apartheid.

The four views corresponded to the division of Africa into the various groups already mentioned. Some of the Foreign Ministers arrived for the meeting with a sincere desire to end the division, but few really believed it could be achieved. While any of the first three views would have been acceptable to all members of the Monrovia group and the Brazzaville Twelve, the fourth view rallied least support and most opposition.

The *Report of the First Committee of the Preparatory Conference of Foreign Ministers,* published later by the Provisional Secretariat of OAU, contains some striking revelations concerning the private debate on African unity. It shows that some of the ministers came to the meeting to discuss at length the principles and structure of African unity, but were not prepared to commit themselves in any way. Some demanded more time for a thorough study of the draft Charter submitted by Ethiopia, and of Ghana's proposal for a Union of African States. Some excused themselves by declaring that they had no mandate from their governments to commit themselves to any text.


However, there were other delegations which considered that the importance of the work to be accomplished was precisely the reason for convening a Conference of Heads of State and Government and that the task of the Foreign Ministers was to draft the best possible agreement about a future all-African organization. The discussion ended with the appointment of a sub-committee composed of representatives from Algeria, Cameroon, Ethiopia, Ghana, Guinea, Malagasy Republic, Nigeria, Tanzania and Tunisia, which subsequently recommended that the task of drawing up the Charter be transferred to the Heads of State. The Foreign Ministers recommended that the Conference of Heads of State and Government of African States should accept as a basis for discussion the Ethiopian draft charter (which was basically the Lagos

Charter) with a view to drawing up the charter of an all-African organization, and suggested that the document be transmitted to all member-Governments so that they could submit their comments and amendments before the meeting of the Foreign Ministers' Conference, which was to be held before the end of 1963 at Dakar. The Foreign Ministers further requested that the provisional secretariat assemble all relevant documents (in particular those pertaining to the Casablanca Charter, the Inter-African and Malagasy Organization, and Ghana's proposed Union of African States), again with amendments and comments, in time for the same meeting. In short, the Foreign Ministers failed to agree on the draft charter and suggested a procedure which would have delayed the establishment of the OAU for at least a year.

While the deliberations of the Foreign Ministers on the issue of African unity were disappointing, better results were achieved in other fields. In particular, the Draft Resolution on Decolonization, prepared by the Second Committee of the Foreign Ministers' Conference, was a powerful document and was subsequently adopted by the Summit without any significant changes.

## 2. THE ADDIS ABABA SUMMIT CONFERENCE OF HEADS OF STATE AND GOVERNMENT OF INDEPENDENT AFRICAN STATES

The Ethiopian capital, Addis Ababa, was astir with activity throughout May 1963 in anticipation of the Summit conference. Huge portraits of African leaders were erected in front of the Emperor's palace. Hundreds of reporters representing the African and world press flocked into the city. The atmosphere was set by the Western mass media which had carried out a consistent anti-Nkrumah campaign. In inciting animosity towards Ghana's President the American press took the lead. *Newsweek* of 20 May 1963, which appeared on Addis Ababa news-stands on the eve of the Summit, included an article entitled 'Ghana Subversion Inc.' smearing the Ghanaian President as follows:

'Since the first of the year, Nigeria and Niger have linked the Bureau of African Affairs (BAA) to treason plots, and Liberia's President William V. Tubman has flatly charged that Ghana was behind a recent attempt on his life. In the Ivory Coast, police claim that a plot to kill President Felix Houphouet-Boigny was financed in Accra, and it is widely believed throughout Africa that the killers of Togo's President Sylvanus Olympio were rewarded by Kwame Nkrumah.

In the understatement of the year, Sierra Leone's Premier Sir

4

Milton Margai had deplored the BAA's "unneighbourly intrusions", and Nigerian Foreign Minister Jaja Wachuku refers cryptically to a "network of subversion". And when 32 African chiefs of State and Heads of Government meet at Addis Ababa later this month, Olympio's assassination is expected to be a major behind-scenes issue. Many are incensed, but they are wary of criticizing Nkrumah — modern Africa's self-styled founding father — in public. "If I sounded the drums about these things", 'shrugs Houphouet-Boigny, "there would be no end to it."

TIME magazine joined *Newsweek* with a similar charade.[7] This outburst was no doubt prompted by Ghana's strong objection to the presence of an Organization of American States expert brought in by Liberia and Ethiopia to help with the drafting of the charter.[8] The British press, though more urbane, was equally critical of Ghana. Considering the weight which the Western press carried in Africa at the time this added much to the tension at the diplomatic lobbies where the signatories of the Lagos Charter fully exploited the anti-Ghana sentiments and succeeded in neutralizing the pro-Ghana lobby of the spokesmen of freedom fighters, various political parties in exile, and African trade unionists.


Never before had so many African leaders gathered in the same place at the same time. Their host, the Ethiopian Emperor, was at the airport to greet each of his arriving guests. A notable absentee was King Hassan II of Morocco. Due to its claims on Mauritania, Morocco boycotted many international conferences attended by Mauritanian delegates, and in this case alphabetical seating arrangements would have placed King Hassan next to the President of Mauritania. King Hassan subsequently signed the Charter on 19 September 1963, and sat next to the President of Mauritania at the 1964 OAU meeting.[9]

On 23 May 1963, the 71-year-old Emperor Haile Selassie opened the conference at Addis Ababa Hall by describing its task as follows:

'. . . What we require is a single African Organization through which Africa's single voice may be heard and within which Africa's problems may be studied and resolved. We need an organization which will facilitate acceptable solutions to disputes among Africans and promote the study and adoption of measures for common defence and programmes of co-operation in the economic and social fields.

. . . Let us, at this conference, create a single institution to which we will all belong, based on principles to which we all subscribe, confident that in its councils our voices will carry their proper weight, secure in the knowledge that the decisions there will be dictated by Africans and only by Africans and that they will take full account of all Africa's vital considerations...[10]

Although the Agenda of the Summit Conference consisted of a wide range of topics, there were two questions which dominated the proceedings: African Unity and the Decolonization of Africa. Dr Nkrumah, speaking on 24 May, put before the assembled Heads of State and Government his proposal for a union Government of Africa and explained what he meant by African Unity: 'African Unity is above all a political kingdom which can only be gained by political means. The social and economic development of Africa will come only within the political kingdom, not the other way round.'

He called for the establishment of Commissions (1) to frame a Constitution for a Union Government of African States; (2) to work out a continental plan for a unified or common economic and industrial programme for Africa, this plan to include proposals for setting up (a) a Common Market for Africa, (b) an African currency, (c) an African monetary zone, (d) an African central bank, and (e) a continental communications system; and (3) to formulate a common foreign policy and diplomacy. He concluded his speech as follows:

'Let us return to our people of Africa not with empty hands and with high-sounding resolutions, but the firm hope and assurance that at long last African Unity has become a reality. We shall thus begin the triumphant march to the Kingdom of African Personality, and to the continent of prosperity and progress...'

The Ghanaian President received support for his call to unity only from the Premier of Uganda, Milton Obote, who advocated the creation of a strong Pan-African executive and an African Parliament, to which African States would be prepared to surrender part of their sovereignty. The Casablanca States let Ghana down. Though sympathetic to Dr Nkrumah's ideas in general terms none of its leaders committed himself to an open support for Ghana's proposal.

Nigeria's Prime Minister, Sir Abubakar Tafawa Balewa, assumed the role of spokesman for the 'moderates', the signatories of the Lagos Charter, and represented what emerged as the majority opinion of the conference. His speech was a clear-cut reply to the main points of Nkrumah's proposal. He rejected the idea of surrendering part of each State's sovereignty for the benefit of the Union of African States by saying:

'Nigeria's stand is that, if we want unity in Africa, we must first agree to certain essential things. The first is that African States must respect one another. There must be acceptance of equality by all the States. No matter whether they are big or small, they are all sovereign and their sovereignty is sovereignty.'

He continued with the remark 'we cannot achieve this African unity as long as some African countries continue to carry on subversive activities in other African countries', an obvious reference to Ghana. He then directly replied to President Nkrumah's proposal for the creation of an African Common Market calling it a 'good but unpractical idea'. He continued by dismissing President Nkrumah's concept of political African unity by maintaining that African unity could only be achieved by taking practical steps in economic, educational, scientific and cultural co-operation and by 'trying first to get the Africans to understand themselves before embarking on the more complicated and more difficult arrangement of political union'. On that the conference appeared to be almost unanimous. Sir Abubakar's cautious approach towards African unity won the support not only of the Monrovia States but, significantly, also of the Casablanca group. President Nasser of Egypt (then the United Arab Republic) joined Presidents Tsiranana of Madagascar, Senghor of Senegal and Bourghiba of Tunisia by advising against haste and saying that 'African unity cannot be achieved overnight'. President Julius Nyerere of Tanzania (then Tanganyika), who at that time had a lot of faith in the East African Federation (which later proved to be misplaced), also preferred the 'step-by-step' approach. As a result, the debate on African unity became more and more a debate about the virtues of regional economic co-operation in which most speakers saw hope for the salvation of the continent. At this point President Ben Bella of Algeria rose to address the conference. During little more than three minutes he brought the delegates to their feet. He told them what, in his view, were the priorities of African unity:

'This Charter will remain a dead letter unless we take concrete decisions, unless we lend unconditional support to the peoples of Angola, of South Africa, of Mozambique and others, unconditional support which these peoples still under the colonialist yoke are entitled to expect from us.

It is my duty to say that if concrete decisions in this sense are not taken, the Charter we are going to adopt will resemble all the Charters which all the assemblies of the world may have adopted. It is my duty to say again that all the fine speeches we have heard here will be the strongest weapon against this unity.'

'Let us all agree to die a little', concluded the Algerian President, 'so that the peoples still under colonial domination may be free and African Unity may not be a vain word.'

Most of those who were present at Africa Hall agreed that this was the conference's finest hour. The Heads of States, aroused by Ben Bella's speech were now seized by an urge for immediate action. Prime Minister Milton Obote of Uganda offered his country as a training ground for African troops to be used to overthrow white governments in Africa. President Sekou Touré of Guinea asked for a date to be fixed after which 'if colonialism were not ended, the African States should expel the colonial Powers'. He also proposed that one per cent of national budgets be allocated for the liberation struggle. President Senghor of Senegal called for an effective boycott of Portugal and South Africa in all spheres of both political and economic life. Most emphatic was the response of President Nyerere of Tanzania who said:

'In our approach to the final liberation of Africa we are all agreed without a single exception that the time for mere words is gone, that this is the time for action, that the time for allowing our brethren to struggle unaided is gone, that from now on our brethren in non-independent Africa should be helped by independent Africa.
... I want to assure our gallant brother from Algeria, brother Ben Bella, that we are prepared to die a little for the final removal of the humiliation of colonialism from the face of Africa.'

Such was the impact of Ben Bella's speech on the delegates that the proposed Charter was interpreted as a common weapon for the liberation of Africa. The growing enthusiasm of the assembled leaders for decolonization and the war against apartheid gave birth to what has been called the *spirit of Addis Ababa*. Herein lies the explanation of the final agreement on the Charter, and it is from here that we can arrive at a correct evaluation of the results of the Addis Ababa Conference and assess the weight of the signatures attached to the Charter.

On the last day the proceedings were slightly disturbed by a clash between the Somali Republic and Ethiopia. President Aden Abdullah Osman of Somalia demanded that the Somali population in Kenya, French Somaliland and Ethiopia be granted the right of self-determination. President Houphouet-Boigny of the Ivory Coast, the Conference President for the day, expressed regret that a subject which should have been discussed in private should have been raised as part of the proceedings. However, the Ethiopian Prime Minister insisted on his right to reply and delivered a belligerent speech: 'If we were to redraw the map of Africa on the basis of religion, race and language', said Prime Minister Aklilu Habtä-Wäld menacingly, 'I fear that many States will cease to exist.'

The duel between the Somali and Ethiopian representatives was quickly put to an end by the joint mediation efforts of several African leaders. The majority of all present supported the statement by President Modibo Keita of Mali, who laid down a rule which subsequently became the guideline for settlement of border disputes:

'The colonial system divided Africa, but it permitted nations to be born. Present frontiers must be respected and the sovereignty of each State must be consecrated by a multilateral non-aggression pact.'

After two and a half days spent in general debate on the United Nations pattern, the conference went into closed session. With very little time left, the meeting was largely confined to canvassing for the unanimous adoption of the Ethiopian draft charter which was to lay down the basis for an all-African organization. Ghana and its few allies finally acquiesced and agreed to sign it in exchange for a few amendments and a promise that the question of a union government would be taken up by the Organization at a later stage.

The political defeat of Ghana, which became clear after President Nkrumah failed to convince the conference of the urgent need for a political union of Africa, was in a way compensated for by the unanimous support for decisive action against colonialism and apartheid initiated by President Ben Bella of Algeria. This gave the meeting a revolutionary stamp in keeping with the earlier stand of the Casablanca group.

Among the resolutions approved by the Addis Ababa conference was *Africa and the United Nations*, which reaffirmed the dedication of the African States to the UN, which they found an important world forum for expressing their views and seeking relief for grievances: so far it was also the most effective instrument in their fight against apartheid and colonialism.

A resolution on *Disarmament* appealed to the great powers to reduce conventional weapons, to abandon the arms race, and to sign a comprehensive disarmament agreement under strict and effective international control. There are two items of major importance in this resolution. First, it is Africa's declaration in favour of a nuclear-free zone, its opposition to all nuclear tests and the manufacture of nuclear weapons, and its support for the peaceful uses of atomic energy. Second, the resolution emphasizes an obligation 'to bring about by means of negotiation the end of military occupation of the African continent, the elimination of which constitutes a basic element of African Independence and Unity'. The resolution, in effect, calls upon states to review military agreements concluded with their former colonizers or with any other non-African powers, by virtue of which foreign military personnel and equipment were accommodated on African soil. The resolution makes it clear that the presence of military personnel of any non-African power on the territory of an independent African state is incompatible with the principle of non-alignment to which most African states claim adherence.[22]

Two resolutions were adopted on the *Area of Co-operation.* The first provided for the appointment of an economic committee charged with the study of the economic problems of African unity.[12] The second called on Member-States to 'maintain The Commission for Technical Co-operation in Africa South of Sahara (CTCA) and to reconsider its role in order to bring it eventually within the scope of the Organization of African Unity which will have as one of its aims an organ for technical, scientific and cultural co-operation.'[13]

The conferences also adopted three supplementary resolutions on social and labour matters, on education and culture, and on health, sanitation and nutrition.[14]


In the early hours of 26 May 1963, in a solemn ceremony, thirty-one African leaders signed the Charter of the OAU. Every one of the assembled leaders must have had reservations about the Charter and its political consequences. However, no objection to any of its provisions could have been strong enough to justify a withdrawal from the signing ceremony. Any leader doing so would have run the risk of being identified as a traitor to Africa's united stand against colonialism and apartheid. So each one, overwhelmed by the historical significance of the conference, felt it his duty to sign the Charter. That in the face of this resolve all personal, regional and ideological differences disappeared, and thirty-one Heads of State agreed to become members of one all-African organization, was the true significance of the Addis Ababa summit meeting. By signing the Charter, the leaders of Africa — feudal, conservative or progressive — showed the world that their determination to free the continent of colonialism and apartheid was sufficiently strong to bind them together. The Ghanaian weekly, *The Spark,* later one of the sharpest critics of the OAU, published an editorial in June 1963, which described the Charter as 'the new voice of Africa which echoes the best tradition of the African revolution since the historic 1958 Accra Conference of Independent African States'. Others hailed it as the greatest accomplishment of the Pan-African movement since it was launched in 1900. The *Uganda*

*Argus*, on 27 May 1963, called the signing of the Charter 'a momentous event' and 'a start of a new phase in African history', and pointed out that 'clearly, the outlook now is for closer and closer co-operation between African States and for a pooling of their efforts in all spheres, but particularly in the ending of colonialism and the freeing of those parts of Africa where the African people are still denied self-determination'.

On the whole, most African press comments were enthusiastic. The Charter was seen as a political and legal instrument for the liberation and unification of the African continent. Perhaps the best assessment of the Charter and of the achievements at the Addis Ababa Summit came from H. M. Basner of *The Ghanaian Times:*

'Charter or covenant, agreement or oath of unity, the document signed at Addis Ababa is a piece of paper, no matter how sacred its contents, how solemn and sincere the intentions of its signatories. Thirty-one signatures on a piece of paper cannot unite a continent of 250 million people. The inspiration and organizational means provided by the document will become a reality only if the masses of Africa are mobilized into action.'[15]

# Chapter II

# THE OAU CHARTER

Perhaps the most striking feature of the OAU Charter is the absence of provisions to enable it to impose its decisions upon its membership. The essence of the OAU is voluntary co-operation between the Member-States for the attainment of common objectives specified in the Preamble, the Purposes, and the Principles.

Great care was exercised in the drafting of the Preamble, which is the rationale for the establishment of the Organization. Such was the importance the African leaders attached to it,[1] that they devoted half the time spent on considering the Charter as a whole just to the Preamble. Its language reveals the influence of other documents: the UN Charter, the Universal Declaration of Human Rights, the Declaration to the Colonial Peoples (Fifth Pan-African Congress, 1945), and the 1958 Accra Conference of Independent African States.[2]

The formal establishment and the name of the Organization is stated in Article I:
- The High Contracting Parties do by the present Charter establish an Organization to be known as the Organization of African Unity.
- The Organization shall include the continental African states, Madagascar and other islands surrounding Africa.

The proposed name 'Organization of African States' was dropped because its abbreviation, OAS, would have been identical with that of the Organization of American States. The second paragraph defines the geographic scope of the OAU and clarifies the concept of the 'continent of Africa'.

## 1. THE PURPOSES

The purposes of the Organization are stated in Article II (1) as follows:
- to promote the unity and solidarity of the African States;
- to co-ordinate and intensify their co-operation and efforts to achieve a better life for the peoples of Africa;
- to defend their sovereignty, territorial integrity and independence;
- to eradicate all forms of colonialism from Africa;

— to promote international co-operation, having due regard to the UN Charter and the Universal Declaration of Human Rights.

The order of purposes has no bearing on the fact that the principal aim of the OAU was to free the African continent of colonialism, apartheid and racial discrimination. This emerged from the debate on the OAU Charter at Addis Ababa in 1963 and was reaffirmed on many subsequent occasions.[3]

To achieve the aims stated in Article II (1), the Member-States pledged themselves to co-ordinate their policies, especially in the following fields:
— politics and diplomacy;
— economics, including transport and communications;
— education and culture;
— health, sanitation and nutrition;
— science and technology;
— defence and security.

Despite the emphasis on defending the sovereignty, territorial integrity and independence of Member-States, the Charter does not provide for collective security in the sense that Member–States are legally obliged to come to the assistance of another Member-State in the event of aggression. This omission was rectified in a document adopted at the 1973 OAU Summit conference at Rabat — *Recommendations of Special Measures to be adopted on decolonization and the struggle against apartheid and racial discrimination.*[4] The Assembly of Heads of State and Government recommended, 'in order to strengthen the means of defence of certain African States, that Member-States apply themselves to making available to those States who request them, units, modern equipment and military assistance, pending the setting up of the Executive Secretariat of Defence.' The Declaration also stated that while the armed struggle of the liberation movements was legitimate, any retaliation by Portugal, South Africa and Rhodesia against the States providing support for the guerrillas would be regarded as 'acts constituting aggression against the whole of Africa'.[5] However, until now no Executive Secretariat for Defence has been set up nor have any measures for collective defence been adopted.


## 2. THE PRINCIPLES

The following are the seven principles of the OAU as embodied in Article III:
— the sovereign equality of all Member-States;
— non-interference in the internal affairs of States;
— respect for the sovereignty and territorial integrity of each State and

13

for its inalienable right to independent existence;
— peaceful settlement of disputes by negotiation, mediation, conciliation or arbitration;
— unreserved condemnation, in all its forms, of political assassination as well as of subversive activities on the part of neighbouring States or any other State;
— absolute dedication to the total emancipation of the African territories which are still dependent;
— affirmation of a policy of non-alignment with regard to all blocs.

All but one of the principles listed in Article III of the OAU Charter are identical to those affirmed in Accra in 1958. The additional principle, namely the 'unreserved condemnation, in all its forms, of political assassination as well as of subversive activities on the part of neighbouring States or any other State' was included at the insistence of Nigeria.

The first four principles are generally recognized principles of present international law and reaffirm the corresponding principles embodied in the UN Charter, as a comparison of both documents will show.[6] The remaining three have a special significance for Africa and were intended to be the guiding principles in the foreign relations of African States.

*Prohibition of subversion*
The fate of President Sylvanus Olympio of Togo, killed during the *coup d'état* in January 1963, was on the delegates' minds when the fifth principle, the 'unreserved condemnation, in all its forms, of political assassination as well as of subversive activities on the part of neighbouring States or any other State' was drafted. In a way it is part of the broader principle of 'non-interference in the internal affairs of States'.

The emphasis on 'assassination' reflects the political situation in Africa, where the concentration of power in the office of Head of State is much greater than, for example, in European countries. The assassination of an African Head of State therefore has far more serious consequences than in a society with a complex administrative structure. The importance attached to this principle by the African leaders was shown by the adoption of a special declaration *on the problem of subversion* at the 1965 Summit in Accra. Ironically, Sir Abubakar Tafawa Balewa, Prime Minister of Nigeria, who was so anxious to insert this principle in the Charter, was himself a victim of political assassination three years later in January 1966.

*Dedication to total emancipation of Africa*
The sixth principle, 'absolute dedication to the total emancipation of the African territories which are still dependent', is a corollary to

the main purpose of the OAU: 'the eradication of all forms of colonialism from Africa'. It reflects the depth of anti-colonial feeling in Africa and the realization that Africa cannot determine its own destiny until its total emancipation is achieved.

Although none of the principles of the Charter imposes a legal obligation on Member-States, the establishment of the OAU Liberation Committee has made the assistance to the liberation movements compulsory.

*Non-alignment*

The seventh principle, 'affirmation of a policy of non-alignment with regard to all blocs', arose from a conviction that, if Africa is to contribute to world peace, it can do so only by a policy of non-alignment. It was largely due to the efforts of President Tito of Yugoslavia, Prime Minister Nehru of India, and President Nasser of Egypt that non-alignment emerged as a new factor in international affairs.

'Non-alignment' assumed an organized form at the five conferences of non-aligned countries, three of which were held in Africa (Belgrade 1961, Cairo 1964, Lusaka 1970, Algiers 1973, Colombo 1976). The first conference in Belgrade in 1961, which was an attempt on behalf of the non-aligned countries to contribute to the international efforts to prevent nuclear war, was attended by representatives of twenty-two countries. Fifteen years later, the conference in Colombo in August 1976 was attended by representatives from eighty-six countries, including forty-six independent States of Africa, with only Malawi absent.[7]

Since the Cairo Conference in 1964 there have been some dramatic developments in international politics, which have had great impact on the Third World. Among the most important were: the Sino-Soviet ideological dispute which broke out in the sixties; China's attainment of the status of nuclear power in 1969, and its admission to the United Nations in 1971; the US intervention in Vietnam (1965-1974); the intervention of the Warsaw Pact forces in Czechoslovakia in 1968; the overthrow of the Chilean Government by its own armed forces and the death of President Salvador Allende in 1974; the 1967 and 1973 wars in the Middle East; the 1967-70 Nigerian Civil War and the 1975-76 war in Angola. The role of the non-aligned countries, which in the sixties was that of intermediary between the eastern and western power blocs, has changed to a search for protection against the super-power tendency to monopolize decision-making on vital world issues. In short the non-aligned countries have refused to entrust the direction of international affairs to the great powers alone, and have insisted on taking part in negotiations and agreements which affect them.

## 3. MEMBERSHIP: RIGHTS AND DUTIES OF MEMBER STATES

Article IV of the Charter states that 'each independent sovereign African State shall be entitled to become a Member-State of the Organization'. The legal interpretation of this gives each independent African State a *right* to membership which it can *claim* — provided however that it pledges 'to adhere to the principles enshrined in the OAU Charter and to work for the achievements of the objectives therein' (a condition not stipulated by the OAU Charter but by the Resolution *On the Admission of New Members* adopted in Kampala in July 1975). By virtue of this qualification the membership of South Africa is ruled out on the ground that its policy of apartheid is contrary to the very purposes for which the OAU was established. The request of the liberation movements for an 'associate membership'[8] was met by granting them an observer's statute allowing the representatives of recognized liberation movements to participate in the OAU conferences without a right to vote.

The Charter draws no distinction between the 'founding members', i.e. those who signed the Charter at Addis Ababa and ratified it in accordance with Article XXIV, and those who deposited the instruments of adherence with the Administrative Secretary-General. Three months after the Charter became operative, the Government of Ethiopia had received instruments of ratification from two-thirds of the signatory states, and the procedure prescribed by Article XXVIII became applicable. It states that membership of the Organization may also be obtained by adherence or accession to the Charter.[9] Any independent State may at any time notify the Administrative Secretary-General that it wishes to do so. On receipt of such notification, the administrative Secretary-General circulates a copy of it to all members, who are required to decide the issue of admission by simple majority. The decision of each Member-State is transmitted to the Administrative Secretary General who, upon receipt of the required number of votes, communicates the decision to the State concerned. This procedure was designed to speed up the administrative process, and not to subject newly independent States to the inconvenience of having to wait for the next annual meeting of the Assembly.

In the case of Guinea-Bissau, which declared its independence on 24 September 1973, the procedure for admission specified by the Charter was totally disregarded. Its membership was proposed by Algeria at the 8th Extraordinary Session of the council of Ministers at Addis Ababa on 21 November 1973 and unanimously approved by the Council. The same procedure was followed by the 12th OAU Summit in Kampala in July 1975 to admit four new members: the Peoples' Republic of Mozambique, the Cape Verde Islands, the Comoro Islands and the

Democratic Republic of São Tomé and Principé. Their admission was approved by the resolution on the admission of new members referred to above.[10]

The most trying case of an admission of a new State has been Angola. However, although the Extraordinary OAU Summit convened in Addis Ababa in January 1976 failed to resolve the issue of Angola's admission, one month later Angola was admitted in accordance with the normal procedure prescribed by the Charter: the Administrative Secretary-General, having been notified by the majority of the OAU Members of their recognition of the MPLA regime in Angola, invited Angola to take a seat in the organization.

The procedure required by the Charter for the termination of membership is similar to the arrangements employed in other international treaties. Any OAU Member-State desiring to renounce its membership must forward written notification to the Administrative Secretary-General. The cessation of membership becomes effective one year from the date of such notification. The period of one year is regarded as being sufficiently long to enable both the Organization and the State concerned to adjust all oustanding rights and obligations. So far no-one has left the organization, although in 1976 Morocco and Mauretania threatened to do so in protest against the OAU's support for POLISARIO.

Article V stipulates that 'all members shall enjoy equal rights and have equal duties'. There is no provision in the Charter to accord any African State 'special responsibilities' similar to those of the permanent members of the UN Security Council. However, certain states like Nigeria, Egypt and Zaire could qualify for such a role by virtue of their size, economic wealth and military strength. The only exception to the strictly observed rule of equality is, understandably, the scale of members' contributions to the OAU's budget. It is determined on the basis of the UN assessment of national income.

Each OAU member, therefore, has the following *rights:*
— to be represented on all principal institutions of the Organization and to stand for election to all special *ad hoc* committees which may be created by any of the principal organs of the OAU;
— to enjoy the right of one vote in each of the organs and committees;
— to request an extraordinary session of both the Assembly of Heads of State and Government and of the Council of Ministers, provided that such a request has the support of a two-thirds majority of the Member-States (Article IX and XII 2);
— to nominate its nationals to any function within the framework of the Organization and its General Secretariat;

- to receive all the certified communications from the Administrative Secretary-General, one of which is expressly specified by Article XXVIII (2) of the Charter: 'Notification of any independent African State of its intention to adhere or accede to the Charter';
- to renounce its membership (Article XXXII);
- to make a request for the amendment or the revision of the Charter in accordance with the procedure stipulated by Article XXXIII of the Charter.

The right of attending all principal institutions does not include the right of participation in the meetings of the *ad hoc* committees charged with a special task, such as was the OAU committee on Nigeria and the OAU Committee on the Middle East.

The *obligations* of each Member-State, as contained in the various provisions of the Charter, can be summarized as follows:
- to implement the purposes of the OAU as enumerated in Article II;
- to observe the principles of the Organization as set forth by Article III;
- to pay its membership contributions (Article XXIII);
- to refrain from interfering with the work of the Secretariat by exercising influence over any member of its staff (Article XVIII);
- to implement the resolutions adopted by the Assembly of Heads of State and Government and by the Council of Ministers, the latter being subject to endorsement by the Assembly. Although this obligation is not expressed anywhere in the Charter, the resolutions themselves are the implementation of the purposes and principles of the Charter to which the Member-States pledge their adherence.

This view is supported by the 'Declaration on the Question of Dialogue' adopted at the 1971 OAU Summit in Addis Ababa.[11] The Declaration points out that 'it was agreed that no Member-State of the Organization of African Unity would initiate or engage in any type of action that would undermine or abrogate the solemn obligations and undertakings to the commitments contained in the Charter.

It was also agreed that any action to be taken by Member-States with regard to the solution of the problems of colonialism, racial discrimination and apartheid in Africa must be undertaken within the framework of the OAU and in full consultation with the liberation movements of the territories concerned.

In other words the right of each Member-State to independent opinion and independent foreign policy does not apply to 'Dialogue', qualified by the Declaration as a policy contrary to the very purposes and principles of the OAU Charter. The Declaration made it clear that henceforth any State pursuing the policy of 'Dialogue' would be acting contrary to the principles of the Charter and defying an expressly and strongly formulated opinion of the majority of OAU members.

# Chapter III

# THE PRINCIPAL ORGANS OF THE OAU

The following are the principal organs of the OAU:

*The Assembly of Heads of State and Government,* which is the supreme organ of the Organization and the only body with decision-making powers. It meets one a year.

*The Council of Ministers,* which has powers to make recommendations only. However, in practice it has become the central political organ of the OAU. It implements OAU resolutions, almost all of which it drafts itself. The Council meets twice a year.

*The General Secretariat,* which is the administrative organ of the OAU, with headquarters in Addis Ababa. It serves the meetings of all the organs and committees of the OAU (except the Liberation Committee), draws up the programme and budget of the Organization, and is responsible for its implementation.

*The Specialized Commissions,* the number of which, enumerated in Article XX, has been changed several times. They meet irregularly, and convening is subject to a quorum of a two-thirds majority.

*The Commission of Conciliation, Mediation and Arbitration.* This was set up by Article XIX as a permanent organ of the OAU but was subsequently changed to an *ad hoc* type of institution. In practice, it was replaced by *ad hoc* mediation and conciliation committees (for settlement of disputes, see Chapter V).

*The Liberation Committee* (Co-ordinating Committee for the Liberation of Africa), which, although not provided for in the Charter, was established in 1963 by the Resolution on Decolonization. The duration of its existence depends on the attainment of the OAU's principal aim: the total liquidation of colonialism in Africa and the elimination of apartheid in South Africa. It is the third most important OAU body after the Assembly and the Council of Ministers.

## 1. THE ASSEMBLY OF HEADS OF STATE AND GOVERNMENT

Article VIII of the Charter describes the Assembly as the 'supreme organ of the Organization'. The functions of the Assembly were laid down in the Charter. Significantly the scope of its power to make recommendations and to take decisions was not specified. The competence of the Assembly is not limited to any particular aspect of the OAU, and the Assembly has the right 'to discuss matters of common concern to Africa'. Thus, it may act on matters of far-reaching consequence in political, military and economic spheres. Its other functions are as follows:

— to review the structure, functions and acts of all the organs and any specialized agencies which may be created in accordance with the present Charter;
— to appoint the Administrative Secretary-General of the Organization and his assistants;
— to establish the specialized and *ad hoc* commissions;
— to decide questions which may arise concerning the interpretation of the Charter;
— to decide on the admission of new members;
— to approve amendments to the Charter;
— to approve the regulations concerning the functions of the Secretariat and of the Commission of Mediation, Conciliation and Arbitration.

The purpose of the Assembly is to provide a forum for discussion. According to Article X of the Charter, any conclusions must be registered in the form of resolutions unless the question at issue concerns appointments, elections, or procedural matters. Article X states that:

— each Member-State shall have one vote;
— all resolutions shall be determined by a two-thirds majority of the Members of the Organization;
— questions of procedure shall require a simple majority; whether or not a question is one of procedure shall be determined by a simple majority of all Member-States of the Organization;
— two-thirds of the total membership of the Organization shall form a quorum at any meeting of the Assembly.

Although Article X elaborates on voting procedures, it does not specify what constitutes a resolution within the context of the Charter. The rules of procedure, while describing the results of deliberations of the Assembly as 'resolutions and decisions', do not define either of these terms. Rule 24 simply states 'All resolutions and decisions shall be determined by a two-thirds. majority of the members of the Organization.'[1]

The agenda of an ordinary session of the Assembly is very flexible. Rule 11 states that the provisional agenda of the ordinary session shall comprise the following:

— items which the Assembly decides to place on its agenda;

- items proposed by the council of Ministers;
- items proposed by a Member-State;
- any other business.

Although it is the Council of Ministers which is charged with the duty of preparing the agenda of the Assembly (Article XIII), the final decision on what is going to be discussed by the Assembly rests with the Assembly itself. For example the Assembly decided to take up the issue of the Nigerian civil war although it was not proposed by the Council.

The agenda of an extraordinary session is limited to the items which prompted its convening (Rule 13). So far, only one extraordinary session of the Assembly has been convened. It dealt with Angola and was held in January 1976 in Addis Ababa. Rule 31 introduces the secret ballot for elections, 'and also in such special circumstances as the Assembly may determine by simple majority'. It is a rule which has been used at almost every session of the Assembly.

Though not mentioned in the Rules of Procedure or the Charter, the results of the deliberations of the Assembly may also take the form of a Declaration. It has been employed for matters of special significance such as subversion, decolonization and apartheid, dialogue with South Africa, etc. One of the most important was the 'Dar-es-Salaam Declaration on Southern Africa' adopted by the Council of Ministers in April 1975 and endorsed by the Assembly at the Kampala summit in July 1975.

*The binding force of Assembly resolutions*

The OAU resolutions were once described by Emperor Haile Selassie as representing 'respect for the basic ideas which bind us together'. However, their binding force has not been clarified in either the Charter or the Rules of Procedure of the Assembly. The omission is striking and indicates a deliberate intention to leave the matter ambiguous. In the absence of provisions in the Charter on the enforcement of the obligations of the Member-States arising from the OAU Charter and the decisions adopted by its supreme body, it follows that OAU resolutions are merely recommendations. As such they do not impose any legal obligations on the States which abstain, nor even on those which approve them. However, it would be incorrect to assess the binding force of OAU resolutions from the legal standpoint alone. OAU resolutions are adopted by the Heads of State and Government. No other international organization of the OAU's size operates at such a high level. The resolutions thus represent the collective consensus of opinion of the Heads of State, reached by exerting influence on one another.[2] They provide guidelines for the foreign policies of Member-States not only in their mutual relations but *vis-à-vis* the whole international community of States. Though lacking legal, binding force by virtue of the fact that they represent political agreements of Heads of State, often reached through tough bargaining, they carry considerable political weight, the more so as most of them are adopted unanimously. Unanimity has always been one of the aims of the Assembly.

An excellent rationale for consensus in preference to a simple majority was offered by the Prime Minister of the Sudan, Saddi El Mahdi, in his address to the 1966 OAU summit at Addis Ababa:

'When people get their proposals defeated, as we ourselves faced on many issues, they tend to get frustrated. We believe that this frustration is only a matter of reality, and it should not at all lead to any cynicism about the Organization or the solidarity of the African peoples. If the proposals of any individual country or a small group of countries are not accepted by OAU, it is because the consensus of opinion is against such proposals. Efforts of all African States must be directed to widen the area of this consensus. The more united the policies of African States, the broader the field of consensus. But what we individually expect of the Organization should not necessarily be what we think is best but what we feel that the Organization can accept as a body.'[3]

Because of the relatively low degree of mutual economic interdependence, the OAU does not possess any means of coercion to make non-complying States conform to collective decisions. However, although lacking the power of enforcement available to the Security Council, the OAU has found other means of dealing with members which refused to comply with its decisions. The display of contempt for States which act against the interests of Africa, and their isolation from the political life of the African community of States, often brings effective collective pressure to bear on the dissidents.

When Malawi, contrary to OAU policy on South Africa, established diplomatic relations with the Republic in September 1967, the wave of indignation from OAU members culminated in Zambia's demand for the expulsion of Malawi from the Organization. This was not legally possible, as the Charter does not provide for expulsion of its members, nor was it viewed by most as desirable. The OAU's policy towards Malawi was that of public condemnation and ostensible dissociation from its policies, which bordered on expulsion. Malawi representatives were conspicuously absent from OAU conferences. Eventually, Malawi returned to the OAU, and in 1973 John Msonthi, Minister of Education, led Malawi's delegation to the 10th Anniversary Summit.[4] Although Malawi did not curtail its relations with South Africa, it ceased to pursue them so openly.

While the Charter deliberately permits the right of dissent on resolutions adopted on political issues, [5] the decisions of the Assembly relating to internal structure or functioning of the Organization presuppose their acceptance by all OAU members. This applies to budgetary matters, to the appointment of an Administrative Secretary-General and his four assistants, to election of the officers of the Assembly, to the creation of *ad hoc* committees and to the following three provisions:
- the power to decide on questions which may arise concerning the interpretation of the Charter (by two-thirds majority);
- the power to decide on the admission of new members (by simple majority);
- the power to approve amendments to the Charter (by two-thirds majority).

*Emergency Session of the Assembly of Heads of State and Government*
Article IX of the OAU Charter concerning the convening of an extra session of the Assembly, was invoked for the first time in OAU history on 10-12 January 1976 when the supreme organ of the OAU met in order to bring the war in Angola between the three liberation movements to an end. The background to the meeting and its proceedings are described in Chapter VIII.


## 2. THE COUNCIL OF MINISTERS

The Council of Ministers, composed of the Foreign Ministers of member governments or such ministers as are designated in their place, acts as a 'cabinet' to the Assembly, in that it is specifically charged with the implementation of the Assembly's decisions. The functions of the Council of Ministers are described by Article XIII of the Charter as follows:
- responsibility for preparing the conference of the Assembly;
- implementation of the decisions of the Assembly of Heads of States and Government.
- co-ordination of inter-African co-operation in accordance with the instructions of the Assembly, and in conformity with Article II (2) of the present Charter, that is, in the following fields:
  - politics and diplomacy;
  - economics, including transport and communications;
  - education and culture;
  - health, sanitation and nutritional co-operation;
  - science and technology;
  - defence and security.

The Council also approves the reports of the Specialized Commissions, the budget, and gifts and donations made to the Organization. It also has power to decide on the privileges and immunities to be accorded to the personnel of the Secretariat when they are on duty in territories of the Member-States. The basic rules governing the functioning of the Council, described by Article XIV, are as follows:

— each member has one vote;
— all resolutions are determined by a simple majority;
— two-thirds of the total membership of the Council of Ministers shall form a quorum for any meeting of the Council.

One of the most important functions of the Council is drafting and adopting resolutions and declarations which are then submitted for the endorsement by the Assembly of Heads of State and Government. The direct responsibility of the Council to the Assembly has been reaffirmed by the Rules of Procedure.[6] Rule 2 states:

'The Council of Ministers is answerable to the Assembly of Heads of State and Government.'

On the whole the Rules repeat the provisions concerning the Council of Ministers as embodied in the Charter. The only additional provision is the power of the Council to establish such *ad hoc* committees and temporary working groups as it may deem necessary (Rule 36).

The Rules further specify that the regular meetings of the Council shall take place in February, which would be an ordinary annual session, and in August, which was to be confined to the preparation of the agenda of the Assembly. While the February meeting takes place with regularity, the other meeting has always been adjusted so as to precede the meeting of the Assembly, the date of which has varied from year to year. The meetings of the Council are closed, and are only held in public exceptionally — on a decision by simple majority. The explanation of the OAU's preference for private sessions lies in its experience with the Western press, which has often displayed its capacity to transform the slightest hint of disagreement into a 'crisis'. In the circumstances, the African leaders prefer to exchange views in closed sessions and make public only the final outcome of their deliberations.

Each session has a chairman, two vice-chairmen and a rapporteur, all elected by secret ballot. The secret ballot does not seem to be so important in the light of Rule 11, which provides that 'these officers are not eligible for re-election until all other representatives have held office'. The provisional agenda of the Council is drawn up by the Administrative Secretary-General and communicated to Member-States at least 30 days before the opening of the Session. The agenda of the Council consists of the report of the Administrative Secretary-General and items decided by the Assembly or the Council as well as those proposed by the Specialized Commissions and by any Member-State.

Great care was devoted to the elaboration of the rules governing the debates. The rules on points of order, time limit, closing of lists of speakers and closure of the debate stem from the experience of lengthy debates at the meeting of foreign ministers which preceded the Addis Ababa summit in May 1963. However, the adoption of the rules has not made the debates any shorter and they have often gone on throughout the night of the last day of the session.

*Emergency sessions of the Council of Ministers*

At times of emergency and need the Council can meet in extraordinary session at the request of any of its members, provided that two-thirds of the members agree. This provision has been invoked frequently. During the first fourteen years of the OAU there were ten extraordinary sessions of the Council. The first, convened in Addis Ababa in November 1963, considered the Algeria-Morocco dispute. The second, in February 1964, was concerned with the situation in Tanzania following the army revolt in January 1964, and with the territorial disputes between Ethiopia and Somalia and Somalia and Kenya. The third, also held in Addis Ababa, considered the situation in the Congo (Zaire), at that time split by the rebellion against the central government of President Kasavubu.

A joint military operation by the United States and Belgium, launched from the British base on Ascencion Island in an attempt to save several hundred expatriates held by a rebel group of the Congolese army, was the topic of the 4th Extraordinary Session of the Council, held at UN Headquarters in New York on 16-21 December 1964. This session finally decided to request the Security Council to consider the situation. The 5th Session was held in Lagos from 10-13 June 1965, and considered the complaint of the OCAM States that Ghana was engaged in subversive activities against them. Two resolutions on Rhodesia were also adopted at the same meeting. The 6th Session, held in Addis Ababa on 3-5 December 1965, dealt with the Rhodesian crisis, which had culminated in the unilateral declaration of independence by the white minority regime.

The 7th Extraordinary Session was held in Lagos in December 1970, and was prompted by Portugal's attack on Guinea on 22 November 1970, when troops were landed close to Conakry by Portuguese warships stationed in Guinea's territorial waters. The 8th Extraordinary Session was held in Addis Ababa on 21 November 1973. It admitted Guinea-Bissau to membership of the OAU and the only other item on the agenda was entitled 'Considerations of the Current Middle East Situation with Particular Reference to its Effects in Africa'. The 9th Extraordinary Session of the Council was convened to Dar-es-Salaam in April 1975 to consider the OAU strategy on Southern Africa. The 10th was held at Addis Ababa in January 1976 to prepare an agenda for the first Extraordinary Session of the Assembly in Angola. And an 11th was held in Kinshasa in December 1976, the first one in the history of the OAU to have been devoted to economic problems, namely the economic co-operation between the African States and their economic relations with the industrialized countries.


## 3. THE GENERAL SECRETARIAT

The title of the head of the General Secretariat of the Organization of African Unity — 'Administrative Secretary-General' — indicates that the Heads of State wished to curb the powers of this official. They feared that, whatever rights and duties were assigned to the function of the Administrative Secretary-General, the person appointed to this post would aspire to become the policy-maker for the African continent. The role assumed by the United Nations Secretary General Dag Hammarskjöld during the various crises of the UN was regarded as a dangerous precedent, so the Charter is cautious in its description of the Administrative Secretary-General's duties, and emphasizes the 'absolute neutrality' of both him and his staff.[7]

*The rights and duties of the General Secretariat*

The Rules governing the functioning of the Secretariat had been formulated long before the Administrative Secretary-General assumed his post. They had been approved under the title of *Functions and Regulations of the General Secretary* at the First Meeting of the Council of Ministers at Dakar in August 1963. The Rules define the Secretariat as a central and permanent organ of the OAU which shall carry out the functions assigned to it by the Charter of the Organization, those that might be specified in other treaties and agreements among Member-States, and those that are established in the Regulations. In practice the Secretariat services all meetings of the Council of Ministers, the Assembly, Specialized Commissions, various *ad hoc* bodies established by the Council of the Assembly and most of the OAU specialized conferences, by providing all administrative and technical staff. It makes and keeps the record of the proceedings of these meetings and circulates them among the Member-States. It is responsible for assisting the Council in the implementation of its own decisions, as well as those of the Assembly. The Secretariat also prepares both the annual report and the OAU budget, which are submitted by the Administrative Secretary-General to the Council of Ministers.[8]

At present, the OAU Secretariat has about 350 staff members, divided into five categories:

— political officers (Administrative Secretary-General, his four

assistants, and President and Vice President of the Commission of Mediation, Conciliation and Arbitration) nominated by the Assembly of Heads of State and Government.
— professional officers (about 50);
— technical staff members of the conference divisions, such as simultaneous interpreters and technicians (about 50);
— general services staff members (about 40);
— locally recruited staff members (about 50).

The budget of the OAU is about US $10 million. The official languages of the Organization are English, French and Arabic. The Administrative Secretary-General is directly responsible to the Council of Ministers. He directs the activities of the General Secretariat and is responsible for its performance. He is also the Accounting Officer of the Organization and responsible for the proper administration of its budget. He drafts the provisional agenda of the meetings of the Council and Assembly, communicated to Member-States. Finally, he has a right to establish or abolish such branches and administrative and technical offices as he deems necessary for the adequate functioning of the General Secretariat, subject, as in all cases, to approval by the Council of Ministers. The formulation of one of the duties described by the Rules governing the General Secretariat as the right to 'call ordinary as well as extraordinary sessions of the Council of Ministers and the Assembly', should be understood within the context of the rules of procedure of the Council and the Assembly. What it really means is that the Administrative Secretary-General calls the extraordinary meeting of the Council of Ministers after the majority of members have so requested, while the ordinary sessions are convened on the date previously agreed upon by the Council itself. In accordance with the Rules of Procedure this should also apply to the meetings of the Assembly. In practice, however, the decision to call both the ordinary and extraordinary meetings of the Assembly has, ever since 1970, rested with the current chairman of the Organization.

From a legal standpoint, the position of the Administrative Secretary-General was weakened by his not being granted the *ex-officio* right to attend the meetings of the Council of Ministers, the Assembly, the Specialized Commissions, or the Commission on Mediation, Conciliation and Arbitration. The *Functions and Regulations of the General Secretariat* avoid the granting of this right by a reference to the respective Rules of Procedure of the bodies concerned. Rule 9 states:

'The participation of the Administrative Secretary-General in the deliberations of the Assembly, of the Council of Ministers, of the Specialized Commissions and the other organs of the Organization shall be governed by the provisions of the Charter and by the respective Rules of Procedure of these bodies.'

There is no mention of the Secretary's participation in the deliberations of the Assembly, of the Council or of the Commissions in the respective Rules of Procedure. It is unlikely that this would have escaped the attention of the Council of Ministers which drafted the Rules of Procedure, and the omission suggests that the Council of Ministers wished to reserve the right to exclude the Administrative Secretary-General whenever it wanted. However, in practice, the Administrative Secretary-General and his Assistants attend all meetings whether public or closed.

The only time the Council invoked the rule and excluded the Administrative Secretary-General from the meeting was during the 14th Session of the Council at Addis Ababa in February 1970. There the Council recommended that 'no recruitment and no upgrading of the staff should be carried out on the sole authority of the Secretary-General. In future, everything should be submitted to the Advisory Committee, which would present a report to the Council of Ministers.'

The Administrative Secretary-General challenged these recommendations in his Report on the activities of the Organization for the period February-September 1970.[9] He pointed out that the Council of Ministers acted *ultra vires* by 'entirely replacing the General Secretariat in the responsibility vested in the latter by the Assembly of Heads of State and Government in all matters pertaining to the recruitment, upgrading and increments of the Organization's staff'. However, Diallo Telli's objections were overruled by the Assembly of Heads of State and Government which approved the Council's Resolution at its 1970 session. In order to guarantee the recruitment of efficient officers, a Recruitment Board within the Secretariat was established to advise the Secretary-General on various applications made for a particular vacant job. Although its powers are only advisory, its recommendations are invariably accepted by the Administrative Secretary-General.*

Because the recruitment of any staff member is made only with the consent of the Government concerned, OAU officials are not truly international civil servants but merely on 'secondment': their governments can recall them at any time they please (and indeed have

*As one of the assistants of the Secretary-General pointed out to the author, failure to do so would create bad feeling in the General Secretariat.

on several occasions). Contrary to the OAU Charter, too many staff members have been encouraged to advance the policies of their own governments at the expense of the OAU.

According to the list of OAU employees at 31 November 1974, the Member-State with the highest number of its nationals in OAU service was Ethiopia (150); but this was largely due to the location of the OAU in Addis Ababa, and out of this number only nine were political officers. More significant is the place of Nigeria, with 37 employees, followed by Tanzania (19) and Cameroon (18); next comes Kenya (15) followed by Egypt (13), Ghana (10) and Zaire (7). Eleven countries — Botswana, Chad, Gabon, Ivory Coast, Lesotho, Libya, Guinea-Bissau, Mozambique, Upper Volta and Malawi — do not have any of their nationals in OAU employ. This is largely because they do not have enough competent staff to release.

The unhappy internal situation in the Secretariat culminated in 1974 when it split into various mutually hostile groups such as the francophone group versus the anglophone group, Arabs versus Africans, and small States versus larger ones. The frustrations of the Administrative Secretary-General, Nzo Ekangaki, who accused one of his assistants of betrayal, and his powerlessness to do anything about enforcing the discipline within his own staff, were the main reasons for his resignation in 1974.[10] But internal dissent within the Secretariat has a history going back to the founding of the Provisional Secretariat in 1963, which at that time was entrusted to the Ethiopian Government, assisted by an expert committee composed of the representatives from Congo, Ghana, Nigeria, Niger, Uganda and Egypt. The malfunctioning of this body was bitterly commented upon by the Ghanaian representative Ambassador Harry Amonoo, and the bickering among its members resulted in a boycott by those who were dissatisfied at not being allowed to play a more important role and assert the policies of their countries at the meetings.[11] Thus from the very beginning the emphasis was always on countries rather than individuals, making a dead letter of the provision of Article XVIII on the impartiality of the staff of the Secretariat and the obligation of non-interference by States with staff in the performance of their duties. Until the appointment of the Administrative Secretary-General in July 1964, the functioning of the Secretariat was sporadic and was little more than an administrative extension of Ethiopia's Foreign Ministry.

*The uneasy choice of Secretary-General*
At the first meeting of the Assembly of Heads of State and Government in Cairo in July 1964, there were two candidates for the post of Administrative Secretary-General, Dr Zinsou, Minister of Foreign Affairs of Dahomey, and Ambassador Diallo Telli of Guinea. Not even

the latter's excellent diplomatic record, the skill he had shown during the preparations for the Addis Ababa Summit in 1963 and his role in the rapprochement between the Casablanca and Monrovia groups would have sufficed, had it not been for the estrangement between Guinea and its former associates in the Casablanca group. Guinea's reconciliation with France also made Diallo Telli acceptable to the Brazzaville Twelve. And Guinea's neutral stand at Addis Ababa put Diallo Telli in a favourable position with the pro-Western states as well as the radical states, to which Guinea claimed to belong.

The choice of Addis Ababa as the seat of the Organization was partly a compromise, on which both the anglophone and francophone groups as well as the Arab states agreed, partly also a tribute to Emperor Haile Selassie's efforts in bringing about the agreement on setting up the OAU, and partly a recognition of Ethiopia as the independent African State of longest standing.

Diallo Telli confirmed in the course of his duties that despite the legalistic limitations imposed on the office of Administrative Secretary-General, the degree of importance and efficiency of any office depends on the capability of the man who runs it. An intimate knowledge of the proceedings of all bodies of the Organization strengthens the position of the Secretary-General in any negotiation with Member-States. In the course of preparing the sessions of the Council of Ministers, he can influence its programme and the insertion of items which he regards as important. The administration of the Organization's finances and the preparation of the budget provides him with an insight into each member's accounts with the Organization. His counsel becomes indispensable and his view on any OAU matter carries weight. Diallo Telli certainly made good use of these advantages for pursuing a radical political line — which won him more enemies than friends.

Diallo Telli's strong views on colonialism and neo-colonialism in Africa, his personal stand on the overthrow of Kwame Nkrumah of Ghana which he openly condemned, and his criticism of the Member-States with large arrears in their contributions,[12] made him unpopular with most of the 'moderate' States, who can always command a comfortable majority at OAU meeting. It therefore took six ballots at the Algiers OAU Conference in September 1968 before Diallo Telli was re-elected for a second four-year term. In two ballots, he was opposed by a Rwandan foreign ministry official, Fidele Nkundabagenzi, whose delegation, earlier in the meeting, had denounced Diallo Telli as a man who 'played politics and was not a neutral civil servant of the OAU'. Under the circumstances, Diallo Telli's re-election showed that even his critics recognized that no other man could discharge his position any better. Another factor which influenced his re-election was his effort on behalf of the OAU at seeking an end to the Nigerian civil war.

In 1972, when Diallo Telli's term expired, the situation was very different. While he still had the support of the radical members, notably the Arab states, he was regarded by the 'moderate' majority as too much of a policy-maker, with influence which exceeded the original concept of his post. The Assembly's choice was the Cameroon Minister of Labour, Nzo Ekangaki, who received 30 votes to Diallo Telli's 10. Aged thirty-eight, Ekangaki had a distinguished political career as his country's Deputy Foreign Minister, Minister of Public Health and Population, and Minister of Labour and Social Welfare. He also had the advantage of being bilingual in French and English. His election was due to two factors: first, that he was nominated by Cameroon's President Abidjo, who had the full confidence of the francophone members (the strongest critics of Diallo Telli); second, that the Assembly of Heads of State placed more emphasis on the administrative than the political profile of the Administrative Secretary-General, in accordance with the terms of the OAU Charter which define his functions. Furthermore, the election of the new Administrative Secretary-General was in line with the new trend in OAU leadership which has evolved since 1970, when the Assembly calls more often on the current Chairman of the OAU to take charge of important political tasks.

Nzo Ekangaki soon proved himself worthy of the trust the Assembly placed in him. The two eventful years of his term in office included his successful efforts at the settlement of disputes between Uganda and Tanzania, Somalia and Ethiopia, Burundi and Rwanda, Guinea and Ghana, Burundi and Tanzania, Guinea and Senegal, Guinea and Ivory Coast, and Gabon and Equatorial Guinea. The highlights of his two years were the Declaration of the Independence of Guinea-Bissau and the great upsurge in the liberation struggle in Mozambique. He worked for the rapprochment between Arab and non-Arab Africa, and for better relations between the OAU and other countries of the Third World. But he too did not escape controversy.

On 9 January 1974, Nzo Ekangaki signed, on behalf of the OAU, a contract with Lonrho, which gave this London-based multinational company the exclusive consultancy to all African countries importing oil. Under the terms of the contract, Lonrho was requested 'to establish direct contacts with the OAU Member-States hit by the oil crisis and to advise, assist and undertake on their behalf in the name of the OAU all necessary steps agreed on by Lonrho and the Member-State's government'. The contract was for a minimum period of three years and Lonrho would have opened an office in Addis Ababa. The OAU agreed to provide a diplomatic *laissez-passer* to Lonrho's executive director and his staff responsible for liaison with Member-States. Lonrho personnel were thus accorded the same diplomatic privileges enjoyed by OAU staff.[13]

As soon as the terms of the contract became public, Nzo Ekangaki was bitterly attacked by the African press, including the Paris-based *Jeune Afrique,* which called for Ekangaki's resignation on the grounds that he had signed a contract with a 'colonialist and racist' company heavily engaged in business in South Africa and Rhodesia. Of the African countries Tanzania, Kenya, Uganda and Congo expressed official disapproval of the agreement. The Administrative Secretary-General firmly rejected accusations that he had overstepped the power bestowed on him by the OAU Charter, and maintained that he was authorized to sign the contract by the OAU Committee of Seven established by the Extraordinary Session of the Council of Ministers in November 1973. He maintained that the Committee, charged with the task of looking after the interests of the African countries affected by the oil crisis, had told him he could sign contracts with the foreign companies. Although the Chairman of the Committee, Sudan's Foreign Minister Mansour Khalid, officially declared that the Committee had empowered Ekangaki to sign such contracts, a member of the Committee, Tanzanian Foreign Minister John Malecela, told the press that he always refused to recognize the validity of the OAU-Lonrho contract. The affair, which had shaken the OAU Secretariat, reached its height in February 1974. It topped the agenda of the 22nd Council of Ministers meeting on 28 February in Addis Ababa. At the last minute the session was suspended, before it had even started, at the request of the Ethiopian Government, which faced a succession of strikes and demonstrations. The OAU was thus temporarily spared a crisis. Two weeks later, on 15 March 1974, Lonrho itself asked for the cancellation of the contract, realizing that the dispute over the contract would lead to publicity surrounding Lonrho's South African and Rhodesian connections and put in jeopardy its extensive interests in Africa.

But the campaign against Nzo Ekangaki continued. He responded by posing the problem of the powers of the Administrative Secretary-General to the 11th Summit Meeting at Mogadishu in June 1974. He called the attention of the Heads of State and Government to the need to review the structure of the OAU with a view to giving the Administrative Secretary-General sufficient powers and authority over his subordinates and limiting the continual interference of Member-States in the running of the General Secretariat. In order to avoid the accusation that he sought 'more powers' for himself, and after disagreement with his own President Ahidjo of Cameroon, he announced his resignation.

The selection of his successor produced a serious crisis and badly shook the African-Arab alliance, which was running out of steam because of the disappointment of the African States at the reluctance of the Arab oil-producing States to alleviate the heavy burden of increased oil prices. The presidents and prime ministers of Africa spent fifty hours in formal session — and many more in private sessions — trying to resolve this single issue, sitting through one entire night, while the principle item of the agenda — Africa's response to the consequences of the collapse of Portugese colonialism — was dealt with by the Council of Foreign Ministers only.

In the event, the African leaders reached a compromise by dropping both the main contenders, Foreign Minister of Somalia Omar Arteh and the Foreign Minister of Zambia Vernon Mwaanga, and unanimously adopted a third candidate, William Eteki of Cameroon, who was for a time Cameroon's Education Minister before becoming President Ahidjo's close adviser. He was sworn in as the new Administrative Secretary-General on 16 June at the close of the 11th OAU Summit.

The appointment of a new Secretary-General did not in any way increase the Secretariat's authority. It is still an organ with very limited powers; a new Secretary-General can ensure its efficiency only if he is given more power to enforce the discipline and improve the service conditions of his staff. This depends on the willingness of the Council of Ministers to part with some of that authority which should, perhaps, have rested with the Secretary-General in the first place. So far there are no signs that the Council is even considering that possibility.

*Branches of the OAU Secretariat*

The growth of the activities of the OAU is best shown by the number of branches of the General Secretariat which were established during the first decade of the OAU's existence:

*OAU Bureau in New York.* This organizes the co-operation of African States at the UN. Among its tasks, specified by a resolution adopted by the Assembly of Heads of State and Government in 1970, is to ensure the implementation at the UN of resolutions adopted by the OAU.

*OAU Bureau in Geneva.* Established in 1972, its task is to see to the implementation of OAU resolutions on decolonization and apartheid in the resolutions of the UN specialized agencies. It is attached to the European headquarters of the UN at Geneva, where it co-ordinates the co-operation of OAU members attending numerous conferences of the UN and its specialized agencies. Its task is also to maintain contacts with international organizations located in Europe (except the EEC, to which the OAU is represented through its group, which conducted negotiation under the chairmanship of the Nigerian Ambassador Olu Sanu) and with

European governments.[15]

*Executive Secretariat of the OAU Scientific, Technical and Research Commission in Lagos.* The Secretariat, though responsible to the OAU Secretariat in Addis Ababa, has developed into a rather autonomous body, something which has often provoked criticism in Addis Ababa. Among its tasks is the direction of the activities of the so-called 'technical bureaux' in Yaoundé, Bangui and Nairobi. The *Inter-African Phytosanitary Council* (IAPSC), based in Yaoundé, Cameroon, assists member-governments to prevent the introduction of disease, insect pests and other enemies of plants into any part of Africa, to eradicate or control them in so far as they are present in the area, and to prevent their spread. The *Inter-African Soils Bureau* (BIS), based in Bangui, Central African Republic, maintains close contact with organizations, services and persons concerned with conservation and utilization of soils both inside and outside Africa. It keeps an up-to-date specialist library and provides an information service. The Bureau also keeps a list of the soil specialists working in Africa. *The Inter-African Bureau for Animal Resources* (IBAR), based in Nairobi, Kenya, collects animal disease statistics from member-governments, follows outbreaks of those diseases and their development, develops methods of their control and prophylaxy, and co-ordinates research work on these diseases.

*Bureau for the Placement and Education of Refugees.* Established in 1968 as an autonomous body in pursuance of a recommendation of the *Conference on the Legal, Economic and Social Aspects of African Refugee Problems* held in Addis Ababa in October 1967, it was integrated within the OAU General Secretariat from 1 June 1974.

The OAU Secretariat also maintains close co-operation with the UN Economic Commission for Africa and the African Development Bank, and with other pan-African institutions (some already in existence and others still in the making) such as the All-African Trade Organization, African Civil Aviation, the All-African Cinema Union, the Pan-African News Agency and the Centre for Linguistic and Historical Studies in Niamey.* The variety and wide scope of the activities of the OAU General Secretariat is best illustrated by the growing number of large African international conferences held under OAU auspices.

*It has offices at Kampala (OAU Inter-African Bureau of Languages) and Niamey (OAU Publication Bureau), and until recently also at Malabo (OAU Co-ordinating Office for Assistance to Equatorial Guinea).

## 4. THE SPECIALIZED COMMISSIONS

Article XX of the OAU Charter envisaged the establishment of the following five specialized commissions:
Economic and Social Commission
Educational and Cultural Commission
Health, Sanitation and Nutrition Commission
Defence Commission
Scientific, Technical and Research Commission.
It also left it for the Assembly to create any other specialized commissions it might deem necessary. Two more were added at the OAU Cairo Conference on 20 July 1964: the Commission of Jurists and the Transport and Communication Commission.

The similarity between the specialized commissions set up in accordance with the OAU Charter and the specialized agencies of the United Nations, provided for by Chapter IX of the UN Charter, (International Economic and Social Co-operation) is not accidental. Taking the UN specialized agencies as a model,[16] the founding fathers of the OAU wished to create their own instruments for promoting inter-African co-operation in the economic, social, cultural, educational, scientific, technical, health and related fields. But the OAU specialized commissions were not designed to *replace* the United Nations specialized agencies operating in Africa: what the Africans had hoped for was co-operation, not competition. This was never properly understood by the officials of the UN regional offices in Africa, who were accustomed to UN monopoly and were not prepared to surrender it in favour of any pan-African schemes. They were quick to point to the duplication of the OAU and UN programmes, and made it clear that if the OAU wished to co-operate with the UN it would have to be on UN terms. Considering that until the Congo crisis in 1961 the United Nations never really took Africa seriously, this attitude was not surprising. The pan-African projects proposed at the first sessions of the specialized commissions were remarkable examples of the OAU's clear thinking on the way the continent should be developed. But because of the clashes of interests between the OAU and the UN nothing came out of it.

When the Economic and Social Commission at its first session at Niamey in December 1963 formulated proposals for a free-trade area among OAU members, a continental system of communications, a payment union and close co-ordination of national development plans, the United Nations Commission for Africa (ECA) regarded it as an infringement of its own responsibilities. Instead of working together for the attainment of the common aims, the two organizations became entangled in bitter rivalry.[17] Similar conflict arose between the Health,

Sanitation and Nutrition Commission,[18] the Food and Agricultural Organization (FAO) and World Health Organization (WHO), as well as between the Educational and Cultural Commission[19] and the Scientific and Research Commission[20] on the one hand and UNESCO on the other.

In criticizing the lack of enthusiasm of the UN specialized agencies for the creation of the OAU specialized commissions, the author does not wish to belittle the work done by the United Nations. Africa receives approximately one half of the total technical aid provided by the United Nations Development Programme (UNDP) and about one third of its total assistance. But there are some who feel that the UN has not done enough, and who question the usefulness and viability of many of the UN schemes.[21]

Unable to match the resources and potential of the United Nations, the OAU specialized commissions never really got off the ground. Since 1964, various attempts to convene ordinary sessions of the Commissions have failed, because the two-thirds quorum stipulated by the Rules of Procedure was not attained. Therefore, at the 4th OAU Conference at Addis Ababa in November 1966, it was proposed to merge the seven existing Specialized Commissions into the following three:

*The Economic and Social Commission*, which would include the Commission on Transport and Communication;

*The Commission on Education, Science and Culture,* which would include the former Health, Sanitation and Nutrition Commission and the former Scientific, Technical and Research Commission;

*The Defence Commission*, which remained unchanged.

The Commission of Jurists reverted to its previous form as a non-governmental organization, and the OAU set up its own Legal Commission.[22]

The regrouping of the Specialized Commissions was approved by the 5th Assembly of Heads of State and Government at Algiers in 1968, and the previous decision on the bi-annual meeting of the Specialized Commissions was upheld. However, these changes did not bring the improvements expected. For example the first session of the re-constituted Economic and Social Commission was held as late as 1970.

Finally, a solution was found in convening specialized conferences of African Ministers. The meetings of African Ministers of Industries and of African Ministers of Trade and Finance[23] convened under the joint auspices of the OAU and ECA proved to serve African interests better than the system of specialized commissions. Perhaps the best example of the new practice was the African Ministerial Conference of Trade, Development and Monetary Problems held in Abidjan in May 1973, which proposed the 'African Declaration on Co-operation, Development and Economic Independence'. It was subsequently endorsed by the 10th Anniversary Summit of the OAU held at Addis Ababa one week later, and became a kind of OAU Charter of economic rights and duties of African States. It embodied most of the pan-African projects proposed by the OAU's specialized commissions ten years earlier.

## 5. THE DEFENCE COMMISSION

The Defence Commission, although formally falling into the category of the specialized commissions, has always occupied a special place within the OAU. Its history offers an interesting insight into the OAU's aspiration to create a security system in Africa with two objectives: to protect the OAU Members against aggression (South Africa and Portugal being regarded as potential aggressors), and to support liberation movements engaged in armed struggle.

The creation of the OAU Defence Commission was one of the few concessions made by the signatories of the Lagos Charter to the States of the Casablanca group. The terms of reference of a 'Joint African High Command' provided for by the Casablanca Charter, which was to 'ensure the Common Defence of Africa in the event of aggression against any part of the Continent and to safeguard the independence of African States',[24] corresponded to similar provisions included in the purposes of the OAU Charter enumerated in Article II (to defend the sovereignty, territorial integrity and independence of African states who agreed to 'co-ordinate and harmonize their general policies', among them co-operation for defence and security).

The idea of the 'Joint African Command' was advocated by President Kwame Nkrumah of Ghana along the lines of his concept of the continental union of African states.[25] Accra, which was the seat of the Permanent Military Staff Committee of the Casablanca states, was also the venue of the first meeting of the Defence Commission in December 1963. The outcome of the Accra session was a document on 'Defence arrangements in Africa', introduced at the OAU summit conference in Cairo in July 1964 by the Ghanaian Foreign Minister Kojo Botsio. The memorandum, called *Rationale for an African High Command,* contained the following main points:

– The primary function of the African High Command will be to ensure the protection of the territorial integrity and independence of all the States of the African continent. In this respect it will be concerned with external threats, in any form, to any African State.
– Another important function of the High Command will be to give

assistance to the freedom fighters of Africa, as properly organized and recognized, to liberate their countries from foreign domination.[26]

The Republic of South Africa was regarded as being the chief enemy, and the Ghanaian memorandum envisaged the possibility of a military clash unless it changed its policy of apartheid. The memorandum rather optimistically expressed a belief that South Africa might do just that when 'confronted with the prospect of a showdown with a well co-ordinated and determined African force representing the collective moral and material force of all African States.'

Assistance to the liberation movements, described as an 'inescapable moral obligation which every African State must face', was, of course, a clearly defined task of the OAU Liberation Committee. This was not an oversight on Ghana's part but a deliberate expression of its mistrust in the Liberation Committee, of which Ghana was not a member and which Nkrumah sharply attacked at the same Summit Conference.

In order to disperse the anxieties some OAU members might have about the possible use of the forces under the African High Command for intervention into their own internal affairs, the memorandum offered the following assurances.

'The African High Command is not intended for use in the maintenance of internal law and order in any Member-State without the expressed request of the duly-constituted Government, deemed to be acting on behalf of the majority of its people. Even so, the conditions for the use of the united armed forces will be clearly defined, so as not to appear in any way to interfere in the internal affairs of any African State.'

The proposal was received very sceptically. The idea of an integrated continental army under a supra-national High Command raised too many questions, such as who would be the supreme commander, where to locate the base for joint training, and what control (if any) each State would have over its participating officers and units. None of them could have been satisfactorily answered. It was felt, however, that rather than reject the proposal altogether and risk 'walk-outs' by Ghana and its friends, it would be better to dispose of it procedurally. It was therefore referred for further study by the Defence Commission.

Most of the OAU members were represented on the Defence Commission by their chiefs-of-staff and other high-ranking army officers, who by definition were regarded as 'non-political'. The British argument 'keep the army out of politics and politics out of the army' was accepted throughout Africa, notably in the Commonwealth countries, as correct and valid. Who would have thought at that time that these 'non-political officers' would soon be running the political affairs of half the African countries?

The lukewarm attitude towards the integration of African armed forces — or any kind of military co-operation, for that matter — was reflected in the activities of the Defence Commission. Its second meeting was held only after two years, at Freetown, Sierra Leone, in February 1965. The recommendation on the unification of military training in Africa and the establishment of an inter-African military academy was approved by the OAU Summit in 1966, but its implementation was beyond the OAU's reach. What model should be adopted for military training? British, American, Soviet, Chinese or French? All these countries have been training the army officers of their respective African partners. Unified military training requires unified weaponry. Which arms to choose? A choice of one of the main suppliers of arms to Africa — the United States, the Soviet Union, China, France or Britain — would inevitably be the political choice of an ally. Smaller arms producers such as Czechoslovakia or Belgium are, through their membership of military blocs (the Warsaw Pact and NATO), politically tied to super-powers, while more independent arms producers such as Yugoslavia or India are in no position to meet requirements for the amount of military equipment needed by the African continental army. Ammunition, trucks, tanks and aircraft need spare parts. The initial purchase always involves further deliveries and hence dependence on the supplier. Other problems stem from the mutual relationships among the OAU States themselves, some of which erupt from time to time into an open hostility and even armed clashes.

The spectre of an external enemy — Portugal, South Africa, Rhodesia — although given much attention in the OAU resolutions, had very little effect on the military thinking of the African leaders. These had always been pre-occupied by a quite different objective common to all political leaders in the world: that of staying in power. As more and more African leaders coming to power by means of military coups were soldiers, they were aware of the risk of allowing their own grip over their armies to slip by placing them under non-national officers from the African High Command, no matter how noble the aims professed by the High Command might be.

The Unilateral Declaration of Independence by the white minority regime in Rhodesia on 11 November 1965 revived interest in the African High Command, but only temporarily. The plan for military intervention in Rhodesia, produced by military advisers from the Member-States — who were called upon by the Council of Ministers sitting in an extraordinary session from 3 to 5 December 1965, in Addis

Ababa, to 'study and plan the use of force to assist the people of Zimbabwe' — was ignored by most. Only Ghana, Egypt, Algeria, Nigeria, Sudan, Ivory Coast, the Congo and Ethiopia pledged to send their armies to fight the Smith regime. President Banda of Malawi openly defied the idea by ridiculing the combat capabilities of the African opponents to Ian Smith. In a speech to the Malawi Parliament he said that if the African states tried armed intervention in Rhodesia, they could not win: 'The Rhodesian army could conquer all the East and Central African countries in a week and the Rhodesian Air Force could reduce every capital in the area to ashes within 24 hours.'[28]

The plan for military intervention in Rhodesia died with the overthrow of Nkrumah and the Nigerian civil war in 1966. By that time the Defence Commission was almost dead too. The Administrative Secretary-General, Diallo Telli, tried to revive it by organizing its session at Addis Ababa in January 1970, but the meeting was cancelled due to lack of a quorum. Diallo Telli angrily attacked the OAU members for their apathy in his Report submitted to the Council of Ministers:[29]

'How could Africa's inertia be explained when the OAU manifesto on Southern Africa has been rejected categorically and defiantly by South Africa and Portugal, when the Ian Smith clique on 2 March 1970 proclaimed a so-called Republic of Rhodesia, when the champion of racial discrimination and apartheid, Prime Minister John Vorster of South Africa, made a revealing trip to Rhodesia, Portugal and France last May, when the Portugese forces have since 6 July 1970 launched violent attacks on the peaceful Senegalese villages at the Senegal/Guinea-Bissau border, and finally, when the countries bordering the occupied territories have been victims of numerous other provocations? It is indeed disturbing that at a time when it is being threatened by calculated dangers, independent Africa is showing what could be termed indifference to its security, instead of expediting the establishment of the most effective means not only likely to intimidate or discourage its enemies, but also to ensure, if need be, its collective defence or the protection of the territorial integrity, sovereignty and independence of all OAU member-states. The Secretariat is still strongly convinced that Africa needs a defence commission, since the prime objective of the Organization of African Unity is the total liberation of the African continent from all foreign domination and the common defence, in a concrete manner, of the vital interests of the African peoples'.

His words were prophetic. In November 1970, three months after his warning, Guinea was invaded by troops landing from Portuguese warships. Guinean armed forces succeeded in defeating the invaders, but the event had a traumatic effect on the OAU. The emergency meeting of the Council of Ministers convened in Lagos on 9 December 1970 called upon the Defence Commission 'to study ways and means of establishing an adequate and speedy defence of African states.'[30] All that the 3rd Session of the Defence Commission, meeting in Lagos later that month, agreed upon was the appointment of an executive committee comprising the Central African Republic, Egypt, Nigeria and Tanzania. The Committee met in Mogadishu in October 1971 to draw up general plans for military measures in such instances, and these were submitted to the 4th meeting of the Defence Commission in Addis Ababa on 14 December 1971.

In his opening message to the meeting, Emperor Haile Selassie admitted that the activities of the Defence Commission had not yet received the priority they deserved. He called the Defence Commission to advance realistic proposals 'as to how independent African States can best collectively safeguard their hard-won independence and at the same time advance the cause of the African liberation struggle'. Other similar speeches were made but little was done. The chairman of the outgoing Executive Committee, Brigadier O. Olutoye of Nigeria, commended African countries for what he called 'their full support for the people of Guinea.' The point was of course that the invasion was repelled by Guinea on its own.

A new concept of a continental African High Command appeared before the Rabat Summit in 1972. Its main features were the following:
— the creation of regional defence systems, comprising units of national armed forces from States in the various regions and linked by bilateral or multilateral defence agreements;
— a military commander for each of these defence systems (who would be subordinate to a Chief of Staff), a deputy and representatives of the national armies of the States concerned;
— a unit of military defence advisers within the OAU General Secretariat, which would not only co-ordinate all matters concerning the security of Member-States but also gather military information and intelligence likely to interest the Liberation Committee. This would comprise a military adviser with the rank of brigadier, appointed for two and a half years: and three officers with the rank of major, appointed for two years. The latter would represent the three armed forces — land, sea and air. Members of the unit would be appointed by the OAU Summit on recommendations from the Defence Commission.
— the creation of a permanent defence committee which would meet

bi-annually or when called into session by the chairman of the Executive Committee. This permanent committee would comprise members, the military adviser in the OAU Secretariat, representatives of the regional executive secretariats, the OAU Secretary-General, and the Executive Secretary-General of the Liberation Committee.[31]

The plan was further discussed by the 5th session of the Defence Commission in Addis Ababa in February 1973. The meeting established a five-nation group to draw up recommendations on co-ordinating African Regional Defence and on policy for the dependent African territories. The military advisers suggested grouping the countries into three military regions — north-east, north-west, and central-east. Each country would decide which of its armed forces would be assigned for 'intervention' in its region. The new plan entailed units being trained for conventional as well as guerrilla warfare. They would be placed under a unified command, on which the countries in the region would agree among themselves. A unit of military advisers was also proposed.

The procedural ritual of the sessions of the experts of the Defence Commission continued with more meetings which, although held more frequently, were as unproductive as before. The idea of an African High Command or even of a limited military co-operation is as remote in 1977 as it was in 1963, despite the tremendous growth of African armies and the vast military expenditure by African States to the detriment of their economic development.[32] The negative attitude of the OAU Members towards the idea of any kind of co-operation over defence was reflected in the 'Recommendation on the item concerning an African Defence System' adopted at the 12th OAU Summit in Kampala in 1975. Although it states that the OAU is 'convinced of the urgent need for the co-ordination and harmonization of the activities of the OAU Member-States in the field of defence and security matters so as to maintain peace and security on the continent of Africa', it confines itself to a call 'to continue in their efforts to co-operate in the field of defence and security in accordance with the provision of Article II of the OAU Charter'. The sad truth however is that there have been no efforts whatever by OAU members to do so. Quite the reverse: those efforts that have been made have tended in the opposite direction.

The tension in the Horn of Africa and East Africa accompanied by the arms race,[33] the invasion of Benin in January 1977, border conflict between Ethiopia and Sudan in April 1977 and the invasion of Shaba province, Zaire, the month before are alarming reminders that the peace and security of Africa is threatened not only by South Africa and the Rhodesian white minority regime, but by some OAU members themselves. The military potential of many African countries is entirely tied down by national military strategies to the detriment of the OAU strategy for the liberation of the continent. This is true of the formidable armies of Egypt poised against Israel, or of the armies of Algeria, Morocco and Mauretania frozen by confrontation over the Sahara, as well as of the armed forces of Tanzania, Kenya and Uganda paralyzed by a possibility of a conflict between the East African States. The division of Africa over the conflict in Angola showed that the OAU Defence Commission has very little chance of prospering beyond the level of rhetoric.

The meeting of the Defence Commission convened on 5 November 1975 by the current Chairman of the OAU, President Idi Amin of Uganda, was yet another example of futile exercise. Apart from condemning South African aggression and expressing 'serious concern over the supply of arms to the warring Angolan nationalist movements', the Defence Commission set up an *ad hoc* Advisory Military Committee consisting of Egypt, Guinea, Kenya, Libya, Nigeria and Uganda 'to assist the current Chairman of the OAU and the Administrative Secretary-General to maintain constant contacts with the Government of National Unity in order to assess the following:

a. Whether there is a necessity to despatch an OAU Peace-Keeping Force to Angola to assist the Angolan Government to maintain peace and security:

b. Whether there is any necessity to despatch an African political military mission to help the Government of National Unity in the establishment of a national army and an administrative structure: and

c. Immediate needs of the independent State of Angola. The Defence Commission has adopted a resolution which is annexed to this report.'

The point was, of course, that there was no Government of National Unity in Angola to whom such assistance could be given. No wonder that many OAU members, who learned of these proposals from the *Memorandum of the Administrative Secretary-General on the Situation on Angola,* circulated to them at the OAU Summit in January 1976, regarded it as 'a charade completely divorced from reality'.

In his 1977 New Year message, the OAU Secretary-General William Eteki called for the founding of a 'deterrent force' to help bring down the white minority regimes in southern Africa. But this idea too was ignored.

# Chapter IV

# THE OAU LIBERATION COMMITTEE

The fact that the OAU Liberation Committee is charged with implementing the principal aim of the OAU — the liquidation of colonialism — has made it one of the most controversial organs of the Organization. The low level of publicity allowed by the OAU and its host-country Tanzania has left plenty of room for speculation about its true function. From the start the Committee acquired the reputation for being the headquarters of clandestine subversive operations, or a military high command conducting the military operations of the liberation movements. Rumours about massive purchases of Soviet, Chinese and Czech arms, emanating largely from South African sources, were designed to label the Committee as a centre of Communist conspiracy against Africa. Contrary to the general belief that the Committee is engaged mostly in arms deals and military strategy, its function has always been primarily diplomatic.[1]

The headquarters of the Liberation Committee in Dar-es-Salaam occupies a modest house in Garden Avenue, a few hundred metres from the city centre and close to the Tanzanian government buildings. The house with the green, white and gold flag of the OAU flying in front of it is often mistaken for the embassy of some unidentified country. Although the address of the Executive Secretariat of the OAU Liberation Committee is listed in the address book of foreign missions in Tanzania, few diplomats in Dar-es-Salaam know anything about it — least of all that the Committee, as a body of the OAU, co-operates closely with the UN and its specialized agencies, which are providing humanitarian assistance to liberation movements, whose armed struggle against colonialism was recognized as legitimate by the Security Council of the UN in 1972.[2] Diplomatic negotiations are also carried out by the Executive Secretariat with African States and 'friendly' non-African States — a description used for the Scandinavian countries, the Soviet Union, China and Eastern European countries. But it is dealings with the liberation movements which mainly preoccupy the Liberation Committee and its Secretariat.

Throughout its history the Liberation Committee has reflected the turbulent changes in Africa and within the OAU: the succession of *coups d'état;* the overthrow of African militant leaders, notably Nkrumah of Ghana; the Nigerian Civil War; the debate about 'Dialogue with South Africa' — all of which diverted the attention of OAU members from their obligations towards the Committee.

Within the framework of the OAU the controversies over the Committee have mainly been the result of the conflict between the States advocating armed struggle against colonial and white minority regimes and those professing 'a peaceful approach to decolonization'. As is often the case, the States with the largest arrears in contribution to the Special Fund administered by the Committee have been its noisiest critics. The constant criticism of the Committee made it subject to never-ending scrutiny by the Assembly of Heads of State and Government, which has continually changed its competence, structure and composition. Most damaging by far to the functioning of the Committee have been the disagreements between the rival liberation movements in Angola and Rhodesia. The long and often frustrating mediation between them has consumed much of the Committee's time. There has also been the problem of guarding the Committee's secrets. An essential condition for the success of any organization dealing with movements engaged in guerrilla warfare is that its communications, reports and recommendations must be kept in absolute secrecy. This was one of the main reasons why the African leaders in Addis Ababa in 1963 granted the Committee an autonomous status. The Committee was directly responsible only to the Assembly of Heads of State and Government. Meetings were closed to non-members, and the powers of the Executive Secretary of the Liberation Committee exceeded even those of the Administrative Secretary General of the OAU. Needless to say this arrangement was resented by both the General Secretariat and non-members of the Committee. When the Assembly of Heads of State and Government in 1966 decided that all the reports of the Liberation Committee were to be distributed to OAU Member-States (except Malawi), it could be safely assumed that these reports found their way to the files of embassies of non-African powers interested in the progress of the armed struggle.

## 1. RELATIONS WITH THE LIBERATION MOVEMENTS

The most important aspect of the work of the Committee is its liaison with the liberation movements. The representatives of the movements have their offices at Dar-es-Salaam and are *de facto* 'accredited' to the Committee. Visiting delegations come, often directly from the front, to discuss their problems with the Executive Secretary and his assistants;

and since the most common problem is arms, the most sought-after man is Major Ahmed Sidky, the Egyptian Assistant Executive Secretary in charge of defence matters.

The Committee deals only with the liberation movements which were accorded official OAU recognition. The recognized liberation movements become eligible not only for aid from the Special Fund but also for representation at the meetings of the Liberation Committee and the Council of Ministers. OAU recognition also provides diplomatic advantages in dealing with non-African States in order to secure further assistance.[3] There are no fixed rules governing the recognition: the main criteria are the degree of support the liberation movements enjoy in their territories and how effective is their struggle. The recognition accorded to Holden Roberto's National Liberation Front of Angola (FNLA) in 1963 was withdrawn in 1964 on the grounds that its armed struggle had waned. It was recognized again in 1972, but *au par* with another Angolan liberation movement, the People's Movement for the Liberation of Angola (MPLA), which challenged the legitimacy of the FNLA as a 'genuine liberation movement'. After ten years of OAU conciliation efforts the dispute was resolved by the military defeat of the FNLA. The same fate met the National Union for the Total Independence of Angola (UNITA), which was hastily recognized by the OAU at the insistence of Portugal wishing to negotiate the transfer of power in Angola with all three liberation movements.

The policy of 'recognition' of the liberation movements was challenged by President Samora Machel of Mozambique in his address to the 26th session of the Committee held at Maputo in January 1976. 'The correct line of action . . .' said Machel, 'was for the OAU to recognize only one organization and exclude the rest, or, in justified cases, to strive to reconcile them before recognition.'[4] Indeed, had this line been adopted, the OAU Liberation Committee could have been spared the frustrations of years of attempted conciliation between the liberation movements in Angola, as well as in Zimbabwe and to a lesser degree in South Africa. While the relations with PAIGC of Guinea-Bissau, FRELIMO of Mozambique, SWAPO of Namibia were always exemplary, the relations with ZAPU and ZANU of Zimbabwe and those between FNLA and MPLA of Angola were the greatest headache of the Committee and of the OAU as a whole. However, the solution of recognizing only one of each pair or group of rival liberation movements would hardly work.

The main obstacle towards the line proposed by Samora Machel was always the preference shown by various OAU members for various liberation movements dictated by reasons of their own policy and interests. Angola was the best example. There, President Mobutu Sese Seko of Zaire backed FNLA, largely because he had hoped that through his brother-in-law Roberto, its leader, he would acquire a strong influence in the affairs of Angola under the FNLA rule. Similarly, Zambia's preference for UNITA over MPLA was motivated by its concern for the fate of the Benguela railway, Zambia's vital export link, which passes through southern Angola. The local population, the Ovambo people, had been the core of UNITA which controlled the area.

But the decisive criterion for the support of any particular liberation movement was ideological affinity. This came out strongly during the Angolan civil war (discussed below), and it was certainly the cause of the OAU's split over the fate of Western Sahara.

In 1976 a conflict arose over the recognition of the People's Front for the Liberation of Saguiet el Hamra and Rio de Oro (POLISARIO) in Western Sahara. POLISARIO was established on 10 May 1973 and on 28 February 1976 declared the independence of the territory under the name of Saharan Republic. At the OAU Council of Ministers, which held its regular session at Addis Ababa at the time, the delegates were split. Algeria called for recognition; Morocco and Mauretania both threatened to withdraw from the OAU if POLISARIO was given the status of OAU liberation movement; seventeen other countries voted for recognition, nine more opposed it and 21 abstained. The Council of Ministers resolved the matter by leaving it to each OAU Member-State to recognize POLISARIO or not, as it chose.

The problem was not, as the Assistant Secretary-General Peter Onu told the press, that of recognizing a liberation movement but rather of recognizing the State POLISARIO had proclaimed. The issue was re-opened at the 13th OAU Summit at Mauritius. At the meeting of the Council of Ministers, which precedes that of the Assembly of Heads of State and Government, Benin introduced a resolution expressing 'grave anxiety over the seriousness of the situation prevailing in Western Sahara'. It also drew attention to 'the principle regarding the self-determination and independence of countries and peoples under foreign domination'. Benin's draft resolution then asked the Council to approve the following points:

— to confirm the right of the people of Western Sahara to self-determination and national independence according to the OAU and UN Charters;
— to ask the Administrative Secretary-General of the OAU to continue his mission until the Saharaouis people are able to exercise their right to self-determination with complete freedom;
— to express unconditional support for the just struggle being waged by the Saharaouis people to regain their national rights,
— to demand the speedy withdrawal of all foreign occupation forces, and respect for the territorial integrity of the Western Sahara and

the sovereignty of its people;
- to request the OAU Administrative Secretary-General to submit a report to the next Ministerial Council meeting about the implementation of the resolution;
- to call on all parties to the Western Sahara dispute, including the Algerian people, to take necessary measures to find a solution acceptable to all and especially to the Saharaouis people within the framework of African unity and in the service of peace, friendship and good-neighbourliness in the region.

After an acrimonious debate at the Assembly of Heads of State and Government, the resolution, although approved by the Council of Ministers, was excluded from the resolutions endorsed by the Assembly. The Assembly adopted a resolution in which it decided 'to hold an extraordinary session at summit level with the participation of the people of Western Sahara with a view to finding a lasting and just solution to the problem of Western Sahara.' No date was mentioned and there were few at that time who believed that it would really take place. The announcement made by the OAU Administrative Secretary-General, William Eteki, in February 1977, that an agreement had been reached to hold the Extraordinary Summit on 18 April 1977, came as a surprise and proved to be premature. The date of the Summit was then moved to July 1977, but there were no signs of any compromise between Algeria on the one hand and Morocco and Mauretania on the other; nor did the latter succeed in defeating POLISARIO, which relentlessly continued to fight.

A different kind of problem was faced by the Liberation Committee on the future of the Territory of the Afars and Issas (French Somalia, called also Djibouti). The OAU recognized the Front for the Liberation of the Somali Coast (FLCS), backed by Somalia, and the Djibouti Liberation Movement (DLM), backed by Ethiopia, but not the three other movements in the country − the African People's League for Independence (APLI), the People's Liberation Movement (MPL) and the National Union for Independence (UNI) − although they all have contacts with the committee.

The Committee's main concern was to guarantee the future security and territorial integrity of the Afars and Issas and to unite all liberation movements in the territory. To stop both Somalia and Ethiopia making their periodic claims on the territory, it tried to make both sign an undertaking to guarantee and respect the independence and territorial integrity of the country.

The OAU Summit at Port Louis in July 1976 approved a resolution, drafted by the Liberation Committee and endorsed by the Council of Ministers, called 'Resolution on the so-called French Somaliland (Djibouti)'. This resolution registered 'the solemn declaration of the leaders of the Ethiopian and Somali delegations before the Council of Ministers ... to recognize, respect and honour the independence and sovereignty of the so-called French Somaliland (Djibouti) and its territorial integrity after its accession to independence.' It also called for a round table conference of all political parties and the two liberation movements recognized by the OAU, to be held before the referendum on independence.

A meeting of all five political movements in the Territory, including the prime Minister Abdullah Kamil, was held under OAU auspices in Accra on 28-31 March 1977. An agreement was reached on forming a common patriotic front for a smooth transfer to independence on 26 June 1977 for which 98 per cent of the Territory's electorate voted in a referendum held on 8 May 1977.

## 2. ORGANIZATION AND STRUCTURE

The original terms of reference of the Liberation Committee set out in the Resolution on Decolonization in 1963 were elaborated in the Rules of Procedure of the Committee which described its functions as follows:
- to be responsible for the co-ordination of all assistance provided by African countries to the liberation movements;
- to manage a special fund set up for that purpose and to submit its own budget to the Council of Ministers for approval;
- to promote unity of action among the various liberation movements in order to make the best use of the assistance given to them;
- to offer its good offices to conflicting liberation movements for the purpose of reconciliation.

The Liberation Committee meets bi-annually. The first meeting ususally examines matters related to financial and material aid, while the second discusses strategy and reviews the achievements and shortcomings of the various liberation movements. Its main organs are: the Standing Committee on Information, Administration and General Policy; the Standing Committee on Finance; the Standing Committee on Defence; and the Executive Secretariat. The Committee works under the overall supervision of the OAU Administrative Secretary-General. It is directly responsible to the Council of Ministers to which it submits bi-annual reports.

The duties of the *Standing Committee on Information, Administration and General Policy* are, *inter alia:*
- to keep the OAU Member-States informed about the state of affairs in the subject territories;

— to collect information from the liberation movements and publicize their achievements;
— to advise the Liberation Committee on all aspects of the liberation movements in Africa.

*The Standing Committee on Finance:* deals with all requests for financial assistance from the liberation movements and authorizes all the expenditure of the Liberation Committee. When the volume of aid is approved, the Committee of Finance pays for the purchase of all materials (e.g. weapons, medical supplies, food) and tries to secure the lowest prices and the best quality. The Finance Committee acts only as a banker and is rarely involved in direct purchases.

*The Standing Committee on Defence* considers all requests for material aid submitted by the liberation movements and forwards its recommendations to the Standing Committee on Finance. It helps the liberation movements to choose suitable weapons and sites for training camps, and eases contact between the liberation movements and the suppliers.

*The Executive Secretariat* in Dar-es-Salaam has a regional bureau in Lusaka, and until the independence of Guinea-Bissau in 1974 it had one also in Conakry. It is the central organ of the Liberation Committee, responsible for co-ordinating the work of the standing committees and for liaison with the liberation movements whose representatives are accredited to the Committee. It also provides an administrative link with the OAU Secretariat in Addis Ababa and with the Council of Ministers and the Assembly. The Secretariat is headed by the Executive Secretary-General, who is assisted by three assistant executive secretaries. The Executive Secretary-General is appointed by the host country, Tanzania, and his assistants are appointed by the Liberation Committee.

The main task of the Executive Secretary-General is to implement the decisions of the standing committees. This involves negotiating with OAU Member-States about the passage of men and arms and the payment of contributions. He travels frequently to the various theatres of operation of the liberation movements, and often conducts delicate negotiations between the host-countries and the liberation movements. He is also involved in mediation between the rival liberation movements. He administers the Committee's accounts and prepares reports for the Council of Ministers. He is responsible for the safe custody of the Committee files and for providing administrative, technical and security services at all meetings of the Liberation Committee and its standing committees.

The post of the Executive Secretary-General was always held by a Tanzanian. The first was S. Chale (1963-6), formerly Acting Permanent Secretary of the Foreign Ministry of Tanzania. He was succeeded in

1966 by George Magombe, formerly head of International Affairs Section of the Tanzanian Foreign Ministry, who served the Committee for six years. His successor, the present Secretary-General Colonel Mbita, was the National Executive Secretary of the Tanganyika African National Union (TANU).

## 3. MEMBERSHIP

In 1977, fourteen years after its establishment, the Committee consists of twenty-one members (Algeria, Angola, Cameroon, Congo, Egypt, Ethiopia, Ghana, Guineau-Bissau, Guinea, Liberia, Libya, Mauritania, Morocco, Mozambique, Nigeria, Senegal, Somalia, Tanzania, Uganda, Zaire and Zambia). Its original composition in 1963 (Algeria, Egypt, Ethiopia, Guinea, Nigeria, Senegal, Tanzania, Uganda and Zaire) had been dictated by the need for compromise between the African groupings (Casablanca, Monrovia and Brazzaville). The criteria for membership agreed upon by the Heads of State were:
— geographical representation;
— proximity to dependent territories; and
— experience in military struggle for independence and in co-operation with the liberation movements prior to the establishment of the OAU.

The membership in the Committee was often a subject of bitter disputes. When Moise Tshombe, who had instigated the Katanga secession, became Prime Minister of the Congo (now Zaire), Uganda challenged the membership of the Congo at the Committee's meeting at Dar-es-Salaam in February 1965.[5] The Committee adopted a resolution condemning the Congo, whose Air Force planes had bombed two Ugandan villages allegedly housing anti-Tshombe rebel forces. The Ugandans released the resolution to the press and the enraged Congolese delegation disrupted the meeting. Nigeria then sided with the Congo accusing Uganda of 'betraying the secrets of the Committee'.

At the 1965 OAU Summit in Accra, Tanzania opposed Malawi's membership on the Liberation Committee which had been proposed by the Council of Ministers. Tanzania charged Malawi with collusion with the Portuguese in Mozambique to sabotage the Committee's work and threatened that if Malawi were admitted as a member, Tanzania would quit. Malawi then withdrew its candidature and Zambia and Somalia were elected members, increasing the membership to eleven. When Tanzania recognized Biafra in 1968, one year after the outbreak of the Nigerian Civil War (1967-70), Nigeria refused to send representatives to the Liberation Committee meetings and they returned to it only after the reconciliation with Tanzania at the 1970 OAU Summit.

The most serious clash over the Liberation Committee occurred at the 1964 OAU Summit in Cairo between Nkrumah, President of Ghana, and President Nyerere of Tanzania. The meeting of the Council of Ministers in Lagos in February had condemned the accusations levelled at the Liberation Committee by the Ghanaian newspaper *The Spark*.[6] But Nkrumah not only upheld the charges against the Committee but attacked it with even more vigour:

'The frequent and persistent reports from freedom fighters about the shortcomings of aid and facilities for training offered to them, make it impossible for the Government of Ghana to turn over its contribution to this Committee until a reorganization has taken place for more effective and positive action.

This is not a situation in which individuals or individual governments can be held to blame. It is our essay at a task of stupendous magnitude and with stupendous difficulties. But some of the failures of the Committee are inexcusable because they were so unnecessary.

It failed, for instance, to make the best use of our resources since some military specialists have been excluded on ideological grounds. If the Liberation Committee had made effective use of the military experience of Egypt and of Algeria, where neo-colonialist interference and espionage have been frustrated and held at bay, we would have given freedom fighters the necessary help in their liberation struggle.

The choice of the Congo (Leopoldville) as a training base for freedom fighters was a logical one, and there was every reason to accept the offer of the Congolese Government to provide offices and accommodation for the representatives of the Liberation Committee.

Africa's freedom fighters should not, however, have been exposed to the espionage, intrigues, frustrations and disappointments which they have experienced in the last eight months.'

At the time this speech was drafted, the author was a member of the staff of President Nkrumah's office and had first-hand knowledge of its contents. The next paragraph of the speech contained the name of a European officer who was responsible for training the guerrillas at one of the training camps of the Liberation Committee. President Nkrumah alleged that this officer was spying for a Western power. At the Cairo Summit, however, he was persuaded by two of his advisers to delete the paragraph. However, he neglected to adjust the text which followed, with the result that it appeared to be directed against Tanzania, where the headquarters of the Liberation Committee were located. It read:

'What could be the result of entrusting the training of freedom fighters against imperialism into the hands of an imperialist agent? Under the Liberation Committee set-up at Addis Ababa, the freedom fighters had no real security and were not provided with the instruments for their struggle, nor were food, clothing or medicine given to the men in training. Thus, their training scheme collapsed within two months under the eyes of the Liberation Committee, and the freedom fighters became disappointed, disgruntled and frustrated.'

This unforgivable slip prompted President Nyerere, raging with anger, to reject Nkrumah's accusations in the following words:

'Some curious accusations have been levelled against the Committee of Nine. Since these accusations are made by a country — the only country — which has not paid a single penny to the Committee since its establishment, I do not propose to pay much attention to them. But I want to disabuse this conference of one or two things.
    The non-payment has nothing to do with the alleged inefficiency of the Liberation Committee. The real reason is extremely petty. The decision not to contribute funds was made at Addis Ababa as soon as the conference committed the unforgivable crime of not including Ghana on the Committee and of choosing Dar es Salaam as its headquarters. This is the petty peevishness which prevents an African country from contributing funds towards the liberation of our suffering brethren in Mozambique, Angola and Portuguese Guinea . . .'

Nyerere paused and then angrily attacked Nkrumah, saying:

'The Great Osagyefo[7] then asked the question: What could be the result of entrusting the training of freedom fighters against imperialism into the hands of an imperialist agent? . . . First, if my interpretation of the statement is right and it really means that the President of Ghana believes that the Liberation Committee should have been housed in Leopoldville, then all I can do is to ask you to imagine what the consequences would have been. Second, if the reference to an imperialist agent refers to my country, or any of its leaders, those who know my country or its leaders and its people, and all those who have any respect for the truth, know that it is a lie.'

Nyerere concluded with sharp criticism of Ghana's proposal for the establishment of a Union Government of Africa. The delegates of the

Assembly, shocked by his outburst, tried to restore the spirit of friendliness and understanding which had hitherto prevailed. Through the personal intervention of the President of Guinea, Sekou Touré, the Ghanaian and Tanzanian leaders made no further comments on the matter. Needless to say, the incident attracted the attention of the Western press, which regarded it as the greatest sensation of the Cairo Summit. Ghana made a gesture of reconciliation by paying its overdue contribution to the Liberation Committee, but its attempt to reorganize the Committee was thwarted.

Ghana continued to resent its exclusion from the Liberation Committee. It felt entitled to membership because of the length of time during which it had provided financial support to the liberation movement before the establishment of the Committee. Ghanaian aid was channelled through its bureau of African Affairs, which operated a training centre at Winneba (Ghana) and organized conferences of freedom fighters, the last of which was held in 1962. While the qualification for membership based on experience in military struggle was recognized in the case of Algeria and Egypt, it was denied to Ghana because of firm opposition by members of the Monrovia group. They maintained that Ghana also used its Bureau of African Affairs for subversive activities against other independent African States. Ghana only became a member of the Committee nine years later, in 1972, when the membership was enlarged from thirteen to seventeen. In January 1973 Ghana was host to the 21st meeting of the Committee, which adopted the 'Accra Declaration on the new strategy for the liberation of Africa'.

## 4. REFORM LIMITING THE POWERS OF THE LIBERATION COMMITTEE

In 1966, the Council of Ministers, at its Addis Ababa Session, put an end to the autonomy of the Liberation Committee. It restricted the Committee's competence to take independent action, and placed the Committee under the overall control of the OAU Secretariat.[8] Examination of the work of the Committee continued at the 12th Session of the Council (in Addis Ababa in February 1969), which asked the '*Ad Hoc* Committee of Experts' to review the strategy in the conduct of the armed struggle.[9] The Council also yielded to the pressure from Member-States criticizing the Committee's secrecy, and decided that all members of the OAU should have the right to attend meetings of the Committee as observers. Accordingly, regular military bulletins on the activities of the various liberation movements, as well as all documents of the Liberation Committee, were circulated to Member-States of OAU having no diplomatic relations with Portugal and the regimes of Pretoria and Salisbury. This excluded only Malawi.

The Council then asked the Administrative Secretary-General to (1) investigate the non-contribution by Member-States to the Special Fund and the reasons for the loss of enthusiasm in the Liberation Committee, and (2) investigate the problems which hinder its proper functioning.

However, the work of the Committee did not improve. In trying to limit the authority of the Executive Secretariat and subject all its dealings to the public scrutiny of the Council of Ministers, reformers failed to understand that there is a fundamental difference in character between the Committee and any other organ of the OAU. Unlike the Council of Ministers and the Assembly of Heads of State and Government, which are organs of *deliberation*, the Liberation Committee is an organ of *action*. Consensus in the Assembly of Heads of State and Government results in the forging of the bonds of African unity. In the case of the Liberation Committee, however, the price of unanimity is often inaction. The dissent among OAU members at the meetings of the Council of Ministers or the Assembly, which results in compromise resolutions, has serious implications when these resolutions have to be implemented by the Liberation Committee.

There were a number of reasons for 'the loss of enthusiasm' about the Liberation Committee. The outbreak of the Nigerian Civil War in 1967, the campaign for 'Dialogue' with South Africa launched by President Houphouet-Boigny in 1970, the failure of sanctions against Rhodesia and the aggravation of the overall economic situation in Africa, made some OAU members regard the Liberation Committee as useless and the contribution to the Special Fund as unnecessary. However, while effectively undermining the authority and efficiency of the committee by this lack of commitment, they continued to blame it for failing to achieve tangible results in decolonization. Success in decolonization requires sustained effort, vigour and above all arms to fight with and money to meet the material needs of the people who do the fighting. The OAU Liberation Committee had none of these things which OAU members were supposed to provide but did not.

A turn for the better came after the 1972 OAU Summit at Rabat. The host of the Summit, King Hassan II of Morocco, who had not previously distinguished himself by support for the liberation movements announced a donation of $1 million to the OAU's African Liberation Committee's Fund. 'Without freedom, there can be no progress, nor prosperity, nor happiness, nor greatness', said the King and concluded his speech by saying: 'All independent countries should allow liberation movements to install military bases on their territories, even if they are bombed day and night by the enemy.[10]

A number of important decisions concerning the Liberation Committee were adopted by the Rabat Summit:

— to increase contributions to the Special Fund by 50 per cent;
— to grant the right of the representatives of liberation movements to speak at the meetings of the Council of Ministers on all matters concerning the liberation struggle, and to attend the closed sessions of the Assembly;
— to enlarge the membership of the Liberation Committee to seventeen members (the new members being Cameroon, Congo, Ghana, Libya, Mauritania and Morocco).

The military approach to the liberation struggle was elaborated in the report the Liberation Committee submitted to the Summit. The report proposed that regional defence commands be set up among liberated countries bordering those ruled by white minority regimes. Subject to the overall direction of the OAU's high command, each regional command would have special responsibility for the liberation of the territories in its area. The proposal never materialized.

The 'spirit of Rabat' was evident also in *Recommendations on Special Measures to be adopted on decolonization and the struggle against apartheid and racial discrimination,*[11] which called for the strengthening of the means of defence of Southern African States. The OAU Member-States were asked to supply those States with modern military equipment and military assistance, including men.

The Portuguese territories were made the first priority in Africa's liberation struggle. A *Resolution on Portuguese colonies,* apart from deciding to increase assistance to the liberation movements of Angola, Mozambique and Guinea-Bissau, called for speeding up total liberation of Angola, Mozambique and Guinea-Bissau 'through concerted and practical actions of all kinds and at all levels'. This implied direct military support of the liberation movements in these territories.

The decision, in principle, to involve African armies directly in the liberation struggle constituted one of the major policy shifts of the OAU. Previously the OAU had strictly upheld that national liberation movements should wage their own guerrilla wars with no greater support than the assurance of material and moral backing from independent African States. It appeared, however, that the proposal for the direct involvement of African armies in the respective liberation struggles in Guinea-Bissau, Mozambique and Angola, as well as in Rhodesia, was not favoured by the leaders of the liberation movements concerned. They insisted that their own guerrilla fighters were quite capable of winning their own battles. They asked only for arms and more arms, money, equipment and shelter for training and operational camps — but *not men*. This, of course, was understandable: while arms and money are anonymous, men are not. The ties established between a liberation movement and the country sending men (whether as volunteers or as members of regular army units) may prove difficult, if not impossible, to cut should the policies of the liberation movements and the donor-country differ. Besides, external military assistance could irreparably damage the credibility of the liberation movements' leaders with their own people and cast doubts on their ability to free themselves from foreign intervention, no matter how well motivated, after the war.

The validity of these arguments, for which the policy pursued by the Viet-Cong in Vietnam was a case in point, was eventually accepted. The principle that the primary responsibility for carrying out armed struggle rests with a liberation movement prevailed and was embodied in all subsequent OAU resolutions on the OAU Liberation Committee.[12]

The only departure from this principle was the assistance of some 10,000 — 12,000 Cuban soldiers who fought (and won) battles for the MPLA in Angola. There were two reasons for the MPLA's decision to employ them: the first was the need for men trained to use the Soviet arms and military equipment supplied to the MPLA on a massive scale as a result of the South African intervention. The second was that the Cubans — fighting for the cause, and not, like the mercenaries in the ranks of FNLA and UNITA, for money — posed a smaller political problem than a contingent of similar strength provided by a single African country. Because of the OAU split over Angola, which ruled out any possibility of an OAU joint force, the Cubans appeared to be the kind of force whose presence the MPLA could justify without compromising its political stand *vis-à-vis* the OAU and Africa. Still only half of the OAU Members approved of the Cuban intervention, and even those who did felt very uneasy about it.


## 5. THE ACCRA DECLARATION ON THE NEW LIBERATION STRATEGY

The Rabat Summit initiated another reform of the Liberation Committee. The task was entrusted to a committee composed of representatives from Algeria, Central African Republic, Ethiopia, Kenya, Morocco, Senegal and Sierra Leone, and its final report was unanimously adopted at the 21st Session of the Liberation Committee held in Accra in January 1973. The recommendations contained in the report were embodied in 'The Accra Declaration on the new Strategy for the Liberation of Africa.'[13] The following are its main points:

— The liberation of Africa is the collective responsibility of all African States. While the responsibilities of carrying on the armed struggle rest with the liberation movements, its intensification presupposes the availability of appropriate resources at their disposal.
— The 'collective responsibility' of OAU Member-States was specified as follows:
(a) to pay immediately their outstanding dues to the Special Fund;
(b) to provide additional, voluntary, material and financial assistance to the liberation movements, which *is a must* in the current situation;
(c) to provide training facilities for the cadres of the liberation movements;
(d) to be ready for collective military and economic assistance to any OAU State in case it becomes the victim of aggression from Portugal, Rhodesia or South Africa.
— The role of the liberation movements was specified as follows:
(a) granting of recognition and of assistance will be only to the 'Fronts' which are politically and militarily united and which can provide evidence of effective operation within the country:
(b) the largest part of the assistance will be given to the liberation movements in the Portuguese territories.
— The Declaration stressed the need to strengthen the institutional structure of the Executive Secretariat in order to enhance its capacity to respond effectively to the urgent needs of the next stage of the liberation struggle.

The Declaration reaffirmed the determination of the Liberation Committee to make the second decade of the OAU a decade of the armed struggle with tangible and decisive victories.


## 6. FINANCIAL DIFFICULTIES

The Special Fund administered by the Liberation Committee started in 1963 on the basis of voluntary contributions. A year later the Assembly of Heads of State and Government at its session in Cairo in 1964 resolved to levy a fixed fee based on UN membership fees. That did not bring the expected improvement, and the non-payment of the membership fees to the OAU became a serious problem for the Organization.

An example of the Committee's financial difficulties in the past was the crisis over its budget for the 1966-7 financial year debated at the Council of Ministers' meeting in Addis Ababa in November 1966. There Tunisia objected to the very high administrative costs, the manner in which funds were managed, and the choice of beneficiaries of these funds. The Tunisian delegate accused the Committee of allocating aid to movements of a certain political ideology, 'even when these were not carrying out liberation activities', and of using most of the sum available to the Committee for its own maintenance so that little was left for other purposes.

In 1966-7 the Committee's budget had been set at £45,000. Nigeria suggested that it should be reduced to £35,000, and after a heated debate the Council of Ministers failed to agree on any budget at all and referred the matter to the Assembly of Heads of State and Government. When a majority of the Assembly appeared to be also in favour of cutting the budget of the Committee, President Nyerere walked out of the meeting in protest. Eventually a compromise was reached — to maintain the same budget for another year — but the Member-States still did not pay their dues.

The financial position of the Liberation Committee became so precarious that at almost every session of the Council of Ministers there was an appeal to the members in arrears — but in vain. The lack of funds created a gap between what the Committee promised to the liberation movements and what it was able to give. It took nine years before the situation improved. Not until 1974 was the Committee in a position to allocate funds to the liberation movements in full accordance with the scale agreed in Accra in 1973.[14] However, the amount channelled to the liberation movements by the OAU Liberation Committee is still less than the volume of aid they receive directly from OAU members and from friendly governments outside Africa.

The bulk of outside aid to the liberation movements comes from the Scandinavian countries, Holland, China, the Soviet Union and Eastern Europe (notably Yugoslavia and Romania). Sweden has always been a leading supporter of the liberation movements, and the amount earmarked for this purpose in the budget of the Swedish International Development Agency (SIDA) for 1977-8 was £7 million — which is about double the amount the Committee received from OAU members.

The volume of Chinese, Soviet and East European aid is not known. However, unlike the Scandinavian and Dutch aid which is described as 'humanitarian' and consists of medical and food supplies, clothing and educational facilities for the civilian population in the liberated areas and for refugees, the Soviet, Chinese and East European assistance consists largely of arms supplies, the quantity of which is not made public. The liberation movements, however, are cautious and do not wish to rely on supplies from the Soviet Union and China, mainly because they are aware of the kind of dependence to which it can lead and which has been experienced by Egypt in relation to the Soviet Union. Of all Communist countries preference is given to aid from Yugoslavia and Romania. This is understandable. Yugoslavia is sympathetic because of its policy of non-alignment; and Romania commands the respect of Africa because it has been promoting a policy of active participation by small and medium-sized States in the settlement of world problems, and because it has succeeded in maintaining considerable independence from the Soviet Union.[15]

One of the reasons why the liberation movements (or the OAU Liberation Committee acting on their behalf) accepted Communist aid was because they had been turned down by the Western powers. The United States, Britain, France, West Germany and Italy justified their refusal by reference to the principle of 'non-intervention in the internal affairs of other States' and by their abhorrence of violence. Curiously enough this did not prevent them from supplying arms to the regimes the liberation movements were fighting. OAU delegations, led in 1970 by the OAU chairman President Kaunda, and in 1971 by his successor President Ould Daddah, toured the NATO countries trying to dissuade them from supplying arms to South Africa and Portugal. They were snubbed in London and Washington, and did not receive friendly receptions in other NATO capitals. The Scandinavian countries, providing non-military aid only, declined requests for arms on the grounds of their 'neutrality' and their disapproval of violence.

Although various liberation movements have drawn heavily on Chinese and Soviet instructors, who have taught them the rules of modern guerrilla warfare, and although some of their leaders are convinced Marxists, the assistance has not given the donors any great influence. Neither Guinea-Bissau nor Mozambique, although both fought their wars with Communist arms, became 'Communist States' or satellites of Moscow or Peking. They both retained the basic African nationalist orientation, firmly opposing any external intervention in their affairs, whether coming from the West or the East. This could also be said for the MPLA which, although it received massive military aid from the Soviet Union, did not turn Angola into a Soviet satellite.


## 7. CONFRONTATION IN SOUTHERN AFRICA

The collapse of the Portuguese colonial empire in 1974 had a profound effect on the work of the Committee, which assumed an important diplomatic role in the ensuing negotiations regarding the transfer of power in Guinea-Bissau, Mozambique and Angola. The Committee drew up a plan of economic assistance to Guinea Bissau based on the report of its fact-finding mission, made prior to Guinea-Bissau's independence. In 1974 the Committee's current chairman Vincent Efan, Foreign Minister of Cameroon, led a delegation of the Committee to Sweden, Norway, Finland, Eastern Germany, Hungary and Yugoslavia to seek assistance for the Programme of Action defining the economic needs of Guinea-Bissau. In close co-operation with FRELIMO the Committee worked out the time-table for the transitional period in Mozambique leading to full independence on 25 June 1975. The members of the Executive Secretariat spent days and nights in session with the representatives of MPLA, FNLA and UNITA trying to find a common platform for the forthcoming negotiations with Portugal about Angola's independence, and finally succeeded in signing the so-called 'Mombasa Agreement' on 5 January 1975.[16]

Since Autumn 1974 the OAU initiative on the liberation of southern Africa, namely Rhodesia and Namibia, has passed into the hands of the 'front line Presidents' — Julius Nyerere of Tanzania, Kenneth Kaunda of Zambia, Seretse Khama of Botswana and Samora Machel of Mozambique (at first in his capacity of President of FRELIMO). In 1976 they were joined by President Angostinho Neto of Angola. Their diplomacy of 'détente' is described in Chapter VIII. The OAU Liberation Committee, and the staff of the Executive Secretariat at Dar-es-Salaam and its office at Lusaka, have effectively been integrated into the diplomatic teams of the five Presidents. However, although fully engaged in the peace initiative of the five Presidents, the Committee has never stopped reminding the African Presidents of the necessity to get ready for the intensification of the armed struggle should the peace efforts fail.

The Committee helped to work out the Lusaka Agreement of 10 December 1974 by virtue of which ZANU, ZAPU and FROLIZI agreed to merge with the ANC of Zimbabwe into one movement accepting the name of ANC. And at its meeting in Dar-es-Salaam in January 1975 the Liberation Committee adopted a new strategy for the liberation of southern Africa, which was subsequently endorsed by the Extraordinary Session of the Council of Ministers convened at Dar-es-Salaam in April the same year and became known as the 'Dar-es-Salaam Declaration' on southern Africa. One month after the adoption of the Dar-es-Salaam Declaration the Committee held a special five-day meeting of the ambassadors of the Member-States of the Committee to discuss contingency plans for the armed struggle in Rhodesia and Namibia.

After the Committee's meeting in Dakar in June 1975 the fighting between the Angolan liberation movements overshadowed all its other activities, and the situation in Angola was the main preoccupation of the Committee until its meeting at Maputo in January 1976.

Since 1976 the OAU Liberation Committee has become more identified with the policies of Tanzania and Mozambique than with those of the OAU; and while during the same period the OAU has become more conservative, indecisive and weak, the Committee has considerably strengthened its position *vis á vis* both the Organization and the OAU Member-States individually, a development which has not been viewed favourably in Addis Ababa. The Committee has been vigorously prodding the OAU Member-States to pay up their dues to the Special Fund, and to give more assistance to the newly independent states and more arms to the liberation movements. It threw its full support (against the protests of Morocco and Mauritania) behind POLISARIO, and behind the Patriotic Front (despite the vehement protests of Nkomo and Bishop Muzorewa); and its close ties with the Palestinian Liberation Movement (PLO) have been further strengthened by the growing co-operation of their respective enemies — South Africa and Israel. It sees PLO as an ally which could induce the Arabs to sever their relations with South Africa and fill the empty coffers of the Committee with funds from which arms for ZIPA and SWAPO could be bought. However, the militant posture of the Committee on the liberation of South Africa, and its pronounced anti-Israeli stand, has led to a conflict with the Organization where the 'moderates' still command a majority sufficient to cut the Committee down to its size as a body formally subordinated to both the Council and the Assembly.

# Chapter V

# HOW THE OAU SETTLES DISPUTES AMONG ITS MEMBERS

Disputes among the OAU members have been settled through direct negotiations between States, good offices offered by third parties, *ad hoc* committees composed of Heads of State, and diplomatic negotiations conducted during sessions of the Assembly of Heads of State and Government. A rather striking feature of the OAU's handling of disputes is that not one has ever been dealt with by the organ created specifically for that purpose, The Commission of Mediation, Conciliation and Arbitration.[1] Established in 1964, it was regarded by the Emperor Haile Selassie of Ethiopia as the *raison d'être* of the Organization.[2] The Commission was to be one of the four principal institutions of the OAU, set up as an autonomous body with its own Protocol which forms an integral part of the Charter of the OAU.[3] It emerged very slowly. The twenty-one members of the Commission headed by Justice M. A. Odesanya of Nigeria were appointed by the OAU Summit in Accra in October 1965. But its first meeting took place in Addis Ababa as late as in 1967. By that time it had already become clear that the OAU had embarked on a totally different course for the settlement of disputes from that envisaged by the Charter and the Protocol of the Commission.

Out of the three means of peaceful settlement of disputes offered by the Protocol — mediation, conciliation and arbitration — only the first two have been employed, but *outside* the framework of the Commission. That the OAU has refrained from resorting to judicial means of settlement or to an option to refer the dispute to the International Court of Justice is not surprising. There are a number of reasons why African States are reluctant to refer their disputes to the International Court.

First, the newly-independent African States are sensitive about their sovereign rights and resent outside interference — hence their refusal to enter into obligations which would be enforceable by a supranational authority. Second, few of them are willing to submit disputes for judicial settlement unless they are absolutely sure of their legal position. They hold the view that since their vital interests are at stake, the problem cannot be reduced to a simple matter of legal interpretation. Third, the rules of customary international law are often so uncertain that many States prefer to rely upon their bargaining position rather than on what they believe may be their rights. Fourth, most African States view the present rules of international law as the outcome of the practice of Western States, not necessarily reflecting the common interest of *all* States. They are unwilling to have their disputes settled by standards to which they have not agreed. In this connection they regard the International Court of Justice as an institution of European judges and therefore not representative of the international community, least of all Africa. It is for the same reason that the procedure of arbitration, presupposing a submission to the arbitration tribunal[4] has also never been employed: 'My OAU experience', said Justice M. A. Odesanya, 'is that States will always show great reluctance in limiting their own political and diplomatic freedom beyond what they regard as absolutely necessary to secure their immediate objectives.'[5]

The approach towards the peaceful settlement of disputes evolved along the following lines:
— The solution to the dispute was sought by an agreement by both parties based on the consensus of the OAU Member-States at large.
— Great importance was attached to the counsel of recognized leaders of African opinion, such as the late Emperor Haile Selassie.
— The search for compromise was regarded as a moral obligation on the conflicting parties to settle their dispute in the interests of African unity.

In the course of the last fourteen years the OAU machinery for the peaceful settlement of disputes has developed this into one of its most important functions and become its main source of strength. The emphasis is on negotiation rather than on the rule of law. The main features are:
— an African framework which excludes external interference;
— the employment of an individual Head of State, or a group of Heads of State, to form an *ad hoc* mediation or conciliation body;
— guiding principles applied in various types of conflict.

## 1. THE AFRICAN FRAMEWORK

The desire to solve problems within an African framework has been connected with that mistrust of external influences which is common among African statesmen. But it also stems from deep reservations about the principles of international law in the western world. With the creation of the OAU, African leaders hoped they would be able to set their own standards for the conduct of inter-State relations, standards which would derive not from the customs and laws of the colonial powers but from the principles of the OAU. In this respect the OAU formulated general principles to be observed by the conflicting parties. It refrained from pronouncing judgements on specific issues or disputes because to do so would have implied that the OAU was acting as a supranational authority, a position the OAU has always declined to adopt. The principle of settling all inter-African disputes strictly within an African framework was first officially announced by Emperor Haile Selassie.[6] It has since found expression in many OAU resolutions.[7]

The competence of the OAU to deal with conflicts involving 'actions with respect to threats to the peace, breaches of the peace, and acts of aggression' — which, strictly, fall within the competence of the Security Council in accordance with Chapter VII of the UN Charter — has been recognized by the Security Council.[8] The Security Council, in its Resolution on the Congo situation adopted on 30 December 1964, stated that it was 'convinced that the Organization of African Unity should be able, in the context of Article 52 of the Charter, to help find a peaceful solution to all the problems and disputes affecting peace and security in the continent of Africa'. Whether this acknowledgement of the primary responsibility of the OAU for African problems was based on pragmatism rather than competence is irrelevant. Ever since 1964 the Security Council has always encouraged States in conflict to refer to the OAU.

In the case of Angola, the Security Council was only asked to handle the aggression by South Africa, not the civil war as a whole. Similarly, an appeal was made to the Security Council to condemn the Israeli raid on Entebbe; but it was not asked also to condemn Kenya, which had been accused by Uganda of complicity — a charge strongly denied by the Kenyan Foreign Minister.

When President Idi Amin of Uganda cabled the UN Secretary Dr Kurt Waldheim in July 1976, asking him to institute an international enquiry into what he described as Kenya's oil embargo imposed on Uganda, the United Nations made it clear that the matter should have been handled by the OAU. This is also how the UN felt about the invasion of Benin by a force of mercenaries in January 1977, and about the invasion of Shaba province, Zaire, in March 1977 by the former Katanga gendarmes.

The competence of the OAU to settle disputes in Africa is not contradicted by the fact that in certain cases — such as colonialism, Rhodesia, the apartheid policy of South Africa, and the latter's illegal occupation of Namibia — the OAU does call on the UN to intervene. These problems are regarded by the OAU not only as having profound international implications but as being UN responsibilities under the terms of its Charter. The UN's involvement in mediation efforts between Algeria on one hand and Morocco and Mauretania on the other, in their dispute over the future of Western Sahara, is a case in point. In the case of Rhodesia there is a direct responsibility on the part of a non-African power, Great Britain, that is recognized both by the OAU and the UN.

## 2. EMPLOYMENT OF SUPREME AUTHORITY

It has been the influence of Africa's elder statesmen, who command the confidence of disputing parties, that has prevented African inter-State disputes from involving others — something that would jeopardize the OAU's very existence. The African tradition of respecting the wisdom of the elders and men of distinction is seen in the frequency with which Emperor Haile Selassie was asked to act as conciliator and mediator. African States appear to rely more on an individual statesman, or on collective advice by a group of statesmen, than on an international body of professional conciliators, mediators and arbitrators.

Thus, when in October 1963 the first dispute between OAU members broke out, over the Algerian-Moroccan border, it was Emperor Haile Selassie and President Modibo Keita who assumed the role of personal peace-makers. The success of OAU intervention in the disputes between Somalia and Ethiopia and Somalia and Kenya was achieved by the collective authority of Africa's foreign ministers, who met in an extraordinary session at Dar-es-Salaam in February 1964. When the dispute flared up again at the 1973 OAU Summit in Addis Ababa, the five Heads of State composing the OAU *ad hoc* mediation committee (Nigeria, Senegal, Liberia, Guinea and Mali) persuaded President Barre of Somalia to co-operate with the committee in a search for a compromise. It was the *ad hoc* committee, consisting of Emperor Haile Selassie and Presidents Tubman of Liberia, Keita of Mali, Nyerere of Tanzania and Nasser of Egypt, which in 1966 resolved a dispute between Ghana and Guinea following the detention by Ghana of a Guinean delegation. Presidents of the Central African States (Presidents Tombalbaye of Chad, Bokassa of the Central African Republic, Bongo of Gabon, and Ahidjo of Cameroon) initiated a reconciliation between President Mobuto of Zaire and President Ngouabi of the Congo, which led to the signing of the 'Manifesto of Reconciliation' on 16 June 1970.

During 1970, Emperor Haile Selassie succeeded in bringing about a reconciliation between Nigeria on the one hand and Ivory Coast, Tanzania and Zambia on the other, three of the four countries which had recognized Biafra. Gabon was the only one of the four African States that recognized Biafra, which refused to normalize relations with Nigeria after the war ended in January 1970. Libreville (Gabon) was used as a staging post for arms supplies to Biafra and a number of

Nigerian war orphans were shipped to Gabon and then returned to Nigeria by relief organizations. Eventually in 1971, Gabon was reconciled with Nigeria through the good offices of Presidents Eyadema (Togo) and Ahidjo (Cameroon). President Diori (Niger) acted as mediator between Chad and Libya when it was decided to re-establish diplomatic relations, which had been severed in August 1971 after Chad accused Libya of interfering in its internal affairs.

The OAU's *ad hoc* Special Mediation Commission, presided over by Emperor Haile Selassie, achieved in 1972 a reconciliation between Senegal and Guinea. The authority of the Heads of State was also sought by the OAU Liberation movements in Rhodesia and Angola. A more recent example is the successful mediation by President Sekou Touré of Guinea between Mali and Upper Volta, concerning a border dispute between the two countries. On 11 July 1975 Presidents Traore of Mali and Lamizana of Upper Volta signed at Conakry a 'permanent peace agreement'.

In connection with this it has been interesting to see how men of the stature of Emperor Haile Selassie of Ethiopia or General Yakubu Gowon of Nigeria, who were instrumental in rallying the OAU ranks against South Africa's 'outward policy', quickly fell into oblivion after they were deposed. It has to be remembered, of course, that the international respect for a Head of State may not necessarily be shared by the people of his own country. The Emperor's Pan-African policies, for example, were in sharp contrast with his feudal rule in Ethiopia. When the demolition of his powers by the Co-ordinating Committee of the Ethiopian Armed Forces, Police and Territorial Army (known as 'Dergue') gradually began in February 1974, Africa looked on with apprehension. But the exposure of the Emperor's career before and after his final deposition in September 1974 was too convincing to be challenged, and the change was accepted almost with relief. In the case of General Gowon, again, his running of the affairs of Nigeria was not in keeping with his performance on the international scene. His failure to keep his promise to hand the country back to civilian rule in January 1976 was regarded by most observers as one of the main reasons for his overthrow in July 1975.

3. GUIDING PRINCIPLES APPLIED IN VARIOUS TYPES OF CONFLICT

The following are the main types of dispute some of which lead to open conflict:
— boundary and territorial disputes
— refugee problems

— charges of subversion

— disputes arising out of non-recognition of a government coming to power by coup d'état.

*Boundary and territorial disputes.*

Among the most explosive of conflicting interests are boundary and territorial disputes. Common tradition has resulted in boundaries not being firmly fixed. In Africa there are few natural frontiers which geographically separate one nation from another, and coherent tribal groupings are often divided between national governments. The Ewe tribes, for example, are divided between Benin (Dahomey), Togo and Ghana, and tribal conflict was the cause of the hostilities between Rwanda and Burundi. Most of these conflicts can be classified as: (a) concerning extension of national territory; and (b) concerning the regrouping of tribal, religious or cultural entities, irrespective of present boundaries.

The present boundaries are the legacy of colonial frontiers, drawn by the rival colonial powers. Some of them were fixed by administering powers which were ignorant of the political, social, economic and ethnic interests of the areas. As a result, independent Africa inherited disputes over boundaries or parts of territories between Somalia and Ethiopia, Somalia and Kenya, Algeria and Morocco; disputes involving a Moroccan claim against Mauritania, and a Tunisian claim to parts of the Algerian Sahara; a dispute between Niger and Dahomey (Benin) over the island of Lette; border disputes between Malawi and Zambia, Malawi and Tanzania, Ghana and Togo, and Chad and Libya.[9]

In February 1976 a startling claim to large areas of Kenya and Sudan was made by President Amin of Uganda.[10] In 1975 a dispute broke out between Algeria on the one hand and Morocco and Mauritania on the other about the future of the Western Sahara. Algeria opposed the tripartite agreement between Spain, Morocco and Mauritania of 14 November 1975, according to which Morocco and Mauritania were to take over the administration of the Spanish Sahara after the termination of the Spanish colonial rule fixed to take place on 29 February 1976. Algeria insisted that the future of the territory was to be decided by its people (a view upheld also by the UN) and supported the cause of the People's Front for the Liberation of Saguiet el Hamra and Rio de Oro (POLISARIO) which declared the independence of the territory under the name Saharan Democratic Arab Republic on 28 February 1976.[11]

Another case was the claim made by Ethiopia and Somalia on the Territory of the Afars and Issas (formerly French Somaliland, also called Djibouti), which they regarded to have been historically linked with their respective countries. The clash between Ethiopia and Somalia was a prominent feature at the 12th OAU Summit in Kampala in July 1975 and at the 13th Summit in Port Louis in 1976. All sessions of the Council of Ministers during 1975 and 1976 as well as those of the Liberation Committee during the same period were also preoccupied by the dispute. A solution was found in 1976 when both countries solemnly declared their respect for the territorial integrity of the Territory of the Afars and Issas after its independence in 1977.

All present territorial and boundary problems of Africa have their colonial past. The nationalist leaders, at the time of their struggle for independence, were strongly critical of the international borders they were about to inherit. Their anti-colonialist feelings led them naturally to resent boundaries arbitrarily imposed by colonial powers. For those who wished to abolish the entire colonial legacy, the logical corollary would have been to reject the colonial boundaries as well. However, most of the independent African States chose to preserve their existing borders. This can be explained as follows:

— The majority of African States had not yet achieved internal stability and cohesion, and would only be further disturbed by boundary revisions.
— The maintenance of the *status quo* began to be associated with the preservation of the State as a political unit. If the right to secede were granted to any region, no matter how well-justified its claim to self-determination might appear in international law, it was felt that this would stimulate secessionist demands in other regions with the resulting disintegration of the parent-State. Hence the reluctance of the majority of OAU members to recognize Biafra, and the plight of the Eritreans seeking independent Eritrea.
— The 'tribal balance' on which the political structure of a State often depends would be upset by any changes of the frontiers which divide tribes between neighbouring States. The annexation of a population could increase the size of a tribe inside a country, which might then quickly lead to internal conflict. Thus, internal political considerations were an important factor in the Nigerian Government's opposition to proposals for the annexation of the Yoruba-populated area of Benin (Dahomey). The cautious policies of Gabon and Cameroon regarding the future of Spanish-controlled Rio Muni arose because its absorption could have involved the incorporation of additional Fang in their respective territories.[1][2]
— The need of the majority of African States to define themselves by means of colonial boundaries led them to the realization that they have a mutual interest in the *status quo*. Since many are vulnerable to external incitement to secession, it was obvious to most OAU members that a reciprocal respect for boundaries, and abstention from demands for their immediate revision, would be to their general advantage. This principle of preserving the *status quo* was recognized

in the resolution 'Border Disputes among African States', adopted at the Cairo summit in 1964.[13]

The resolution declares that 'all Member-States pledge themselves to respect the borders existing on their achievement of national independence'.

Kenya's *Daily Nation* of 10 June 1970, commenting on the signing of a treaty between Kenya and Ethiopia which defined the border between the two countries,[14] supported the *status quo* in arguments which sum up the prevailing views on boundary problems in Africa:

'Most African States are now, through the Charter of OAU, generally agreed as to the vital need to maintain the boundaries as they had been carved out by the Berlin Conference of the imperialist powers. Several factors are behind this. One of them is that once countries begin conceding to demands for whole tracts of land — whatever the cultural, religious or ethnic justifications — there would be no end to the exercise. Claims would heap upon claims and anarchy would be the result. But the most important factor is that even were there a case for regrouping ourselves according to tribal or ethnic affinities, the implementation would logically result in the proliferation of small units and the balkanization of the continent into entities that could not possibly be viable economically.'

However, an exactly opposite view was put forward by the Togolese Information Minister Kwaovi Benyi Johnson in an editiorial in *Togo-Presse* of 21 January 1976. Praising President Leopold Senghor of Senegal for adjusting the frontiers between Senegal and Gambia by handing to Gambia an area comprising twenty-six villages in the Kantona region, the minister challenged what he described as 'the sacrosanct principle of the immutability of African frontiers'. He called the OAU principle 'a wise idea at the time of OAU's inception' but one which at present 'does not stand up to an objective historical analysis' as it avoids 'the fundamental question of human groupings separated by colonial treaties'. This was a reference to Togo's own dispute with Ghana over the Western Togolese area (a former German colony) which was handed over to Ghana in 1946 after a UN referendum.

*Refugee problems.*

There are two categories of refugees in Africa, those from dependent territories and those from independent African States. The first category is closely linked with the liberation efforts directed against the white minority regimes in southern Africa, and previously against the Portuguese colonial regime. Within this category of refugees are the freedom fighters engaged in political activity or armed struggle against the colonial power. Others are refugees in search of economic and social betterment, and young people dissatisfied with the colonial conditions and inferior educational opportunities. Fugitives from justice do not qualify as refugees within this context. According to the report of the United Nations High Commission for Refugees (UNHCR) of October 1976 there were more than one million refugees in Africa in need of immediate assistance. Zaire topped the list of host countries by giving asylum to 460,000 Angolans, 24,000 Burundians and 26,000 other displaced persons. Tanzania had 171,900 refugees, Uganda 112,500, Sudan 98,000 and Zambia 36,000.[15]

The most delicate problems are posed by the refugees from independent African States, who are either victims of political or tribal persecution or are engaged in activities aimed at the overthrow of existing governments. Independent African States often hesitate to grant recognition to this class of refugee for fear that, in granting them asylum, they would be suspected of subversive activities against the refugee's home State.

While all governments are agreed on the need for something to be done for the refugees as a whole, not much has been achieved so far, largely because the question of the classification of refugees has not yet been satisfactorily resolved. On the one hand there are humanitarian considerations, but on the other there is the demand to refrain from subversive activities on the part of neighbouring States or any other State, as stipulated by Article III of the OAU Charter. The concern of the OAU has been clearly shown in a resolution adopted at the OAU Summit in Accra in 1965. There the Assembly of Heads of State and Government adopted a resolution entitled *The Problem of Refugees in Africa*,[16] in which it 'reaffirms its desire to give all possible assistance to refugees from any Member-State on a humanitarian and fraternal basis', yet at the same time 'recalls that Member-States have pledged themselves to prevent refugees living on their territories from carrying out by any means whatsoever any acts harmful to the interests of other States, members of the Organization of African Unity', and 'requests all Member-States never to allow the refugee question to become a source of dispute amongst them'.

The problem of refugees has always been of particular concern to the East African States, and in February 1964 they called for a special OAU commission to consider the matter. When this commission was set up, it was proposed that certain principles governing the treatment of refugees be established, and a general African Fund set up to help support refugees throughout the continent. These aims were largely met by the *OAU Convention Governing the Specific Aspects of Refugee Problems in Africa*,[17] signed in Addis Ababa on 6 September 1969. The Convention is a carefully drafted compromise between the recognized need to 'alleviate the misery and suffering of the refugees and provide them with a better life and future' and a determination not to allow the refugees to become a source of friction among OAU Member-States.

The Convention defines the refugee as 'every person who, owing to well-founded fear of being persecuted for reasons of race, religion, nationality, membership of a particular social group or political opinion, is outside the country of his nationality and is unable or, owing to such fear, is unwilling to avail himself of the protection of that country, or who, not having a nationality and being outside the country of his former habitual residence as a result of such events, is unable or, owing to such fear, is unwilling to return to it'. The Convention applies the term 'refugee' also to every person who, 'owing to external aggression, occupation, foreign domination or events seriously disturbing public order in either part or the whole of his country of origin or nationality is compelled to leave his place of habitual residence in order to seek refuge in another place outside his country of origin or nationality'.

Article IV of the Convention, enumerating the circumstances under which the Convention ceases to apply to a person claiming refugee-status, includes the case where the person 'has been guilty of acts contrary to the purposes and principles of the Organization of African Unity'. This would exclude any person involved in 'subversive activites on the part of neighbouring States or any other States' — which would nullify the Convention's provision for asylum to be granted in precisely these circumstances, i.e. as protection from extradition to the State claiming the refugee's return. This likely interpretation is further clouded by Article II's insistence that asylum should be regarded as a 'peaceful and humanitarian act, and shall not be regarded as an unfriendly act by any Member-States' — which does not establish whether the persons fleeing their countries because of charges of subversion are the ones entitled to the benefit of the asylum. The rule designed to prevent any disputes or friction between the country of origin of the refugees and the country granting them asylum is laid down in Article III and entitled *Prohibition of subversive activities:*

— Every refugee has duties to the country in which he finds himself, and they require in particular that he conform with its laws and regulations as well as with measures taken for the maintenance of public order. He shall also abstain from any subversive activities against any Member-State of the OAU.

— Signatory-States undertake to prohibit refugees residing in their respective territories from attacking any Member-State of the OAU by any activity likely to cause tension between Member-States, and in particular by use of arms, through the press, or by radio.

The *OAU Convention Governing the Specific Aspects of Refugee Problems in Africa* came into force on 20 June 1974 when Algeria, as the fourteenth OAU member, deposited its instruments of ratification. However, the Convention has had very little effect on the fate of refugees, who continue to be treated by each African State in accordance with its own laws and political interests. The 'Resolution on Refugees' adopted by the 13th OAU Summit at Port Louis, Mauritius, in July 1976 begged Member-States to provide more employment and educational opportunities for the refugees and make it easier for them to obtain travelling documents. It also called on all States concerned to declare a general amnesty which would enable many of the refugees to return to their countries. The OAU also invited its members to take an active part in the UN Conference convened in January 1977 to elaborate a Draft Convention on Territorial Asylum, which constituted a major international effort to alleviate the refugee problem: it impressed upon Member-States that they should give priority to humanitarian rather than political considerations in dealing with people driven by various causes out of their own countries.

However, life is still a nightmare for most of Africa's one million refugees. In many African countries the refugee, if admitted at all, is merely tolerated and lives off the charity of the host-government, usually in conditions of squalor and misery in a settlement-camp in a remote part of the country. Treated as an alien — with little or no chance of employment, which is scarce even for the nationals of the host country — he is rarely integrated into the new society, and stays a refugee for ever.

*Charges of Subversion.*

At different times, before and since the establishment of the OAU, serious political and ideological differences between various States or groups of States have led to mutual charges of subversion. The founders of the OAU, fully aware of this problem, expressed their 'unreserved condemnation, in all its forms, of political assassination as well as of subversive activities on the part of a neighbouring State or any other State' as one of the principles of the Charter. This did not put an end to the political quarrels which continued to erupt from time to time between the OAU Members, often thus causing major crises within the OAU.

The first serious crisis of this kind was the conflict between the OCAM States and Ghana in 1965. The charges of subversion made by the members of the Organisation Commune Africaine et Malagache (OCAM),[18] in particular by Ivory Coast, Niger and Upper Volta, against Ghana was the reason given by the OCAM States for boycotting the OAU Summit in Accra in 1965. However, the roots of the hostility of the OCAM States towards Ghana went deeper than that. The francophone States had always resented Ghana's militant posture in African politics, its relations with the Communist countries and in particular Kwame Nkrumah's criticism of OCAM's support for Moise Tshombe, the secessionist leader of Katanga who later became the Prime Minister of the Congo (Zaire). They wanted to use the OAU Summit in Accra to drive Ghana into political isolation.

The OCAM States gave as their reason for not coming to Accra the presence in Ghana of political dissenters from their countries, whom the Ghanaian Government allegedly assisted in their subversive activities against the OCAM countries. With the Rhodesian crisis looming up, the majority of the OAU Member-States were reluctant to support OCAM and cause a rift among African States. The handling of the Rhodesian crisis made unity more essential than ever before. Besides, Kwame Nkrumah's firm stand on Rhodesia, and his challenge that Great Britain should be held responsible for its solution, won him great respect in the Organization. As a result, it was OCAM and not Ghana which found itself in isolation. Support for Ghana gained ground at the Extraordinary Meeting of the OAU Council of Ministers in Lagos in June 1965, convened to resolve the problem of the venue of the Summit conference. At the meeting, Ghana surprised the OCAM States by agreeing to deport all persons regarded by the latter as 'undesirable'. Ghana also invited the Chairman of the Council of Ministers and the Administrative Secretary-General of the OAU to visit Ghana before the Summit to ascertain the measures to be taken to ensure the success of the conference.

Eight days before the OAU Conference was due to begin, President Kwame Nkrumah travelled to Bamako to meet Presidents Houphouet-Boigny of Ivory Coast, Diori of Niger and Yameogo of Upper Volta and gave them personal assurances of their safety in Accra. Although the 'undesirable persons' were removed from Accra, a fact confirmed by the OAU Administrative Secretary-General, the three Heads of State and five other OCAM members (Cameroon, Chad, Dahomey (Benin), Gabon and Malagasy) declined to attend the Assembly meeting there. They maintained that the undesirable persons were not deported from Ghana as had been promised at Lagos. In order to appease the OCAM States the Assembly of Heads adopted a *Declaration on the Problem of Subversion.*[19] The Declaration pledges all African States:

— not to tolerate any subversion originating in their countries against any member of the OAU;

— to refrain from conducting press or radio campaigns against any African State;

— not to create dissension within or among Member-States by fomenting or aggravating racial, religious, linguistic, ethnic or other differences;

— to observe strictly the principles of international law with regard to all political refugees who are nationals of any Member-State of the OAU.

The principles of the Declaration were applied, for example, to the dispute between Guinea and Senegal, resolved in 1972 at the OAU Summit at Rabat. The dispute dated from 1971 when Guinea accused Senegal of harbouring refugees implicated in a Portuguese-sponsored invasion of Guinea in December 1970. A special *ad hoc* mediation commission, composed of seven Heads of State and chaired by Emperor Haile Selassie, drafted an agreement subsequently signed by Presidents Sekou Touré of Guinea and Senghor of Senegal. The application of the principles laid down by the Accra 'Declaration on Subversion' was linked with an appeal for unity against the current common enemy, Portugal. It contained, *inter alia,* the following points:

— non-interference in the internal affairs of States, and respect for their sovereignty.
— an undertaking by both parties to prohibit the use of their respective territories as a base for aggression or for hostile acts against each other;
— cessation of all hostile propaganda through the information media.

Two months later, on the initiative of the African States at the UN and supported by the Asian and Latin American States, the General Assembly reaffirmed the Principles enunciated in the Accra declaration by adopting a *Declaration on the Inadmissibility of Intervention in the Domestic Affairs of States.*[20] Ironically, it was Ghana, the country which had for years been accused of such intervention by its francophone neighbours, who evoked the principles of the Declaration in a charge against Guinea. The charges were made by the military regime of General Ankrah which had deposed President Kwame Nkrumah in February 1966. Nkrumah had by then taken refuge in Guinea, and had been declared by President Sekou Touré to be co-President of Guinea. The regime of General Ankrah in Ghana felt constantly threatened by Nkrumah and Guinea.[21]

*Disputes arising out of non-recognition of governments coming to power by coup d'état.*

The question of the legality of a government coming to power by military *coup* was raised in Africa for the first time in connection with the over-throw of President Sylvanus Olympio of Togo, who was killed in the course of the *coup* on 13 January 1963. The OAU was not then in existence, but preparations for the Addis Ababa Summit in May 1963 were already well on the way. Ghana was suspected of having initiated the *coup* because of its strained relations with Togo over the harbouring of Ghanaian political refugees. The preparations for the Summit were brought almost to a standstill as enmity between the Monrovia and Casablanca groups flared up again.

Allegations concerning Ghana's role in the *coup* were publicly voiced by the Nigerian Foreign Minister Jaja Wachuku, who convened an emergency meeting of the Foreign Ministers of the Inter-African and Malagasy Organization (Monrovia group) in Lagos in February 1963 to announce the condemnation of Ghana and to consider the legality of the new regime in Togo headed by President Grunitzky. At this meeting, Jaja Wachuku asked the Conference:

'Should automatic recognition be accorded to the provisional government of Monsieur Grunitzky, without taking into account the suspension of the Constitution, or the dissolution of the Assembly and the abrogation of the electoral laws of the Republic of Togo? . . Can recognition be decided without taking account of the external influence and of the military constraint which contributed to bring to power and reinforce the new regime?'

The conference did not provide any answer to Jaja Wachuku's questions and the recommendation of the conference was that 'where there is sufficient evidence that internal subversion has been engineered by another State, diplomatic relations with that State be severed by all members of the Inter-African and Malagasy Organizations'. However, none of the countries represented at the conference (Cameroon, Zaire, Chad, Central African Republic, Ethiopia, Gabon, Ivory Coast Dahomey (Benin), Liberia, Mauritania, Madagascar, Niger, Nigeria, Senegal, Sierra Leone and Upper Volta) followed the implied suggestion of severing relations with Ghana. A five-member commission appointed by the conference to enquire into the circumstances of the *coup* was disbanded five weeks later. However, the Togo affair reverberated at Addis Ababa in May 1963. The Summit condemned political assassination and subversive activities as incompatible with the OAU Charter. At the time of the Addis Ababa Summit, Nigeria and Ivory Coast still withheld their recognition of President Grunitzky's regime and as a result Togo was absent from the conference.

However, the futility of the principles of recognition of a government preached by Jaja Wachuku at the Lagos conference was soon exposed in a series of *coups*, of which the one in Togo had only been the beginning. During 1966, six *coups* took place, two of them, ironically, in Nigeria. Except after the overthrow of Ben Bella in Algeria (1965), Kwame Nkrumah in Ghana (1966) and Milton Obote in Uganda (1971) the legality of the military governments which came into power was never questioned. Even in these three cases, 'legality' gave way to 'reality'. Experience had shown that when the *status quo*, although brought about illegally, acquires the character of permanence, its acceptance by other members of the international community is merely a matter of time. Recognition, which is a political and not a legal act, is accorded by States for political or economic reasons of their own, or simply because there is nothing they can do about it. The illegal usurpation of power by the white settler minority in Rhodesia in 1965 is a solitary exception to the rule. The problem of the recognition of the MPLA regime in Angola, although of entirely different origin, became the central issue of the Extraordinary Session of the Assembly of Heads of State and Government in January 1976 (examined in Chapter VIII).


To illustrate how 'legality' gave way to 'reality' the following is a brief account of how the OAU handled the disputes which arose after the overthrow respectively of Kwame Nkrumah in Ghana (1966) and Milton Obote in Uganda (1971). Both split the ranks of OAU Members into two camps: one refusing to recognize the new regime, the other insisting that any such change is entirely an internal matter of the country concerned

*The Coup in Ghana (1966)*

After the *coup* in Ghana on 24 February 1966, a Ghanaian delegation led by E.T.K. Seddoh, representing the new regime headed by a National Liberation Council, arrived at Addis Ababa to attend the 5th Session of the Council of Ministers. Its credentials were questioned by Mali, Guinea, Tanzania and Egypt, all of whom objected to its presence. After a lengthy debate, the meeting decided to accept the Ghanaian delegation as a full participant, adding a rider that this was not to imply the recognition of the new Ghanaian government. The following three days of session were full of suspense in expectation of the announced arrival of the Ghanaian delegation sent by the deposed President Nkrumah from Peking where the news of the *coup* in Ghana reached him. He was on his way to Hanoi in an attempt to mediate in the conflict in Vietnam. Nkrumah sent to Addis Ababa his trusted Foreign Minister Alex Quaison-Sackey. The latter, however, chose to travel to Accra instead and placed himself at the service of the National Liberation Council: he was immediately arrested. The case of the OAU Members opposing the presence of the delegation led by Seddoh was thus considerably weakened. But the crisis was yet to come.

On the third day of the session, when the leader of the Ghanaian delegation rose to speak, he was stopped by the chairman of the Political Committee, Mohamed Khalil of Sudan, who ruled that the Ghanaian delegation would not be allowed to speak. Immediately afterwards, the chairman of the session, Ethiopia's Ketema Yifrou, convened a plenary session at which the delegate of Guinea, Diallo Abdulaye, told the delegates that he had been instructed by his government to withdraw Guinea's delegation from the session. 'The continued presence of the Ghanaian delegation,' he said, 'is contrary to OAU principles', and added: 'some delegates have become the voices of imperialism. Guinea will not stay in a conference where delegates no longer fight against imperialism, but against the peoples of Africa.' When the Guineans left, the Mali Foreign Minister, Ousman Ba, leapt to his feet. 'Mali cannot sit down with this Ghanaian delegation', he declared. 'We also are leaving the conference.' 'We want unity, but unity has principles', said Oscar Kambona, the leader of the Tanzanian delegation; and he joined the Guinean and Malian delegations in walking out of the meeting. Egypt then proposed that the session be adjourned to allow time for tempers to cool, but this recieved little support.

The next day, the Egyptian delegation withdrew. Its Foreign Minister, Ibrahim Khalil, announced that Egypt had withdrawn for two reasons: Ghana's continued presence and the 'unfortunate atmosphere' between delegates. 'We believe the conference should be adjourned for a month or six weeks to allow tensions to abate', he said. When Algeria left the conference, it was for a different reason. Its resolution on Rhodesia was rejected by the majority of members of the Political Committee.

Three more delegations were to leave before the conference ended — Somalia in protest at a 'submissive resolution' then being prepared on Rhodesia, the Congo because of the 'deteriorating atmosphere' of the talks, and Kenya. Leading Kenya's delegation out of the talks, a Minister of State, Joseph Murumbi, said that the delegation had been ordered to withdraw by President Kenyatta. He added: 'We are protesting against the recognition of the Ghanaian delegation. The Kenya Government is against military *coups* and the disregard of constituted authority. Military *coups* are a menace to the peace and stability of Africa.'

OAU policy on the crisis was revealed only after the meeting by the Zambian High Commissioner to Tanzania, A.M. Sembule. He said: 'It was agreed by the heads of the delegations attending the conference that the attendance by the Ghanaian representatives did not amount to the recognition by OAU of the new regime, and it was agreed that if another Ghanaian delegation arrived, the matter would be rediscussed with a view to excluding both delegations.'[2 2]

A distinction between feeling sympathy for Nkrumah and establishing a *policy* towards the new regime in Ghana was made in clear terms by President Nyerere of Tanzania at a press conference on 11 March 1966: 'But after our sympathies, what do we do? Do we organize subversion in Ghana? Do we promote or provoke civil war in Ghana? . . . When there is a change of government in a country it is up to the people of that country to help in effecting another change of government, because we believe in constitutionality.'[23]

In the absence of any effective challenge to its authority, the military regime of Ghana was gradually recognized by almost all OAU Members. Apart from Guinea, only Zambia withheld its recognition throughout the four years of military rule in Ghana. President Kaunda, a personal friend and admirer of Nkrumah, waited until in 1970 Ghana reverted to a civilian regime headed by Dr. Busia. When Dr. Busia himself was overthrown by the military in 1972, the change was accepted without a whisper of protest at OAU.

*The military coup in Uganda (1971)*

When General Idi Amin deposed President Milton Obote on 25 January 1971, a military *coup* was no longer an unusual event. By that time thirteen out of forty OAU members were governed by the military who had seized power unconstitutionally.[24] It is therefore extraordinary that the effect of the coup in Uganda on the Organization was as shattering as it was.

The first occasion on which the OAU was directly confronted with the *coup* was when two Ugandan delegations arrived at the 16th Session of the Council of Ministers of 16 February 1971 in Addis Ababa — one sent by General Amin and the other by ex-President Obote. The Ministerial Council, unable to resolve the question of Ugandan representation, adjourned *sine die* on 1 March and referred the matter to the OAU Summit scheduled for June. The decision was without precedent in the history of the OAU. The situation was complicated by the fact that Kampala was to be the venue of the 1971 meeting of both the Council of Ministers and the Assembly of Heads of State and Government. The current chairman of the Council of Ministers, Omar Arteh of Somalia, and the Administrative Secretary–General Diallo Telli, made known their strong disapproval of the overthrow of President Obote. Time, however, worked in favour of General Amin, and the rule that the recognition of a new government was for each sovereign State to decide and should not be of concern to the OAU eventually prevailed. It was felt, however, that holding the conference in Kampala would inevitably give rise to a showdown between General Amin's supporters and his opponents. It was therefore decided to hold the conference at the OAU headquarters in Addis Ababa.

Following intense diplomatic activity, in which Nigeria acted as conciliator between Uganda and its adversaries, President Kaunda, as the current chairman of the OAU, wrote to all Member-States proposing that it would be 'in the highest interest of the OAU' to convene the 8th Session of the Assembly of Heads of State and Government on 21 June 1971 in Addis Ababa and the Session of the Council of Ministers ten days earlier, on 11 June, in the same place. As a result, thirty-three Heads of State and Government expressed themselves in favour of holding the meeting in Addis Ababa, and accepted the dates. Uganda accused President Kaunda of violating the OAU Charter on the grounds that in order to change the place of meeting, the correct procedure was to convene an extraordinary session of the OAU, which is the only competent body to take a decision on the matter. The Charter, however, does not specify how the necessary majority is to be obtained, and President Kaunda, by securing the consent of a majority of more than two-thirds, had acted in conformity with the Charter.

When the Council resumed its meeting on 11 June 1971 in Addis Ababa, the credentials of General Amin's envoys were recognized but the Ugandan delegation withdrew from the subsequent meeting of the Council and of the Assembly in protest at the change of venue. The absence of the representatives of the new regime reduced the tension at the meeting. It also gave President Amin one more year in which to consolidate his power — which he did.

The recognition of General Amin's regime did not remove the frictions between Uganda and Tanzania, which offered asylum to the deposed President Milton Obote. In September 1972 the supporters of ex-President Obote launched an armed attack from Tanzanian territory against Uganda. The invasion failed but brought the two countries to the brink of war. At the OAU Anniversary Summit in Addis Ababa in May 1973, ex-President Obote circulated a letter addressed to all African leaders in which he accused General Amin of the murder of 80,000 Ugandans.[25] However, Obote's appeal to the OAU 'that a large-scale slaughter of Africans in any part of Africa must concern the OAU' fell on deaf ears. The principle of non-interference in the internal affairs of Member-States prevailed.

The tension between the Ugandan and Tanzanian delegations was temporarily eased at the OAU Anniversary Summit in Addis Ababa in May 1973 when General Amin proposed to add the name of Dr Milton Obote to the list of distinguished Africans to be awarded a special medal marking the OAU's tenth anniversary. Tanzania seconded his move. Amin then publicly called Nyerere his brother against whom he bears no grievance and offered him a handshake, which Nyerere accepted. An agreement between Tanzanian and Uganda was concluded under the auspices of Emperor Haile Selassie.[26]

This truce between Tanzania and Uganda did not last long. Soon after the 1973 Addis Ababa Summit the war of words in the mass media of the two countries was resumed. In July 1975 the choice of Kampala for the 12th OAU Summit and of Field-Marshal Idi Amin Dada as its chairman was challenged by Tanzania, Zambia, Botswana and Mozambique, which boycotted the meeting. Their reasons were stated in a strongly worded memorandum issued by the Tanzanian government on 25 July entitled *Africa's New Danger*.[27] The statement warned that Africa is in danger of becoming unique in its refusal to protest at crimes committed against Africans provided such crimes are committed by African leaders and African governments. The statement continued:

'This refusal to protest against African State crimes against African people is bad enough, but until now Africa has at least refrained from giving public support to the worst perpetrations of such crimes. Now, by meeting in Kampala, the Heads of State of the OAU are giving respectability to one of the most murderous administrations in Africa. For this meeting will be assumed to have thrown the mantle of OAU approval over what has been done, and what is still being done, by General Amin and his henchmen against the people of Uganda.'

The statement concluded with the strongest condemnation of President Amin so far officially pronounced by any African government. In summing up the reasons for Tanzania's absence from the OAU meeting the statements says that:

'Tanzania cannot accept the responsibility of participating in the mockery of condemning colonialism, apartheid, and fascism in the headquarters of a murderer and oppressor, a black fascist and a self-confessed admirer of Hitler.'

Although the statement does not raise the question of the legality of President Amin's regime it cast serious doubts on the legitimacy of Uganda's membership of the OAU. Furthermore, the statement exposed the fallacy of the rule of 'non-intervention into internal affairs of another State', by drawing a comparison between Uganda and South Africa in the following words:

'The agreement not to interfere in the internal affairs of another State is necessary for the existence of the OAU. A similar condition is accepted by members of the United Nations. But why is it good for States to condemn apartheid and bad for them to condemn massacres which are committed by independent African governments? Why is it legitimate to call for the isolation of South Africa because of its oppression but illegitimate to refuse co-operation with a country like Uganda where the government survives because of the ruthlessness with which it kills suspected critics?'

However, the majority of the OAU members chose to ignore the

Tanzanian appeal and went to Kampala;* the conflict between Uganda and its neighbours continues to this day.

The years 1975 and 1976 witnessed a serious decline in the OAU's role as peacemaker in Africa. The OAU had very little to do with ending the civil war in Angola, which was terminated not by negotiation but by a military victory of the MPLA. In 1976 at the 13th OAU Summit at Port Louis the display of disputes between OAU Members and the vigour with which the disputing parties fought each other completly overshadowed the crucial problems which faced the organization — the deadlock of the peace talks concerning majority rule in Rhodesia, the future of Namibia, and the strategy against South Africa which was being swept by racial riots. Morocco and Mauritania threatened to terminate their membership if the OAU continued to support POLISARIO; Uganda accused Kenya of complicity in the Israeli raid on Uganda's Entebbe airport;* Ethiopia sought a firm stand by the OAU on what its delegation described as 'expansionist plans of Somalia on the territory of the Afars and Issas'; President Numeiry of Sudan, whose arrival at the Summit was delayed by an attempted *coup d'état* in Sudan, accused Libya of plotting it; and Zaire and Angola were not on speaking terms because Angola had still not repaired the Benguela railway bridges, blown up during the Angolan civil war in which Zaire supported MPLA's enemies. Angola was a notable absentee at the 11th Extaordinary Session of the Council of Ministers at Kinshasa in December 1976.

While the present African conflicts and disputes are still kept within the African framework and the OAU continues its efforts to solve them peacefully, the Organization is not in a position (and for that matter it never really was) to prevent any of the disputes breaking out into war. This has been clearly shown by the outbreak of hostilities between Ethiopia and Sudan along their borders in April 1977. Although both countries filed their complaints with the OAU the only thing the organization could do was to register them. Even less was done about the conflict in the Zaire province Shaba, despite the direct involvement of outside powers, notably Morocco which sent troops and France which transported them. The same goes for the war in Eritrea to which the OAU has become an idle by-stander.

*When the news broke that General Gowon had been deposed, several heads of State hastily withdrew — his decision to attend the Kampala Summit had originally made even those who were hesitating follow his example.
*to rescue the hostages of the hi-jacked Air France plane.

# Chapter VI

# THE CONGO CRISIS (1964-1965)

Unlike the Algerian-Moroccan conflict, which was essentially an internal African affair, the Congo crisis[1] from its outset in 1960 became an international conflict which dragged Africa into cold war politics. The situation in the Congo had been of concern to independent African States before the Congo's independence in 1960. The division of opinion among African States about the role of the UN in the Congo was one of the main causes of the split of Africa into the Casablanca, Monrovia and Brazzaville Twelve groupings referred to in Chapter II. The initiative in the Congo crisis lay with President Nkrumah of Ghana, who was in daily contact with the Congolese Prime Minister, Patrice Lumumba, and later with UN headquarters. He was Lumumba's close personal friend and adviser, as the correspondence between the two reveals.[2] Nkrumah played an important part in persuading Lumumba, who was leader of the Mouvement National Congolais (MNC), to accept his political rival, Joseph Kasavubu, leader of ABAKO ('Association des Bakongo pour l'Unification, l'Expansion et la Défense de la langue Kikongo'), as the first head of State. Nkrumah also advocated a UN presence in the Congo. Later, he believed that the establishment of an African high command was the only remedy for the failure of the UN operations.

The background to the 1964-5 Congo crisis goes back to the colonial history of the Congo and the rule of Leopold II which had reduced the Congo to a reservoir of slave labour exploited with a ruthlessness which crippled the country for several decades.[3] The events following the declaration of independence on 20 February 1960 have been described in great detail in many writings.[4] For the purpose of this book it suffices to mention the situation in the Congo at the time when the OAU came into existence, and the reasons which made the organization intervene.

At the Addis Ababa conference in 1963 the Congo was represented by its Prime Minister Cyrille Adoula. Although the secession of the Katanga — the primary cause of the conflict in the previous three years — had been brought to an end four months earlier on 12 January 1963, the political turmoil in the country did not recede. From the beginning of 1964, there were reports that the former secessionist leader of

Katanga, Moise Tshombe, was assembling mercenary forces in Angola as well as training former Katangan *gendarmes*. In his report of 16 March 1964 to the Security Council, the UN Secretary-General, U Thant, drew attention to the new threat to peace in the Congo. He estimated that there were 1,800 former Katangan *gendarmes* undergoing training in Angola under the command of twenty white mercenaries. Tshombe was residing in Spain, apparently organizing his return to the Congo.

The authority of Adoula's government was challenged by a military revolt in Kwilu province in June 1964. It was led by Pierre Mulele, a former minister in Gizenga's[5] government, and a National Liberation Committee (CNL). The latter had been formed in Brazzaville on 3 October 1963 by Christopher Gbenye, Edige Bocheley Davidson and Gaston Soumailot. In February 1964 a CNL branch was formed at Bujumbura, Burundi, by Soumailot.

During the last days of June 1964, Tshombe left Madrid to begin a triumphant journey back to the Congo. He arrived in Leopoldville on 26 June. Symbolically, within twenty-four hours of Tshombe's return, his bitterest enemy, Jason Sendwe, Provincial President of North Katanga, was assassinated in Albertville with two other leaders. Adoula's government, having completed its term of office on 30 June 1964, resigned. Four days later Tshombe invited Kasavubu to form a caretaker government. On 10 July 1964 Moise Tshombe was sworn in as Prime Minister of the Congo.

African leaders were shocked. For them Tshombe symbolized everything they abhorred: secession, collaboration with the Belgian colonialists, defiance of the UN and foreign intervention. They also held him responsible for the murder of Lumumba[6] and detested his recruitment of white mercenaries from Rhodesia and South Africa. In African eyes Tshombe was, as President Ben Bella of Algeria put it, 'the incarnation of all the elements which constitute neocolonialism'. In the Congo the reaction was equally strong. The CNL armies formed by General Nicholas Olenga into a People's Liberation Army (APL), launched an offensive against the Congolese armies, the highlight of which was the capture of Stanleyville on 4 August 1964, which became the headquarters of a People's Republic of the Congo, proclaimed by CNL on 5 September 1964, with Christopher Gbenye as its President. The ensuing civil war revived the rivalry between East and West, with NCL representing the aspirations of the East, and Kasavubu and Tshombe those of the West. However, the military aid provided by the Soviet Union and China to CNL was small compared with the massive military assistance given to the Congo in response to Tshombe's requests.[7]

# 1. OAU INTERVENTION IN THE CONGO CRISIS

Intervention by the OAU was proposed in March 1964 by President Nkrumah of Ghana in a letter to the Congolese Prime Minister, Cyrille Adoula, when reports of Tshombe's return had been confirmed. Nkrumah suggested that Adoula call on the OAU to replace the departing UN troops by an all-African force, but Adoula ignored the advice.

The call for an emergency meeting of the OAU Council of Ministers came from the Mali Government on 22 August 1964. With the consent of the majority of OAU Members, the meeting was arranged for 5 September in Addis Ababa. Two proposals were submitted to the Council: the first was Ghana's proposal for a political conference of all Congolese political leaders, including the Stanleyville regime. The object was 'to find ways and means of bringing to an end the fratricidal strife in the Congo'. Ghana also proposed a special commission of mediation, composed of representatives of Algeria, Ethiopia, Ghana, Nigeria and Sudan, to make preparations for such a conference. President Nkrumah specified his proposals as follows:

— the proclamation of a cease-fire forthwith and the neutralization of all the armies in the Congo;
— the convening of a conference in Addis Ababa of the leaders of the main political parties (including President Kasavubu and Moise Tshombe) in the Congo, the sole objective of which would be to organize fair and peaceful elections under the auspices of the OAU;
— for the duration of the conference and the general election, the OAU to maintain a peace force in the Congo (its main responsibility would be to assist the Provisional Government in the preservation of law and order, and it was to be withdrawn as soon as the conference and the general election were concluded and a truly democratic government established).

President Nkrumah also wrote to Presidents Kasavubu and Tshombe, but neither replied. The second proposal was put before the Council on 5 September by Mali. The Mali Foreign Minister, Boucoum, suggested that the OAU should urge:

— the immediate withdrawal of all foreign troops and all mercenaries;
— an immediate cease-fire throughout the country;
— the formation of a caretaker government of national unity;
— free elections under OAU control;
— the establishment of a commission to implement the proposals;
— the despatch of a delegation of foreign ministers to the foreign powers that were interfering in the Congo problem with a request to them to discontinue their interference.

The Congo's Prime Minister, Moise Tshombe, whose participation in the deliberations of the Council of Ministers was a major diplomatic victory, quickly grasped the mood of the meeting, which was most of all concerned with the presence of the white mercenaries. He assured the Foreign Ministers that he was ready to dispense with their services, provided they be replaced by a contingent of African troops. He appealed to Ethiopia, Liberia, Malagasy, Nigeria and Senegal to send military units to the Congo. But Ghana's Foreign Minister, Kojo Botsio, warned the delegates that if troops were sent to the Congo, they might be required to fight African nationalists. Kenya's Foreign Minister, Joseph Murumbi, supported Ghana's proposal for a conference, but Tshombe turned it down. He defended the Congo's relations with the United States and Belgium, both in the supply of military aid and as a strictly internal matter. The OAU refused to accept this view; it saw the problem of mercenaries as identical with that of the foreign intervention in which the United States and Belgium played a major part. This was stated in the Resolution adopted by the Council on 10 September 1964, in which it made clear its opinion:

'that foreign intervention and the use of mercenaries has unfortunate effects on the neighbouring independent States as well as on the struggle for national liberation in Angola, Rhodesia, Mozambique and the other territories in the region which are still under colonial domination, and constitutes a serious threat to peace in the African continent.'[8]

In the operative part of the Resolution, the Council endorsed the Mali proposal for an *ad hoc* commission. It was to be composed of representatives from Cameroon, Egypt, Ethiopia, Ghana, Guinea, Nigeria, Somalia, Tunisia and Upper Volta. The chairman was President Kenyatta of Kenya. It was given the following mandate:

(a) to help and encourage the efforts of the Government of the Democratic Republic of the Congo in the restoration of national reconciliation;
(b) to seek by all possible means to bring about normal relations between the Democratic Republic of the Congo and its neighbours, especially the Kingdom of Burundi and the Republic of the Congo (Brazzaville).

The Resolution also appealed to all powers active in the Congo to cease their interference.

The outcome of the conference sealed Tshombe's political victory. Six countries abstained from voting on the resolution; and Tshombe had succeeded in preventing Gbenye's supporters from being heard, and rejected the proposals for a round-table conference to be attended by Gbenye's representatives. The OAU *ad hoc* Commission on the Congo held its first meeting in Nairobi from 18 to 22 September 1964. Tshombe was present in the capacity of a 'consultative member'. The Commission succeeded in reconciling the Congo and its two neighbours, Congo (Brazzaville) and Burundi, and made proposals for national reconciliation in the Congo. This included a request for the release of 3,000 political prisoners.

Tshombe continued to oppose the requests of the OAU *ad hoc* Commission to negotiate with the Stanleyville regime. He called its leaders 'robbers, rapists and butchers who burned schools and churches'. However, he promised safety to 'all rebels who lay down their arms'. His pledge was endorsed in the resolution adopted by the Commission. As at the session of the Council of Ministers, the problem of white mercenaries dominated the Commission's proceedings. The OAU Secretary-General, Diallo Telli, was quoted in the *East-African Standard* of 22 September 1964 as saying that the OAU considered it of paramount importance for all mercenaries to leave the Congo immediately. In answering a question on the Commission's priorities, he linked the cease-fire with the departure of mercenaries. 'The presence of mercenaries might be considered the initial cause of trouble', said Diallo Telli, 'because one could not be blind to the fact that they were another aspect of foreign interference';[9] but he went on to describe foreign interference *per se* in the Congo as the key problem facing the Commission. His views were confirmed by the Chairman of the Commission, President Kenyatta, who told a press conference on 22 September that the Commission felt that without the withdrawal of all foreign troops from the Congo, it could not find the right atmosphere for a solution.[10] Kenyatta also announced that the Commission was sending a delegation to Washington to ask President Johnson to stop shipments of war materials to the Congo.

News of the proposed OAU mission to Washington was received in Leopoldville (Kinshasa) with great alarm. Without consulting Tshombe, President Kasavubu announced the Congo's withdrawal from the OAU on the grounds that the mission represented interference in the Congo's internal affairs. Meanwhile, in Washington, President Johnson refused to hold discussions with the OAU mission unless the Congolese government took part in them. Eventually, Dean Rusk, the American Secretary of State, met members of the mission at a working luncheon and gave some vague assurances of the United States' sympathetic understanding of the OAU's peace efforts. But the position remained the same as before. The attitude of the President was viewed by the OAU delegation as evidence of how little importance the United States attached to the OAU.[11] US military aid for Tshombe continued to flow into the Congo.

The Conference of the non-aligned States, held in Cairo on 5-10 October 1964, supported the OAU initiative on the Congo, and endorsed the appeal to stop the armed hostilities and foreign interference. It also called for the expulsion of the mercenaries.[12] But the fighting between the Congolese army and the *Simbas* of General Olenga continued with even greater ferocity.


## 2. THE 'STANLEYVILLE DROP', 24 NOVEMBER 1964

The culmination of the Congo crisis was a joint military action by Belgium, the United States and Great Britain, known as the 'Stanleyville drop'. It was executed on 24 November 1964 and, presented to the world as a humanitarian operation, attempted the rescue of about 1,300 European hostages held in Stanleyville by the Gbenye regime.

The conditions of Europeans living in the areas controlled by the APL changed drastically when it became apparent that the employment of white mercenaries had reversed the fortunes of war in favour of the Congolese army. Unable to contain the thrust of the combined forces of the mercenaries and the Congolese army, supported by US fighter-bombers flown by Cuban exiles, General Olenga of APL used Europeans as an 'umbrella' against air raids. He refused the Red Cross permission to evacuate Europeans from the war zone and announced that he regarded Europeans as hostages whose fate would depend on the outcome of the negotiations about the cease-fire and the withdrawal of all foreign military personnel from the Congo. These conditions were unacceptable to Tshombe, who refused to be deprived of the spoils of victory. The announcement by the leaders of the People's Republic in Stanleyville on the 15 November that they would execute an American missionary doctor, Dr Paul Carson, accused of espionage and of being a major in the United States army, added to the tension. Michael Hoare, a mercenary commander, commented as follows on the problem of the hostages:

'Why had three of the great nations of the world allowed themselves to be messed around by a handful of semi-literate savages? ... My solution to the hostage problem would have been the landing of an airborne battalion damn quick regardless of diplomatic niceties ... Queensbury rules when you are fighting gentlemen; no holds barred when you are up against savages. They do not think any more of you if you use kid gloves and soft talk. Less, as a matter of fact; these are the traditional signs of weakness in Africa.'[14]

The 'three great nations of the world' — Belgium, the United States and the United Kingdom — did not in fact waste much time on diplomatic niceties. When the United States offered to negotiate in Nairobi on the status of Americans held among the European hostages in Stanleyville, it was only to gain time to complete the preparations for a paratroop drop on the city. The Belgian paratroop units were flown to the British base on Ascension Island on 17 November. The day after the talks in Nairobi between the US Ambassador William Attwood, Thomas Kanza (representing Gbenye's government in Stanleyville) and President Jomo Kenyatta (chairman of the OAU *ad hoc* Commission on the Congo), Belgian paratroops were moved to the Congolese army base at Kamina in the Congo. The operation was carried out in the early hours of 24 November under the command of a Belgian, Colonel Vandewalle, assisted by Colonel Laurent, Colonel Burgess Gradwell, (the US Air Force commander), Colonel Clayton Isaacson of the US Strike Command, Colonel Frank A. Williams (chief of the American military mission to the Congo), and Colonel Monmaert, (the Belgian military attaché in the Congo). The 'British liaison' was provided by Colonel Kirk, a military attaché at the British Embassy in Leopoldville.

The perfect timing of the drop of Belgian paratroopers, which coincided with the arrival of mercenary commandos and units of the Congolese army on the outskirts of Stanleyville, was at variance with the claim by Belgium and the United States that the task of the paratroops was 'not to engage rebel forces in combat nor to seize or hold territory'.[15] The 'Stanleyville drop' was swift and effective. Of the 1,300 Europeans hostages, all but sixty were rescued. Those who died were killed by soldiers of APL who opened fire at the hostages minutes before the arrival of the paratroopers. The *simbas* were blamed for the bloodbath. Commenting on the death of Dr. Paul Carson, who was among the victims, *Time* magazine of 4 December 1964 expressed the following view:

'His death did more than prove that black African civilization — with its elaborate trappings of half a hundred sovereignties, governments and UN delegations — is largely a pretence. The rebels were after all, for the most part, only a rabble of dazed, ignorant savages used and abused by semi-sophisticated leaders.

But virtually all other black African nations, including the more advanced and moderate ones, supported the rebels without even a hint of condemnation for their bestialities. Virtually all these nations echoed the cynical communist line in denouncing the parachute rescue as "imperialist aggression"! When this happened, the sane part of the world could only wonder whether black Africa can be taken seriously at all, or whether, for the foreseeable future, it is beyond the reach of reason.'

Considerably less publicity was given to the massacre of the civilian population of Stanleyville, which was almost wiped out by the looting mercenaries and Congolese soldiers. The killing did not stop with the capture of Stanleyville. It went on until January 1965, when the Congolese army finally established its control over most of the area formerly controlled by Olenga's army. It was estimated that of about 1 million Congolese killed since 1960, 40,000 were shot by mercenaries and Congolese soldiers in the Stanleyville area.

African reaction to the joint US-Belgian intervention was explosive: on no other occasion was there such an upsurge of anti-West sentiment. Even the most moderate pro-Western African leaders denounced it as an 'imperialist, unjustified intervention'. The invitation to intervene, which the Congolese Premier Moise Tshombe extended to the US Ambassador in the Congo on 21 November 1964, was seen by the African leaders only as further proof of Tshombe's conspiracy with the enemies of Africa.[16] There is no doubt that the plight of the hostages was real, and that reports of their ill-treatment by their captors greatly disturbed the American and European authorities. However, the same authorities were almost totally indifferent to the sufferings of the Congolese. The fundamental racism was unmistakeable: the paratroops came to rescue the Whites from the Blacks. The Africans saw this as a demonstration of the forces of neocolonialism: an open threat to all African countries that if they 'misbehaved' the great powers would 'civilize' them.[17]

The last act of the Stanleyville drama was staged at the UN when the Security Council debated the situation in the Congo from 9 to 30 December 1964. In a letter of 1 December, the representatives of twenty-two countries had asked for an urgent meeting of the Security Council to consider the situation in the Congo. They described the Stanleyville operation as being in complete defiance of Article II (7) of the UN Charter, a deliberate affront to the authority of the OAU, an intervention into African affairs, and a threat to the peace and security of the African continent.[18] Replying to the Belgian Foreign Minister, Paul-Henri Spaak, who described the Stanleyville operation as purely 'humanitarian', the Kenyan Minister of Foreign Affairs, Joseph Murumbi, said:

'I put it to the Council that the Belgian and the United States aggression was wholly and directly responsible for all the excesses that were committed in the Congo. How can one speak of a blood-bath which one has designed and caused, in one breath, and of humanitarianism in the other? Where is this humanitarianism when the white mercenaries are allowed full licence to murder innocent African men, women and children? Where was this humanitarianism when Patrice Lumumba, later brutally done to death, was held hostage? What happened to this self-same humanitarianism when innocent Africans were butchered in Sharpeville in South Africa? Where is this humanitarianism when American Negroes are brutally done to death in Mississippi and elsewhere? This type of humanitarianism is partial — thousands of African lives lost to rescue a few whites who could have been saved in any case through peaceful negotiatons — and it gives rise to journalistic sensationalism . . .'[19]

Concurrently with the session of the Security Council, an emergency session of the OAU Council of Ministers was held in New York from 16 to 20 December 1964. Even though the delegates were expressing their abhorrence of the 'Stanleyville drop', they became divided in their attitudes to the Tshombe regime. Its legality was defended by the Nigerian Foreign Minister, Jaja Wachuku, and by most of the delegates from the francophone African countries. The discord was evident in the Resolution adopted at the meeting, which refrained from deploring the Belgian-United States military intervention in Stanleyville. It merely 'disapproved'; and it indirectly endorsed the legality of Tshombe's regime by requesting its co-operation to work with the OAU Commission on the Congo towards national reconciliation. The Resolution also reaffirmed its faith in the *ad hoc* Commission, which was encouraged to continue its work.

In February 1965, the military assistance supplied to the Gbenye regime by some of the OAU members after the 'Stanleyville drop', (notably Algeria, Sudan and Egypt) began to be felt. It was evident that government forces in the Congo had, for the time being, lost the initiative. There were concentrations of anti-government troops near every government-held town, and the raids of the revolutionary forces became more frequent and daring. This view of the military situation was confirmed by the three members of the OAU sub-committee who visited the Congo at the beginning of February 1965. The members (from Ghana, Guinea and Nigeria) spent three days in Leopoldville in talks with government officials, and then went on to Brazzaville and to Bujumbura in Burundi before returning to Nairobi to report to the OAU *ad hoc* Commission on the Congo.

Unfortunately, just at the point when the leaders of the Stanleyville regime, Christopher Gbenye and Gaston Soumailot, were within reach of military victory over Tshombe's forces and recognition by the OAU, they became entangled in an internal struggle for leadership. In turn their dissent eroded the morale of the army. Tshombe exploited the situation by mounting a counter-offensive led by mercenary units, the number of which was rapidly increasing. The split within the Congolese revolutionary forces barred the way to recognition by the OAU.

After several postponements, the *ad hoc* Commission finally met in Nairobi on 25 February 1965 under the chairmanship of President Kenyatta. In his opening address, Kenyatta told delegates that the Commission had been unsuccessful in its efforts in the Congo, and that the situation had gone from bad to worse. The number of white mercenaries seemed to have increased, in spite of his appeal for their withdrawal. The representatives of the Gbenye regime were not permitted to put their case to the Commission. When the Sudanese Foreign Minister, Nahgoub, suggested that they be invited to the plenary session to answer certain questions, thirteen countries voted in favour and seven against, with fourteen abstaining. As a majority of all delegations present was required, the motion was rejected. This reluctance to agree to the proposal was largely due to the disunity of the revolutionary forces.

Tshombe, who represented the Congolese Government at the discussions, welcomed the exclusion of the revolutionary leaders from the proceedings of the Commission as an expression of the OAU's faith in his government. He announced that a general election would take place in the Congo, and that the round-table conference proposed by the OAU was therefore unnecessary. He suggested that the OAU send a team of observers to the Congo, and said that he would allow the team freedom of movement provided that the revolutionaries had laid down their arms. After five days of discussions, on 9 March, the Council of Ministers of the OAU adjourned, agreeing only to refer the Congo question to the African Heads of State.[20] Significantly, the OAU Summit held in October 1965 deliberately omitted the Congo problem from its agenda and refrained from adopting any resolution. Thus ended the OAU chapter on the Congo.

The support for the Tshombe regime from the francophone States, which had been evident at the emergency session of the Council of Ministers in New York in December 1964, was consolidated further at the Nairobi meeting, where these States openly supported Tshombe against the majority of OAU Members. On 25 May 1965 the Congo was admitted as the fifteenth member of OCAM at its meeting at Abidjan. The Tshombe regime thus became a fully-fledged member of the 'French Club'. In the meantime, the mercenaries liquidated the last stronghold of the forces of Gbenye's regime. The bitter internal disputes within Gbenye's government considerably weakened its stand with the independent African States from which they asked military assistance and diplomatic recognition. At the beginning of August 1965, the Congo revolutionary leaders met in Cairo to try to settle the leadership problem. But the meeting produced a split when Gaston Soumailot formed a new government and announced the dissolution of the government led by Christopher Gbenye.

Tshombe's triumph was soon overshadowed by the deterioration of his alliance with President Kasavubu, who was doing his utmost to restrict Tshombe's political influence. On 13 October 1965, Kasavubu forced Tshombe to resign as Prime Minister and asked Everiste Kimba, the former Foreign Minister of Katanga, to form a new government. Tshombe, however, still remained on the scene and began to rally support against President Kasavubu. The end of the Tshombe era came in November 1965, when General Mobutu overthrew Kimba and assumed power. Tshombe went into self-imposed exile in Spain but did not abandon hope of a return to power. There were rumours about a new concentration of the former Katangan *gendarmerie* in Angola. On 30 June 1967, a British aircraft in which Tshombe was travelling from Ibiza to Mallorca was forced to land in Algeria and Tshombe was imprisoned by the Algerian government. On 30 June 1969, he was reported to have died in prison.

## 3. LESSONS FROM THE CONGO CRISIS

The OAU did not and could not bring peace to the Congo and resolve its political problems. This was due above all to foreign intervention in the conflict. If the OAU *ad hoc* Commission on the Congo had been given more time, it might have succeeded in its primary objective, which was to forestall external intervention. The conclusion of the African leaders was that the only safeguard against the occurrence of a similar situation was for them never to allow themselves to become involved in the confrontation between East and West.

The 'Stanleyville drop' was the most important single event in the Congo crisis that led African States to establish a policy of non-alignment as the basis of their foreign policy. The consensus of opposition to foreign interference, notably in the form of employing white mercenaries, was expressed in a 'Resolution on Mercenaries' adopted by the OAU Assembly of Heads of State and Government in Kinshasa in 1967. The Resolution defined in general terms the dangers that mercenaries represent, and offered the Congo help in dealing with the remaining mercenary units which in 1967 were still active in the Eastern Congo under the command of Colonel Schramme. The Resolution stated that the presence of mercenaries would inevitably arouse strong and destructive feelings, and jeopardize the lives of foreigners in the continent. It appealed to all States to enact laws making the recruitment and training of mercenaries a punishable crime and to deter their citizens from enlisting as mercenaries.[21]

The Congo Crisis also forced Africa to realize the danger of disintegration exemplified by the secession of Katanga. As no part of any country — whether it is called a region, a province or a State within a federation — seeking its own independence can achieve it without international recognition (and often foreign help), secession is synonymous with foreign intervention. It was largely due to this lesson of the Congo Crisis that the overwhelming majority of OAU Members supported Nigeria and opposed Biafra, despite the sympathies they might have felt for the plight of the Ibos.

Finally, the Congo Crisis taught the African leaders that their interests would be best served if these were entrusted to the collective opinion of their own organization, the OAU, rather than to the UN. Since the Congo, no African crisis (except for those involving the white-minority regimes) has been allowed to be dealt with outside the African framework.

## 4. NEW 'KATANGA' CONFLICT

However, none of these lessons has had a lasting effect. Africa was not spared foreign intervention in Angola, and this turned the war in there into a major international conflict. Nor have the OAU Members abstained from recruiting mercenaries: they were employed in Angola, in the invasion against Benin, and most recently in Zaire.[1]

Ironically, in March 1977, Katanga (now called Shaba) became the scene of fighting bearing strong resemblance to the events twelve years ago. On 8 March 1977 a force led by 300 mercenaries had invaded south-eastern Shaba province. Within a month the conflict grew into a war between the Zaire army and the troops of the Congolese National Liberation Front (FNLC) led by General Nathanial Mbumba, former Commissioner of Police in Katanga. Most of the invaders were Zairean dissidents who had lived in Angola since the collapse of the late Moise Tshombe's regime. The reported aim of General Mbumba's campaign was not the seccession of Shaba but the overthrow of Mobutu and the setting up of a government of national unity. Although Zaire did appeal to the OAU, its first call for help was addressed to the United States and France. The US responded with a grant of $1 million non-military aid, but stayed out from the conflict. France rushed in Mirage jet bombers, helicopters and transport planes. Out of the blue came the Moroccan offer to send troops, which were subsequently transported to the battlefield by French planes. Apart from Morocco only Egypt and Sudan expressed support for President Mobutu Sese Seko, offering both arms and men. Despite Mobutu's charges of Angolan, Cuban and Soviet involvement no evidence was ever offered to substantiate the accusations.

Africa's reaction to the conflict was best summed up by Dr Bolaji Akinyemi, Director-General of the Nigerian Institute of International Affairs, in his interview with the *Daily Times* (Lagos) of 16 April 1977:

'I should have thought that in 1977 Africa should consider outside military interferences absolutely unacceptable. The OAU has got to be prepared to move away from the ostrich role whenever there is an African action it does not approve of. If the OAU had condemned Africans who prolonged the sufferings of the Angolans, then it should have been in a position to act now. On a second level, the OAU is going to be irrelevant if it cannot cope with problems like this.'

With the outside help, President Mobutu Sese Seko succeeded in halting the advance of the invading force and by the end of May it had been pushed back behind the Angolan border. However, his readiness to use troops of a foreign power to supress a revolt of his own people, and the OAU's failure to initiate steps which would forestall an intervention by its own members will, no doubt, have serious repercussions both for Mobutu's regime and for the Organization.

# Chapter VII

# THE NIGERIAN CIVIL WAR (1967-1970)

The historical origins and actual course of the war between Nigeria and the secessionist Eastern Region, which declared independence under the name of Biafra, have been extensively treated in a number of books.[1] The purpose of this chapter is to show the impact of the Nigerian war on the Organization of African Unity and on the relationships of its members. Two main principles of the OAU Charter were put to the test: the principle of non-interference in the internal affairs of Member-States (Article III, 2), constantly referred to by Nigeria; and respect for the inalienable right to independence (Article III, 3), insisted upon by Biafra,

Fighting started between the troops of the Nigerian Federal Army and of Biafra on 6 July 1967. This soon developed into a war of international dimensions. The war lasted 920 days. The number of Ibos and other Nigerians who died in the conflict is unknown; neither side kept accurate records of military casualties, and there are no reliable records of the civilian victims whose numbers far exceeded those of the former. The figure is estimated at between one and two millions.

Biafra was defeated for a variety of reasons. Starvation and the superiority of the Nigerian Federal forces in manpower were significant factors, but most decisive was the massive supply of arms from Great Britain, which by December 1969 had reached a value of £10 million, and which was more than enough to wipe the Biafrans off the face of the earth. Had there not been a surrender on 12 January 1970, this is precisely what would have happened.

## 1. THE MOTIVES FOR OAU INTERVENTION IN THE NIGERIAN CONFLICT

Despite the attempts of the Federal Military Government to treat its war against Biafra as strictly an internal Nigerian affair, three elements made it of great concern not only to Africa but to the whole world:
— The supply of arms, including aircraft and heavy artillery, by the governments of the United Kingdom, the Soviet Union, Czechoslovakia, and Egypt to the Federal Government, and from French,

Portuguese and other undisclosed sources to Biafra.[2]
— The recognition of Biafra as an independent State, thus according it
  the status of a full member of the international community, by the
  governments of Tanzania (13 April 1968), Gabon (8 May), Ivory
  Coast (14 May), and Zambia (20 May). France too came very close
  to recognizing Biafra.[3]
— The starvation of Biafra's population, which was cut off from the sea
  and encircled by Federal troops. A world wide campaign to help the
  civilian population of Biafra was launched by the International Red
  Cross, the Churches, and other international bodies. A further,
  related element was the presence of a group of foreign military
  observers investigating Biafra's allegations of 'genocide'.[4]


## 2. SUMMIT AT KINSHASA IN SEPTEMBER 1967

The first initiative by the OAU on the Nigerian war took place at the
OAU Assembly meeting at Kinshasa in September 1967. At that time,
the war had already become one of Africa's major problems. The
meeting of the OAU Council of Ministers, which always precedes that
of the Assembly of Heads of State and Government, did not propose
the Nigerian situation for the Assembly agenda. It was felt, however,
that if the African leaders had dispersed without a word on the Nigerian
conflict, they would have provided the OAU's critics with strong
arguments against its usefulness.

The decision to discuss Nigeria was a very difficult one to make. On
the one hand, the Heads of State and Government were faced with
the repeated warnings of the Federal Government of Nigeria that the
war was merely a matter for Nigeria. General Gowon held very firmly
to the view that any intervention, even in the form of a discussion at
OAU level, would be in violation of Article III (2) of the OAU Charter,
which prohibits any interference in the internal affairs of States. On the
other hand, the Biafran regime was pressing for 'internationalization' of
the conflict, which could come about through outside mediation,
especially by the OAU. Several days before the Conference began,
Colonel Ojukwu sent a high-level delegation to Kinshasa to acquaint the
African Heads of State with the Biafran case.

The Resolution adopted by the Assembly was carefully drafted so as
not to create the impression that the OAU was interfering in Nigeria's
internal affairs. In the Resolution, the Heads of State and Government
recognized the situation as an 'internal affair, the solution of which is
primarily the responsibility of the Nigerians themselves', and resolved
to send a consultative mission of six Heads of State (Cameroon, Congo,
Zaire, Ethiopia, Ghana, Liberia and Niger) to the Head of the Federal

Government of Nigeria to assure him of the Assembly's desire for the territorial integrity, unity and peace of Nigeria. The mission was later called a Consultative Committee on Nigeria.

The composition of the mission represented a careful balance of the different attitudes towards the Nigerian conflict. President Ahidjo of Cameroon was known for his sympathy with the Biafran cause and was believed to have co-operated with Biafra in breaking the Federal blockade in the field of telecommunications. Many Ibo people trade and work in Cameroon, especially in the Western region which was once part of Eastern Nigeria. President Diori of Niger, in considering the Nigerian crisis, had to bear in mind the dependence of Niger on the Northern Nigerian Railways as a vital link between his country and the sea. The economic aspect aside, the people of Niger have a natural affection and attachment to Northern Nigerians as fellow-Muslims, and because they claim the same ancestry. Two other members of the mission, Emperor Haile Selassie of Ethiopia and President Tubman of Liberia, were senior statesmen wielding great influence in African diplomacy. The choice of General Ankrah was motivated by the fact that he had been a host of the Aburi meeting and because he knew both General Gowon and Colonel Ojukwu personally. The mission arrived in Lagos on 23 November 1967. General Gowon, though giving the mission warm welcome, told its members very firmly: 'You are here not to mediate'.[5]

The communiqué issued by the mission at the end of its visit to Lagos expressed full agreement with General Gowon's views by reaffirming that 'any solution of the Nigerian crisis must be in the context of preserving the unity and territorial integrity of Nigeria'. The outcome of the OAU mission was a bitter disappointment for the Biafrans. Until the Kinshasa Summit, they had advocated OAU mediation, provided that Biafra's sovereignty should not be negotiable and that Biafra would be invited to the peace talks as a sovereign State and not as a part of Nigeria. An official broadcast by Radio Enugu on 24 November 1968 stated that 'by deciding to consult with only one party to the dispute, the mission has demonstrated its lack of objectivity and doomed itself to failure right from the start'. The OAU was accused of 'condoning genocide' and of proving itself 'a rubber stamp by merely endorsing General Gowon's warning that their own countries would disintegrate if they did not rally to his support.'

## 3. THE KAMPALA PEACE TALKS, MAY 1968

The Biafran rejection of the OAU initiative was the reason why the first peace talks between the two parties were held under the auspices of the

Commonwealth Secretariat rather than those of the OAU. On 6 May 1968 preliminary talks between Chief Anthony Enahoro, the Commissioner for Information, and Sir Louis Mbanefo representing Biafra, were held in London. It had been agreed that peace talks should begin in Kampala, Uganda, on 23 May 1968 and that on the agenda would be the questions of foreign observers, the conditions for ending the hostilities, and the arrangements for a permanent settlement.

The peace talks in Kampala were opened by President Obote of Uganda, who called for an early agreement on the cessation of hostilities as a basic preliminary for a broader understanding. The following were the proposals for a settlement put forward by Biafra:
— unconditional cease-fire and withdrawal of the Federal troops to their pre-war positions;
— that the maintenance of order and respect for law should remain the responsibility of the Biafran Government;
— that the Biafran Army should remain under the control and command of the Biafrans and not the Federal Government;
— that Biafra would join international organizations in its own right and preserve a capacity for concluding international treaties and agreements;
— that Biafra would control its currency and its economic resources, and determine its own policies on economic development.

The Federal Government's conditions for a settlement can be summarized as follows:
— the withdrawal of the declaration of independence by the Eastern Region;
— public acceptance and recognition of the authority of the Federal Military Government over the Eastern Region;
— public acceptance of the twelve new States created in Nigeria;
— the acceptance of civilians as Commissioners in the Federal Executive Council and as members of the State Executive Councils, as a major step in the return to civilian rule;
— agreement to the holding of talks on the future of Nigeria by accredited and equal representatives of the twelve States.

While both proposals offered a great deal of scope for manoeuvring, there remained a fundamental disagreement — namely, that while the Federal Government's principal condition was renunciation of secession by Biafra before a cease-fire, the Biafrans wanted an immediate cease-fire with no such conditions attached.

The difficulty of reconciling the three objectives implicit in the Nigerian crisis — stopping the fighting, preserving the unity of Nigeria, and giving effective assurances of safety to the Ibo people — appeared, both in the peace talks held before the war and during the war itself, to be the absolutely insurmountable obstacle to any settlement. Soon after the peace negotiations began, the issue was no longer whether the Biafran Republic could survive or not. The Federal advances into Biafran territory made it certain that it would not survive within the frontiers set out on 30 May 1967. The practical question (known as the 'permanent settlement') was on what terms the Ibo peoples would be able to live with their neighbours in the future.

On 31 May the Kampala peace talks broke down. Sir Louis Mbanefo accused the Federal delegation of exploiting its military position, trying to dictate rather than to negotiate the terms, using the talks as a propaganda exercise and pinning the blame for the breakdown on the Biafran delegation. He further accused the Nigerian delegation of employing obstructive tactics, of not wanting to talk peace, and of putting forward totally unacceptable proposals. Chief Enahoro described the Biafran demand for an unconditional cease-fire as unrealistic, and the demand for the withdrawal of Federal troops to their pre-war positions as totally unacceptable.


4. NEW INITIATIVE — TALKS AT NIAMEY, JULY 1968

The appalling condition of the Ibo population in the war areas aroused world-wide concern and made further African inaction impossible. Humanitarian considerations were behind the initiative of Emperor Haile Selassie to revive the work of the OAU Consultative Mission on Nigeria by convening a meeting of its members in Niamey (Niger) on 15 July 1968. Colonel Ojukwu made it known that he was prepared to come to Niamey if invited. All six members of the mission were represented, five of them — Cameroon, Ethiopia, Ghana, Liberia and Niger — by the Heads of State. Only President Mobutu of Congo sent a delegation led by a Deputy Foreign Minister.

The assembled members of the mission first heard General Gowon, who told them that 'the rebel leaders and their foreign backers are playing politics with the whole question of human sufferings to their diplomatic and military advantage'. He declared that, in military terms, the rebellion was 'virtually suppressed already'; and that a unilateral cease-fire by the Federal Government without any prior commitment from the rebel leaders to give up secession would offer the secessionists the opportunity to regroup and rearm, and prepare for the continuation of the conflict. He added that 'a unilateral cease-fire on humanitarian grounds would not in any way relieve the sufferings of the innocent victims of our tragic war'. General Gowon did, however, show more understanding for the Ibo fears for their safety than his delegation had done at Kampala, and he agreed to the introduction of outside observers to ensure that Federal troops would not massacre the

Ibo. But he was very firm on the terms of reference of the observers, who were not to be concerned with peace-keeping operations but should observe and bear testimony only.

Colonel Ojukwu's speech to the Consultative Mission, made on 18 July, was not made public, but to judge from his press conference at Abidjan (Ivory Coast) on 21 July, he appeared to be impressed by the way the OAU had dealt with the most important issues of the conflict. He said: 'Provided the spirit of sincerity and honesty which was so very evident in Niamey continues, provided Africa is left on its own to grapple with the problems posed by our difficulties, I think there is a hope. Judging from the way the conference started moving, I think there would be permanent peace or at least temporary peace.'[6]

The OAU Consultative Mission on Nigeria, although continuing to support the Federal Government on the need for preserving Nigeria as one entity, adopted a resolution in which emphasis was put on the relief operations in the distressed areas of Biafra rather than on the reconciliation of the two parties. They were merely invited 'to do everything possible to resume the negotiations as soon as possible in order to achieve a peaceful solution to the crisis'. Although very little information about the proceedings of the mission was made public, it seems that arrangements for relief were the main preoccupation.[7]

Following the meeting of the Consultative Mission, the representatives of Biafra and Nigeria held talks under the chairmanship of President Diori of Niger, and agreed on peace talks in Addis Ababa with the following agenda:
— arrangements for a permanent settlement;
— terms for the cessation of hostilities;
— proposals for the transport of relief supplies to the civilian population in the war areas.


## 5. THE ADDIS ABABA PEACE NEGOTIATIONS (AUGUST— SEPTEMBER 1968)

The talks were opened by Emperor Haile Selassie on 5 August 1968, and he appealed to both parties not to fail. After that the meeting went into closed sessions. It soon became evident that an agreement for political settlement of the dispute between Biafra and the Federal Government was virtually unobtainable. The only field in which the talks could possibly succeed was relief. The Emperor seized this opportunity to get the two sides to agree on some workable arrangements for getting the relief supplies to the war-ravaged areas. He continued his talks with the delegations in his palace and received both delegations on more than thirty-five occasions. His efforts and humanitarian approach to the conflict were commended by Pope Paul, and supported by the International Red Cross. The Red Cross special envoy, August Lindt, came to Addis Ababa and tried to get the two sides to agree on a 'mercy corridor', which would speed up relief supplies. Without any agreement being reached, the meeting was adjourned for a week, on 15 August, to give time to the delegations to study various proposals.

When the negotiations were resumed on 22 August, an agreement seemed to be within reach. Both sides had agreed in principle to a compromise proposal, put forward by the Emperor, for air and land mercy corridors to aid the civilian victims of the war. The Federal Government had requested that the Biafrans should place one of their strategic airfields under Red Cross control so that it could receive freighter aircraft with food and medical supplies from a demilitarized Federal airport.

However, all glimmers of hope proved to be premature. On 25 August, General Gowon, without waiting for the outcome of the Addis Ababa talks, announced the launching of a 'final offensive'. As a result, Aba, one of the few remaining towns still held by the Biafrans, fell into Federal hands on 4 September, and this in turn put more pressure on the Biafrans at Addis Ababa. But they refused to yield. Finally, on 9 September 1968, after nearly five weeks of negotiations, the Addis Ababa peace talks were adjourned.


6. SUMMIT AT ALGIERS, SEPTEMBER 1968

When the Assembly of Heads of State and Government met on 4 September 1968 at the Club des Pins in Algiers, the political fate of Biafra seemed to be sealed. The four countries which recognized Biafra were unable to muster any meaningful support for the Biafran cause. Although many African leaders sympathized with the humane motives behind the recognition of Biafra by four OAU members, and shared their concern, they rejected President Nyerere's thesis that unity achieved by conquest is worthless.[8] Despite the support given to President Nyerere's arguments by President Houphouet-Boigny of Ivory Coast,[9] the fear of similar conflicts in their own countries, many with similar tribal and ethnic problems, was a decisive influence on nearly all the delegates to the Algiers Summit.

It must have disappointed Emperor Haile Selassie that he could not report more solid achievements. Although the OAU Consultative Mission on Nigeria had no easy task in trying to help the parties to the dispute to settle their differences in peaceful negotiation, it had come closer to solving the problem than had any of the other initiatives made at different times by the Commonwealth Secretariat and other countries, notably Great Britain. In its report to the Summit Conference, the Federal Government maintained its insistence on the principle of a united country, but recognized the right of the many minorities in Nigeria to safeguards. The Biafran delegation insisted equally strongly that the Ibo could not live with the rest of the Nigerians, and held that secession was the only solution.

The meeting adopted a resolution which appealed to the Biafran leaders to co-operate with the Federal authorities in restoring peace and unity in Nigeria through the cessation of hostilities. The OAU recommended that the Federal Military Government of Nigeria should declare a general amnesty and co-operate with it in ensuring the physical security of all the people of Nigeria, until mutual confidence could be restored. The Resolution further called upon all Member-States of the UN and the OAU to 'refrain from any action detrimental to the peace, unity and territorial integrity of Nigeria'. Finally, it invited the Consultative Committee to 'continue its efforts with a view to implementing the resolutions of Kinshasa and Algiers'.[10]

Thirty-three delegations voted for the Resolution, which gave them an outright victory. This can be attributed to the following factors:

— The host-country, Algeria, strongly sustained the Federal thesis, and would not admit a Biafran delegation, even if the Federal delegation and the conference might have been disposed to concede the possibility. President Boumedienne, in his opening address, fiercely denounced 'plots from all sides directed against Nigeria, aiming to disintegrate and shake to its foundations this great African State, of whose unity and cohesion we were and are proud'; and this set the course of the conference which the majority of the delegations followed.[11]

— The support for the Federal stand from the UN Secretary-General, U Thant, who spoke to the Conference on 13 September 1968.[12]

— The desire of most leaders to be on the winning side and thus cement diplomatic relations with Nigeria, which seemed about to reassume a most influential role in Africa.

The feelings of the great majority of States siding with the Federal Government of Nigeria were well expressed by the *East African Standard* of 3 September:

'Recognizing Ibo concern, nonetheless is should be reiterated that Biafra took the initative in secession, though the OAU specifically supports unity. Even if any hope of success existed in the beginning, none is left, and for Col. Ojukwu to continue resistance when the ring is closing is reminiscent of Hitler in his Berlin bunker. Sacrifice of life and the prolongation of suffering are reasons more potent than any OAU resolution *per se* for accusing him of useless and callous disregard for his people. Biafra has lost the war and the terms for a cease-fire should have been accepted months ago. Every day has added death and suffering — needlessly sacrificed to personal obstinacy in the face of OAU condemnation.'

On the question of the independent existence of Biafra, the majority of the OAU members adhered to a policy of non-recognition of Biafra.[13]


## 7. MONROVIA MISSION ON NIGERIA

The last meeting of the OAU Consultative Mission on Nigeria was held in Monrovia on 17 April 1969, attended by President Tubman of Liberia, Emperor Haile Selassie, President Ahidjo of Cameroon, and I. K. W. Harlley of Ghana. The OAU Secretary-General, Diallo Telli, was present. The Mission ended its three-day meeting on 20 April 1969 without making any progress towards reconciliation between Nigeria and Biafra. The Mission proposed that 'the two parties of the Civil War accept, in the supreme interest of Africa, a united Nigeria, which ensures all forms of security to all citizens'. It further suggested that 'within the context of this agreement, the two parties accept an immediate cessation of fighting, and the opening without delay of peace negotiations'. Furthermore, the Consultative Mission offered its good offices to facilitate these negotiations. The Mission 'noted with satisfaction that the Federal Government of Nigeria accepted the proposals', and expressed regret that the Biafran delegation did not.

The Biafran delegation was later reported to have stated that, if the words 'a solution' had been used in place of the words 'united Nigeria', they would have been willing to accept the declaration in principle. They were not prepared to discuss an OAU concept of territorial integrity without some discussion on what this would entail.


## 8. SUMMIT AT ADDIS ABABA, SEPTEMBER 1969

The last OAU initiative on a settlement of the Nigerian conflict was made at the 6th Assembly of Heads of State and Government in Addis Ababa on 6 September 1969. The Conference adopted a resolution urging both sides in the Nigerian Civil war to call a cease-fire and negotiate for a united Nigeria. The four countries which had recognized Biafra (Gabon, Ivory Coast, Tanzania, Zambia) abstained, as did Sierra Leone. The Resolution appealed 'solemnly and urgently to the two parties involved in the civil war to agree to preserve, in the overriding interests of Africa, the unity of Nigeria and accept immediately the suspension of hostilities and the opening without delay of negotiations intended to preserve the unity of Nigeria and restore reconciliation and peace that will ensure for the population every form of security and every guarantee of equal rights, prerogatives and obligations'.[14]


## 9. END OF PEACE EFFORTS AND THE COLLAPSE OF BIAFRA

Colonel Ojukwu, in an address to the Biafran Consultative Assembly on 1 November 1969, reiterated his preparedness to meet Federal representatives in any place and at any time. However, he excluded the OAU as a possible forum. Biafra had lost faith in the OAU, 'due to its lack of foresight, objectivity, courage and conviction'.[15]

A few days later, a Biafran policy statement was issued by the Markpress Agency in Geneva, indicating a major concession:

'Since our attachment to sovereignty is functional and not sentimental, Biafra will be prepared to accept, at the suggestion of no matter who, any alternative arrangement that can guarantee the non-recurrence of the massacres of the past twenty-five years.'[16]

The announcement was taken to mean that Colonel Ojukwu was prepared to abandon his hitherto unyielding demand for secession from Federal Nigeria. Twenty-four hours later, however, the head of the Markpress Agency, William Bernstein, declared that the statement had been completely misinterpreted. He said it was:

'absolutely ridiculous to say that Biafra is prepared to give up her independence. Biafra has always demanded safety guarantees for the Ibo people, whose mistreatment was the principal cause of secession. But this would have to be done within the framework of an economic federation of autonomous states. Sovereignty can be interpreted in many ways. The way it is understood by Biafra is an economic federation of independent States, with Biafra keeping her army.'

Ojukwu's attempts to secure mediation in the conflict through Switzerland, Austria, Sweden and Yugoslavia, in preference to the OAU, yielded no positive results. None of these countries made an official approach to the Federal Government of Nigeria, which stressed repeatedly that the OAU was the only body authorized to mediate.

The last round of peace talks between Biafra and the Federal Government were agreed to take place in December 1969. Both parties were invited to Addis Ababa by the Emperor Haile Selassie. The question of whether the Emperor was making his initiative privately or in his capacity as chairman of the OAU Consultative Mission on Nigeria gave rise to some controversy. The Biafran interpretation was that it was a private initiative, as Biafra had refused to have anything more to do with the OAU. The Nigerian Ambassador to Addis Ababa, Olu Sanu, asked for clarification, and on 17 December 1969 he announced that he had received assurances from the Ethiopian Foreign Minister, Ketema Yifru, that the talks were organized by the Emperor within the framework of the OAU. As a result of this impasse, the talks never took place and the Biafran delegation, led by Pius Okigbo, which had already arrived in Addis Ababa, returned home on 18 December 1969. By that time the war was almost over.

By the end of 1969 the morale of the Biafran Army was rapidly declining, and desertions were rife. The famished soldiers threw away their arms and disappeared into the bush or into the crowds of distressed refugees. In what remained of Biafran territory, refugees clogged the roads, and the refugee camps and villages were overcrowded. The frequent strafing of the retreat routes by the MIG's of the Nigerian Air Force added to the panic, which was increasing from day to day. According to an official Federal announcement on 11 January 1970, Owerri had fallen on 9 January.

On the morning of 10 January the last meeting of the Biafran Cabinet was held. Colonel Ojukwu announced that he would leave Biafra 'in search of peace', and appointed his Chief of Staff, Colonel Phillip Effiong, to administer the government. Meanwhile, Federal troops were within three miles of Biafra's only remaining airstrip at Uli. One of the last people to use it was the Biafran leader, who arrived there at about 03.00 hours local time on 11 January.[17] The following day, on 12 January, Colonel Effiong offered General Gowon the unconditional surrender of Biafra.

The surrender ceremony took place at army headquarters, Dodan Barracks, Lagos, on Thursday, 15 January 1970. Colonel Phillip Effiong formally presented a document to General Gowon, before members of the Supreme Military Council, the Administrator of the Central Eastern State, A.U. Asika, and top-ranking military and government officials. The document contained a declaration that the so-called 'Republic of Biafra' had ceased to exist and that:

— the authority of the Federal Military Government of Nigeria was accepted;
— the existing administrative and political structure of Nigeria was accepted; and
— constitutional arrangements would in future be worked out by representatives of Nigeria.

General Gowon concluded his speech by saying to the Biafran delegation: 'Gentlemen, let us join hands to rebuild this country, where no man will be oppressed.'[18] The two soldiers, General Gowon in uniform and Colonel Effiong in civilian clothes, then posed for photographs, embracing each other several times.


## 10. CONCLUSIONS

Ojukwu grossly miscalculated the impact of the Biafran case on the international scene, where he hoped for both recognition and material assistance. Biafra did not obtain recognition soon after his secession, because of three main factors:
— the assumption by the Federal Government of the political initiative in the crisis, following the creation of twelve States;
— the Federal Government's firmness and its gaining of the support of Chief Awolowo, who became a member of Federal Executive Council; and
— the rapid and effective institution of an economic blockade on Biafra.
By these three moves, coupled with a very sharp warning to the outside world not to interfere in what was described as a purely internal problem, the Nigerian Federal Government rapidly showed its determination to oppose the secession. The Portuguese connection and the help which Biafra received from South Africa lost the Biafrans a great deal of African goodwill.

The recognition of Biafra by Gabon, Ivory Coast, Tanzania and Zambia strengthened Biafra's claim to independent existence and its demand to be treated on an equal basis with the Federal Government at the peace talks. But it never amounted to anything more than moral support of the Biafran cause — support given purely for humanitarian reasons. There is no need to go deeper into the recognition of Biafra by the four African States, or the effect of the implied recognition by France, which was believed to have provided Biafra with more than moral support: within the context of the Nigerian crisis, Biafra's existence depended above all on the outcome of the armed conflict between the two sides and not on the legitimacy of the Biafran cause. The significance of the policy of non-recognition of Biafra, which was endorsed by the OAU Summit Meeting at Algiers when it called upon 'all Member-States of the United Nations and OAU to refrain from any action detrimental to the peace, unity and territorial integrity of Nigeria', was that it upheld the principle of African unity. This might be seriously undermined if secessions of the Biafran type were allowed to pass.

The Federal Government never asked for UN intervention. Biafra's plea for UN mediation was ignored, and UN involvement was limited to the humanitarian relief carried out and organized with the Federal Government's consent. In the absence of a Federal request for UN help, there was no legal basis for the UN to adopt any measures aimed at restoring peace in Nigeria. The consent of a legitimate government is the only basis on which the UN peace-keeping force can operate in a country. This applies not only to military operations, but also to 'humanitarian intervention' for relief of civilian victims of war. The dilemma of those who, deeply moved by the mass starvation of the Ibo, were urging their governments to mount an airlift to Biafra against the wishes of the Federal Government, was that such action would constitute a violation of Nigeria's sovereignty.

The loss of more than 1 million lives was the most horrible aspect of the Nigerian war. However, two important lessons emerged from the conflict. The Nigerian experience persuaded all OAU Members to accept the authority of the OAU concerning the settlement of their disputes of whatever origin and magnitude. And the outcome of the war was that 60 million Nigerians found a common political and economic future within the framework of twelve States.[19] The functioning and prosperity of such a large Federation demonstrates the advantages of a close co-operation on an inter-State basis.

# Chapter VIII

# OAU POLICY AND STRATEGY ON SOUTHERN AFRICA

'There are two main areas of conflict in Southern Africa. The first is the confrontation with colonialism. The second is the conflict with the system of apartheid which has rightly been declared by the United Nations as a crime against humanity. But whether we are dealing with the struggle against colonialism in Rhodesia or illegal occupation of Namibia or racist domination in South Africa, the main opponent of Africa is the same: the South African regime and the power it wields in the three areas. Thus the Southern African problem is firstly South Africa as a colonialist power, and secondly South Africa as a racist society.'

This is how the situation in southern Africa was defined by the Declaration on Southern Africa adopted at the 9th Extraordinary Session of the Council of Ministers at Dar-es-Salaam on 10 April 1975. The Declaration is one of the two most important policy pronouncements by the OAU on southern Africa since the adoption of the OAU Charter in 1963. The other is the Lusaka Manifesto, endorsed by the OAU in 1969. Both documents are to be examined here.

The foundations of OAU policy on southern Africa — which encompasses the white minority regimes of South Africa and Rhodesia, and which, at the time when the OAU came into existence in 1963, also included the largest part of Portugal's colonial empire — were laid down by the OAU Charter, which declared as one of its purposes 'to eradicate all forms of colonialism in Africa'. They were elaborated in the resolutions adopted on the problems of decolonization of southern Africa and apartheid, which featured prominently at all deliberations of the OAU main bodies.

## 1. SOUTH AFRICA

When the Heads of State and Government of independent African States, assembled at Addis Ababa in May 1963, were debating 'apartheid', the word was already twenty years old. An Afrikaans word meaning 'separateness',[1] it was first used on 28 March 1943 in the Cape

Town newspaper *Die Burger*, to refer to the policy of the Nationalist party. It was described by the architect of apartheid, Prime Minister Malan, in his address to the South African parliament on 25 January 1944, as the policy 'to ensure the safety of the white race and of Christian civilization'. Since then, South Africa has implemented apartheid by forcing the removal of at least 3 million people and breaking up hundreds of thousands of families in the process of reversing the development of a multi-racial society of almost 22 million people.

In considering measures which would put an end to the 'South African criminal policy of apartheid', the Addis Ababa conference took its inspiration from a resolution of the General Assembly of the United Nations adopted the previous year.[2] The resolution called on the UN Members to force South Africa to abandon its racist policies by:

- breaking off diplomatic relations with the Government of South Africa, or refraining from establishing such relations;
- closing their ports to all vessels flying the South African flag;
- enacting legislation prohibiting their ships from entering South African ports;
- boycotting all South African goods and refraining from exporting goods, including all arms and ammunition, to South Africa; and
- refusing landing and passage facilities to all aircraft belonging to the Government and companies registered under the laws of the Republic of South Africa.

The OAU made an identical demand on its Members,[3] and delegated the Foreign Ministers of Liberia, Madagascar, Sierra Leone and Tunisia to inform the Security Council of how the independent African States saw the situation in South Africa. The four African Foreign Ministers told the Council:

- that the OAU Members regarded apartheid as a threat to international peace and security;
- that it was obvious that the South African Government had no intention of abandoning its apartheid policies despite numerous urgings from the United Nations;
- that the independent African States would not sit passively by while Africans were subjugated to sub-human level; and
- that the Security Council should follow the OAU example by implementing the General Assembly Resolution 1761, of 1962.

It is worth noticing that the OAU also asked the oil-producing countries 'to cease as a matter of urgency their supply of oil and petroleum products to South Africa' — an idea which, eleven years later, the Arab oil-producing countries turned into an 'oil weapon' used against the supporters of Israel.

The Security Council Resolution S 5386 of 7 August 1963[4],

adopted on the initiative of the OAU, was the beginning of a sustained OAU diplomatic offensive at the United Nations against South Africa, with two objectives:

— to convince the members of the United Nations that the situation in South Africa constituted a threat to international peace and security, and that the Security Council should therefore resort to actions provided for in Chapter VII of the UN Charter ranging from an economic blockade to military intervention by the UN forces; and

— to push South Africa into isolation from the international community, and to work for its expulsion from the United Nations and all other international organizations.

These objectives were only partially achieved. While the General Assembly of the United Nations endorsed the African view that the policies of apartheid of the Government of South Africa are 'a negation of the Charter of the United Nations and constitute a crime against humanity', and that the explosive situation in South Africa and in southern Africa as a whole results from the inhuman and aggressive policies of apartheid pursued by the Government of South Africa, which constitute a threat to international peace and security — the Security Council never went beyond the mere description of the situation in South Africa as 'seriously disturbing international peace and security in southern Africa'. It not only refused to concede that the situation constituted a *threat*, but also maintained that the peace was being disturbed in a limited area only, that is southern Africa. The OAU was close to its second objective in 1974, but South Africa's membership was saved by the triple veto cast by the United States, Great Britain and France.[5] When they repeated their veto in June 1975, stopping the Security Council Resolution requesting a mandatory arms embargo on South Africa and calling for actions under Chapter VII of the UN Charter, the OAU Summit at Kampala in 1975 called it a testimony 'to their well-known commitment on the side of the South African racist regime.'[6]

Before long, the OAU had to accept that their anti-apartheid offensive was virtually powerless. The Administrative Secretary-General Diallo Telli, in his report submitted to the 1964 OAU Summit in Cairo, said that the offensive 'did not have the slightest effect on the regimes concerned', and after summing up the developments in South Africa concluded that 'all venues for peaceful and legal means to alleviate the intolerable conditions have been progressively eliminated by the South African Government'. The findings of the International Conference on Economic Sanctions against South Africa held earlier that year in London, which concluded that 'the adverse effects of a policy of collective sanctions on world trade, finance and on the economies of individual countries having a significant share in the South African economy would be small and marginal',[7] also proved to be of an academic value only.

The Cairo Summit repeated the call for a boycott of South African goods, and asked the major trading partners of South Africa to cooperate. Unfortunately, many of the African countries were themselves still trading with South Africa; South African vessels enjoyed the facilities of African ports, and the South African Airways used African airports. Jomo Kenyatta, then the Prime Minister of Kenya, told the Cairo Summit: 'We shall have a duty now to marshall world support for sanctions and especially to see how best our own efforts in Africa could be made effective. We cannot expect the world to take us seriously if we do not ourselves make the maximum sacrifice in this matter.'

In 1976, the OAU still found it necessary to urge those of its members 'which have not yet done so to refrain from all relations with the reactionary and inhuman regime of apartheid'.[8] The fact that this was thirteeen years after they were first asked to do so speaks for itself. The majority of the OAU States had gradually complied with OAU measures against South Africa, but a small number of recalcitrant members had sabotaged collective OAU efforts. In defiance of the OAU policy the President of Malawi, Dr Kamuzu Banda, announced on 10 September 1967 the establishment of formal diplomatic relations between his country and South Africa. Ironically, on the same day, the OAU Assembly of Heads of State and Government in Kinshasa adopted a Resolution on Apartheid and Racial Discrimination which condemned the political, economic and military collaboration of the Western powers with South Africa and requested all African States to be vigilant in boycotting South African products.[9] Most OAU Members condemned Malawi, with Zambia taking the lead in proposing its expulsion from the OAU;[10] but they were fairly restrained, and there was even some sympathy for Malawi's policy from the Ivory coast, the Central African Republic, Chad, Dahomey (Benin), Gabon, Ghana, Lesotho, Malagasy, Mauritius, Rwanda, Togo, Uganda and Upper Volta. This foreshadowed the subsequent division of Africa over 'dialogue', described below.

Much more disappointing to the OAU was the attitude of the Western powers who were trading with South Africa with no excuse beyond profit. The point which the OAU put again and again to the Western powers was that their economic links with South Africa are responsible for the survival of that country and its apartheid policies. The Western powers never really took the OAU seriously and their attitude towards the African pleas and demands was that of arrogant disregard. Rather than blame the 'communist penetration' into Africa, it is in this arrogance of theirs that the Western powers should see the cause of those anti-Western feelings which have, in many African countries, grown into open hostility.[11]

At all times the African leaders have been fully aware of the fact that the success of their campaign against South Africa ultimately depends on the attitude of the great powers, permanent members of the UN Security Council, who by virtue of their economic and military strength have a decisive say on any international issue both inside and outside the United Nations. Two of the permanent members of the Security Council — Great Britain and France — were the chief architects of colonialism in Africa. Three of them — Great Britain, France and the United States — were, in the Sixties, South Africa's main trading partners and the principal investors in South African business. They were joined later by West Germany, which since 1975 has become South Africa's number-one trading partner and its third largest investor. All four were also allies of Portugal through common trading and business interests.[12] It was to them that the OAU delegation of Foreign Ministers stated their case in August 1963.

The OAU Summit in Cairo in 1964 appealed to the great powers 'to discontinue the encouragement they are giving to the maintenance of apartheid by their investments and commercial relations with the Pretoria Government.' One year later, in Accra, the Assembly of Heads of State and Government singled out arms deliveries to South Africa as the first target of embargo policy. It urged all States to institute a strict embargo on the supply of arms to South Africa, and asked France in particular to end forthwith its supply of military equipment. The Accra Summit also reminded the Western powers that 'their economic collaboration with the South African Government encourages it to defy world opinion and to accelerate the implementation of the policy of apartheid'.[13] None of the South African trading partners took any notice of OAU's plea, repeated in much stronger language at subsequent OAU meetings.

At the 1968 OAU Summit, the African leaders showed their anger by condemning 'unreservedly' Great Britain, the United States, France, West Germany and Japan for their 'continued political and military collaboration with the South African regime' which made it possible for South Africa to persist with its racial policies. West Germany, Italy and France were also condemned for selling military equipment and assisting South Africa in the production of ammunition and poisonous gas.[14]

An important African initiative on decolonization and apartheid was the 'Lusaka Manifesto on Southern Africa', a joint statement agreed upon by representatives of Burundi, Central African Republic, Chad,

Congo, Ethiopia, Kenya, Rwanda, Somalia, Sudan, Tanzania, Uganda, Zaire and Zambia at the Conference of East and Central African States at Lusaka in April 1969.

The purposes of the Manifesto were to explain Africa's reasons for its united opposition to the racialist policies of the Government of South Africa; to outline Africa's objectives in southern Africa (decolonization and the elimination of racial discrimination); and to refute South African claims that its apartheid policies are an internal matter into which no State has the right to intervene. The signatory States explained their concern with southern Africa as follows:

'Our objectives in Southern Africa stem from our commitment to the principle of human equality. We are not hostile to the administrations of these States because they are manned and controlled by white people. We are hostile to them because they are systems of minority control which exist as a result of, and in the pursuance of, doctrines of human inequality. What we are working for is the right of self-determination for the people of those territories. We are working for a rule in those countries which is based on the will of all the people, and an acceptance of the equality of every citizen.'

The Manifesto asserts that the Republic of South Africa is an independent State;[15] but while recognizing that 'on every legal basis its internal affairs are a matter exclusively for the people of South Africa', it points out that the policy of apartheid exceeds the limits of 'internal affairs' and is of rightful concern to the international community.

'The purpose of law is people, and we assert that the actions of the South African Government are such that the rest of the world has a responsibility to take some action in defence of humanity.'

African aims are then summed up as follows:
— that the people in the territories still under colonial rule shall be free to determine for themselves their own institutions of self-government;
— that the individuals in Southern Africa 'shall be freed from an environment poisoned by the propaganda of racialism, and given an opportunity to be men — not white men, brown men, yellow men or black men'.

While the African objectives outlined in the Manifesto reaffirmed the previous stand expressed by OAU resolutions, it was the following statement which brought an entirely new element into African policy on southern Africa:

'We would prefer to negotiate rather than destroy, to talk rather than kill. We do not advocate violence, we advocate an end to the violence against human dignity which is now being perpetrated by the oppressors of Africa. If peaceful progress to emancipation were possible, or if changed circumstances were to make it possible in future, we would urge our brothers in the resistance movements to use peaceful methods of struggle even at the cost of some compromise on the timing of change.'

It was to this section of the Lusaka Manifesto that the Western press drew most attention, interpreting it as 'the abandoment of the armed struggle'; and it seriously disturbed the liberation movements in southern Africa who objected strongly to being pushed into a 'compromise' with the regimes they were fighting.

The Manifesto also constituted a departure from the OAU policy of deliberately avoiding any direct contact with the Pretoria regime. None of the OAU resolutions on apartheid and South Africa, although regularly condemning it, were ever addressed to it; no appeal was ever made to the South African Government, despite the fact that the existence of South Africa as an independent sovereign State and member of the international community was recognized by all OAU members. The OAU pressure for a change in South Africa had always been applied through the United Nations and those Western countries maintaining close relations with the South African Republic. It was the Manifesto's wish 'to negotiate rather than destroy' that finally opened the doors to 'détente'.

The Lusaka Manifesto was endorsed by the Assembly of Heads of State and Government in 1969 in Addis Ababa. Its chairman, then President Ahmadou Ahidjo of Cameroon, was asked to present it to the 24th Session of the General Assembly of the United Nations. On 20 November 1969 the UN General Assembly adopted Resolution 2505 (XXIV) welcoming the Manifesto and recommending it to the attention of all States and peoples. The Resolution was adopted by a roll-call vote with 113 countries in favour, 2 against (South Africa and Portugal) and 2 abstentions (Malawi and Cuba).

The proposal for a 'Dialogue with South Africa' was made by President Houphouet-Boigny of Ivory Coast on 6 November 1970.[16] It was based on the belief that mutual contact between the independent African States and the South African regime would eventually cause a 'change of heart' on the part of the South African whites and bring about the end of apartheid. He proposed the establishment of diplomatic relations, trade missions and an exchange of delegations with South

Africa. He invited African Heads of State to join him in launching a 'peace mission' to 'help the South African Whites to enter into dialogue with their own blacks'. However, he added cautiously that he would take no independent intiative towards Pretoria, and that he would act only in co-operation with the OAU after consulting first the members of the Organisation Commune Africaine et Malagache (OCAM). He elaborated on his fears over the danger to peace in the African continent, which he saw to be threatened by Communism. The key point in his statement was:

'I believe the dialogue with the White citizens of South Africa is feasible, if it is carried out in a perspective of peace through neutrality . . . which is of concern to all Africans, to the White population of South Africa as well as ourselves.'[17]

The President's initiative was supported by the members of the 'Entente Council' (Upper Volta, Dahomey (Benin), Niger and Togo) as well as by Gabon, the Central African Republic, Lesotho, Madagascar, Swaziland and Malawi. But each of the Heads of State and Government of the countries emphasized that 'while we condemn racial discrimination and apartheid, another way besides armed struggle should be found to achieve our objective'.[18] Thus the debate over a Dialogue began.

The views of the advocates of Dialogue can be summed up as follows:
— the armed struggle of the national liberation movements had failed;
— the African States did not possess the military and economic resources to challenge South Africa decisively;
— the trade embargo was certain to fail: non-African powers, including the USA, Britain, France, West Germany and Japan would not stop trading with South Africa, and a number of African States could not afford to do so;
— if the independent African States engaged in a dialogue with the South African Government, this would encourage moderate White opinion and influential business pressure groups within South Africa to make peace with the Black majority and put an end to apartheid. Alternatively, it might bring about a change in the South African regime itself by methods which only those who live in the country could legitimately use.[19]

The challenge of the 'Dialogue policy' forced the African leaders to define their policy towards South Africa, as a matter of urgency. First to act were General Gowon of Nigeria and Emperor Haile Selassie of Ethiopia who met in May 1971 and laid down the OAU rules for dealing with the 'Dialogue policy'. In their joint communiqué of 8 May

1971, they stated that there could be no meaningful dialogue which was not based on that respect for human equality and dignity demanded by the Lusaka Manifesto[20] — a view also subscribed to by President Jomo Kenyatta whom General Gowon saw after his visit of Ethopia.[21]

A showdown between the supporters and opponents of Dialogue occurred at the OAU Summit held on 21–23 June 1971 in Addis Ababa. It was preceded by the meeting of the Council of Ministers which began on 11 June. After it the Chairman of the Council, Omar Arteh, the Foreign Minister of Somalia, issued a statement saying 'whatever differences we may have, the ultimate goal is one — African Unity'. The unity was evident when the Council began its deliberation of the agenda for the Summit. When the discussion opened, thirty-seven delegations were present and four — Zaire, Uganda, Mauritius and the Central African Republic — were absent. The prevailing mood on Dialogue with the South African Government was shown in the debate on the wording of this item on the agenda. The proposal of Ivory Coast, to have the matter described as 'peace through neutrality', was defeated in favour of the Tanzanian proposal: 'the principles of OAU and the Lusaka Manifesto: Dialogue and the future strategy of Africa'. The delegations of Ivory Coast and Gabon walked out in protest. Those of Upper Volta, Togo and Dahomey (Benin) also left the meeting, but only to show solidarity with the senior member of the Entente rather than as a direct expression of disagreement with the proposal. Their departure did not deter those who formulated the 'Declaration on the Question of Dialogue'. It was drafted by a committee composed of representatives of Algeria, Burundi, Egypt, Ghana, Liberia, Nigeria, Senegal and Tanzania. The Declaration rejected Dialogue with South Africa, describing it as a 'manoeuvre by South Africa and its allies to divide African States, confuse world opinion, relieve South Africa from international ostracism and isolation, and obtain an acceptance of the *status quo* in South Africa'.[22]

The Declaration reiterated the commitment to the principles of the OAU Charter, stating that the Lusaka Manifesto was the only basis for a solution to the problems of apartheid, racial discrimination and colonialism in Africa. If there was to be any dialogue at all, it should be between the minority regime of South Africa and the people they are oppressing and exploiting. Perhaps its most important provision was the obligation that no Member-States of the OAU should initiate or engage in any type of activity that would undermine or abrogate the solemn undertakings of the OAU Charter, and that such activity should be undertaken only with the guidance, consent and approval of the OAU. This implied that the right of each Member-State to independent opinion and independent foreign policy did not apply in the case of Dialogue with the South African Government. The Declaration made it clear that, from then on, any State pursuing the policy of Dialogue would be acting contrary to the principles of the Charter and defying an expressly and strongly formulated opinion of the qualified majority of OAU Members.

The Declaration was endorsed by twenty-eight States. Ivory Coast, Gabon, Lesotho, Malagasy, Malawi and Mauritius voted against it, while Dahomey (Benin), Niger, Togo, and Upper Volta abstained. Although Ivory Coast expressed disapproval of the Declaration and President Banda of Malawi defied it by paying an official visit to South Africa in August 1971 (the first Head of an independent State to do so), the principles laid down in the Lusaka Manifesto prevailed.

The OAU's rejection of Dialogue with South Africa was reaffirmed by the signatories of the Lusaka Manifesto who met in Mogadishu in October 1971. In a document called 'Mogadishu Declaration',[23] the Heads of State of East and Central Africa reviewed the developments since the adoption of the Lusaka Manifesto. The document dealt at length with the so-called 'outward looking policy',[24] launched by South Africa in support of the Dialogue, and described it as follows:

'The "outward looking policy" should not fool anyone about South Africa's intentions. Indeed, Vorster has time and again told the South African White population that his policy in no way deviates from the official apartheid policy. Vorster's so-called policy of friendship with independent Africa has been motivated by his government's growing isolation in the whole world and the necessity therefore to want to change that situation without, however, removing the cause of that isolation. With promises of aid or with the threat of "hitting them so hard that they will never forget it" Vorster is using blackmail to divide the African States. While the South African Government rejected and continues to reject the idea of dialogue with the African people in South Africa, the African governments should not have been deceived about the real reasons for the "outward looking policy" of Pretoria.'

After analysing the situation in Southern Africa, the Declaration concluded that 'there is no way left to the liberation of Southern Africa except armed struggle to which we already give and will increasingly continue to give our fullest support', which was the reassurance demanded and received by the liberation movements that the OAU had not abandoned them. The effect of the Declaration was soon felt in the intensification of fighting on all fronts, in Mozambique and Angola as well as within Rhodesia itself and Namibia.

The sudden reversal in policy by President Amin of Uganda, from a position favouring a Dialogue to one of fervent opposition; the overthrow of the Busia regime in January 1972; and the fall of President Tsiranana of Malagasy, finally sealed the fate of the Dialogue. When the OAU Assembly of Heads of State and Government met in Rabat in June 1972, it was already a dead issue and was not even mentioned.

In 1971, the OAU repeated its call for world-wide action against South Africa with the following objectives:

— the cessation of all military co-operation with South Africa;
— the boycott of South Africa in economic, cultural, and other fields;
— the ending of torture in South African prisons and the release of all political prisoners;
— the application to freedom fighters of the relevant articles of the Geneva Conventions of 1949 on the treatment of prisoners of war; and the definite participation of liberation movements in the drafting and application of international law applicable to the internal conflict;
— the imposition of sanctions on companies investing in South Africa; and
— the prohibition of forced emigration, especially in respect of skilled workers, to South Africa.[25]

The year 1972 also showed a rising level of consciousness and organization among the opposition in Rhodesia (where the British-Rhodesian agreement on the settlement was rejected) and in Namibia (where there was a general strike of workers in Ovamboland). These developments indicated that if internal opposition were reinforced by guerrilla warfare carried from outside, the white minority regimes would be faced with serious security problems. The OAU Summit held in 1972 at Rabat was, so far, the finest example of African unity in the history of the OAU and it was entirely dominated by the issues of Africa's total decolonization. It adopted one of its most militant resolutions, the 'Recommendations on special measures to be adopted on decolonization and the struggle against apartheid and racial discrimination" discussed in Chapter VI above.

The Resolution on South Africa adopted at the 10th OAU Summit in Addis Ababa in May 1973 reiterated its concern over the 'repressive measures of the South African minority racist regime against the African people in this territory' and its view that the 'massive military build-up of South Africa constitutes a threat to peace and security in Africa'. The continued economic and military assistance to South Africa by NATO powers was condemned on the grounds that 'it enabled the Pretoria regime to maintain and even expand its apartheid policy.' The Resolution rejected the contention that 'economic, financial and cultural links with South Africa could lead to a rescindment of the apartheid policy'.* The 'Resolution on sanctions against the white minority regimes in Southern Africa', adopted in 1975 at the 12th OAU Summit at Kampala was very explicit in voicing Africa's disappointment with the attitude of the Western powers, and held them directly responsible for the survival of the regimes in South Africa and Rhodesia.[26]

When the 13th Assembly of the Heads of State and Government met in July 1976 at Port Louis, Mauritius, South Africa was engulfed in racial riots at Soweto and other African townships, which were suppressed with a brutality which set the whole African continent ablaze with anger. The Port Louis Summit responded with a 'Resolution on the Soweto Massacre in South Africa',[27] which described the Soweto events as a challenge to the conscience of the world and condemned the Western powers for 'buttressing and arming the racist regime responsible for the massacres'. The 'Resolution on South Africa' is the longest of all adopted by the Summit; it reiterated the OAU commitment to the liberation of South African people from racist oppression, and in very strong language condemned the trading partners of South Africa, notably the United States, Great Britain, France and West Germany, whose co-operation with the Pretoria regime was declared 'a hostile act against South Africa'. But the most effective proved to be the 'Resolution on the Non-recognition of South African Bantustans', which referred to the 'so called independence of Transkei to be proclaimed on the 26 October 1976', and declared that a recognition of Transkei or any other Bantustan in the future would be seen as a 'betrayal of not only the fighting people of South Africa but the entire continent'.

The OAU's appeal for non-recognition of Transkei was fully respected by the whole international community and now no State recognizes it. However, the facade of the seven resolutions on South Africa adopted at Port Louis in 1976 could not cover up the fact that OAU policy on South Africa had been gradually eroded by its own members. Malawi still maintains diplomatic relations with Pretoria; Ivory Coast continues exchanges of delegations with South Africa at ministerial level; the Central African Empire draws on South African loans; Zaire exports its copper through South African ports; LUFTHANSA, PANAM and other international airlines co-operating in pool with South African Airways still land at the airports of independent African States. A considerable number of trans-national companies (such as Lonrho) and

*An opinion put forward by the advocates of dialogue with South Africa (such as the Ivory Coast), and shared by the non-African trading partners of South Africa.

banks (such as Barclay) who are known for their South African connections still operate freely in Africa. This is in addition to the 'necessary ties' which countries like Botswana, Lesotho, Swaziland, Malawi and Mozambique still are bound to maintain with South Africa in order to exist.

## 2. RHODESIA

The British colony called Southern Rhodesia[28] has dominated African politics ever since the breakdown of the Central African Federation in 1962. The Rhodesian Government insisted on its right to independence, which had been granted to the two other members of the defunct Federation: Northern Rhodesia and Nyasaland both became independent in 1964 in the names respectively of Zambia and Malawi. Rhodesia featured prominently in the 1963 Addis Ababa 'Resolution on Decolonization', which asked Britain 'not to transfer the powers and attributes of sovereignty to a foreign minority government imposed on African peoples by the use of force and under cover of racial legislation'.

The Resolution also revealed the anxiety of the African leaders at the possibility of a unilateral declaration of independence, or British consent to Rhodesia's independence under white minority rule. This fear was well founded, as on 11 November 1965 the white minority regime, led by Ian Smith, unilaterally declared the territory independent of British rule. Although the British Prime Minister Harold Wilson termed UDI a rebellion, he refused to suppress it by force. As if to underline the racial implications of this decision, he announced that he would consider the use of force only in the event of a breakdown in law and order. This meant, in effect, if the Africans posed a challenge to the security of the white minority regime.

Because of Britain's direct responsbility for Rhodesia (which, as a non-self-governing territory, comes also under the umbrella of the UN within the meaning of Chapter XI of the UN Charter), the Rhodesian crisis was brought before the UN. The involvement of the UN in the Rhodesian question did not, however, diminish the interest of the OAU in finding a solution to the problem. The importance which the OAU attached to the task of securing African majority rule in Rhodesia is best shown by the fact that during the first thirteen years of its existence it adopted twenty-five resolutions on Rhodesia. The resolutions reflect various phases of OAU policy corresponding to the internal developments in Rhodesia and to international developments in southern Africa.

The OAU plan on the settlement of the Rhodesian independence issue was outlined in the resolutions of the Council of Ministers adopted at its sessions in Lagos in February 1964,[29] in Cairo in July 1964,[30] in Nairobi in February-March 1965,[31] in two resolutions adopted in Lagos in June 1965[32] and in Accra in October 1965.[33] These resolutions were endorsed by the Assembly of Heads of State and Government, which in addition adopted a resolution on Rhodesia at its first session in Cairo in 1964[34] and at its second in Accra in 1965.[35] The OAU proposed the following measures:
- the suspension of the 1961 Constitution in Rhodesia and of all discriminatory legislation;
- the holding of constitutional talks to be attended by representatives of all the people of Rhodesia with the aim of adopting a new constitution which might pave the way to majority rule;
- the release of leaders of the African political movements, namely Joshua Nkomo and Ndabaningi Sithole.

As the colonial power responsible for Rhodesia, Britain was asked to see that these demands be met. When the Unilateral Declaration of Independence became imminent, the OAU Summit in Accra in 1965 called the situation in Rhodesia 'a serious threat to world peace'[36] and insisted that Britain should take all steps, including the use of armed forces, to resume direct administration of the territory. The OAU also declared that it was ready to use 'all possible means including force to oppose UDI'. But the hope persisted that Britain would succeed in solving the crisis. When UDI was proclaimed on 11 November 1965, the general mood among Africans was that Britain had let them down.


An emergency meeting of the OAU Council of Ministers was held in Addis Ababa on 3-5 December 1965. In a strongly worded resolution, the Council of Ministers stated that '. . .if the United Kingdom does not crush the rebellion and restore law and order, and thereby prepare the way for majority rule in Southern Rhodesia by 15 December 1965, the Member-States of OAU shall sever diplomatic relations on that date with the United Kingdom. . .'[37] In the event, only nine of the thirty-six Members of the OAU actually did so — thus, in the words of President Nyerere of Tanzania, 'dealing a death blow to the Organization'.

To understand the atmosphere in which the Foreign Ministers of the Member-States drafted the Resolution on Rhodesia, one has to recall their efforts at the OAU and the UN, as well as the representations made to Great Britain and its allies, to prevent the establishment of a new racist State in Africa. The African leaders felt that the ideals expressed in the OAU Charter had been flagrantly violated by the usurpation of power by 200,000 whites in a country of 5 million

Africans. They were deeply hurt by Smith's assumption that the African States would do nothing about it, the more so as this assumption proved to be correct. In Addis Ababa, the possibility of using African armies against Rhodesia was openly discussed. However, not all members were prepared to follow this course of action. While some of them, notably Algeria and Ghana expressed their readiness to do so, others were hesitant and some openly opposed it. The momentum was soon lost.[38]

When the supreme organ of the OAU — the Assembly of Heads of State and Government — met in 1966 at Addis Ababa, the atmosphere was one of gloom. Although the Resolution on Rhodesia adopted at the meeting stated that 'the programme of sanctions will not and cannot bring down the illegal regime in Salisbury', the African leaders chose to support the UN sanctions simply because in the absence of any effective African resistance in Rhodesia, and with the dissent between the Rhodesian liberation movements making their unity impossible, the sanctions were the only measures left. Zambia, which would feel the fullest weight of the UN sanctions, was promised assistance through a 'Committee of Solidarity with Zambia' set up by the Assembly for that purpose and consisting of Egypt, Ethiopia, Kenya, Sudan and Tanzania.[39]

The UN adopted a very tough line. By its Resolution 2024 (XX) of 11 November 1965, adopted immediately after the Declaration of Independence, the General Assembly
— condemned the unilateral declaration of independence, calling the Ian Smith regime a 'racialist minority in Southern Rhodesia';
— asked Great Britain to put an end to the rebellion 'by the unlawful authorities in Southern Rhodesia'; and
— called on the Security Council to consider the situation as a matter of urgency.
The Security Council, at its 1258th meeting, on 12 November 1965, adopted a resolution by ten votes to none with one abstention (France), condemning 'the unilateral declaration of independence made by a racist minority in Southern Rhodesia' and calling upon all States 'not to recognize this illegal racist minority regime in Southern Rhodesia and to refrain from rendering any assistance to this illegal regime'.[40]

On 20 November 1965, the Security Council adopted another resolution, requesting Great Britain to restore legality in Rhodesia.[41] However, despite pressure from the African group at the UN, the Security Council refrained from using the term 'force' and merely asked Great Britain to 'take all appropriate measures which would prove effective in eliminating the authority of the usurpers and in bringing the minority regime in Southern Rhodesia to an immediate end'. Instead of using force the UN resorted to the economic sanctions policy on Rhodesia, which reached its peak on 28 May 1968, when the Security Council (acting under Chapter VII, Articles 39 and 41, of the Charter) resolved unanimously to impose comprehensive mandatory sanctions on Rhodesia. The Resolution proclaimed an almost complete ban on all trade with Rhodesia, on the supply of funds to that country, and on direct or indirect airline services maintained by companies established in other States. It also declared Rhodesian passports invalid for international travel.*

The mandatory sanctions, however impressive in terms of the UN Charter, did not bring about the expected breakdown of Rhodesia, nor did they make the Smith regime renounce UDI and negotiate a new independence constitution. In that respect they completely failed, principally because of the non-compliance of South Africa and Portugal, whose trade and economic relations with Rhodesia never ceased.

In all OAU resolutions adopted after UDI, as well as in all proposals put by the African delegation before the UN, Great Britain was repeatedly asked to restore legality in Rhodesia by all means including the use of force. Rhodesia was still held to be a British colony in a state of rebellion (a view repeatedly confirmed by Britain itself) and Britain was blamed, in terms which became stronger over the years, not only for having allowed UDI to happen, but for having done nothing *when* it happened. When the Smith government declared Rhodesia a Republic in 1970, the OAU condemned Britain for 'its betrayal of the African majority in Zimbabwe' and 'for the explosive situation in the territory': the Republic had been successfully established because of the 'ineffectiveness, complicity and duplicity of the United Kingdom'. Britain was condemned for her consistent refusal to use force as the only means to establish legality in Rhodesia, and was once again asked to do so immediately.[42]

The African group at the UN continued to remind Britain of her responsibilities towards her colony, by proposing measures agreed at the meetings of the OAU Council of Ministers and Assembly of Heads of State and Government. An example of the African initiative was a resolution adopted by the General Assembly on 13 November 1973 asking Britain:

— to expel all South African forces from Rhodesia;
— to release all political prisoners in Rhodesia;

*Under Article 41 of the Charter, the Security Council could also have ordered the complete or partial interruption of postal, telegraphic and radio communications between Rhodesia and other States, but it did not.

- to repeal all repressive discriminatory legislation, remove all restrictions of political activity and establish full democratic freedom and equality of political rights; and
- to convene a constitutional conference attended by legitimate political representatives of the people of Zimbabwe to work out a settlement of the future of Rhodesia to be submitted for endorsement to the people of the country.

The British delegate Marcus Worsley described these proposals as totally unrealistic and therefore unacceptable.[43]

The OAU was increasingly frustrated by the violation of sanctions against Rhodesia. The OAU Summit in Mogadishu in 1974 adopted a special resolution on the matter,[44] calling on OAU Members to 'blacklist those persons, companies and institutions in their countries which in pursuance of colonial and racial interest continue to have dealings or business with the illegal regime in Southern Rhodesia', and to take measures against those firms which operate simultaneously in independent African countries and in Rhodesia and South Africa. In a resolution 'On investments in Mozambique, South Africa and Rhodesia',[45] an appeal was made to OAU Members to impose heavy tariffs on the exports of those countries which persistently ignored OAU appeals against investing in Southern Africa. Sanctions against the white minority regimes were discussed also at the OAU Summit at Kampala in 1975. The emphasis was on South Africa but Rhodesia was mentioned in OAU appeals to the industrialized countries — in particular the United States, Great Britain, France, West Germany, Switzerland and Japan — 'to respect the UN resolutions on sanctions'.[46]

Although the UN sanctions failed in their primary objective to topple Smith's white minority regime, the OAU recognized the need to maintain them:
- In the absence of any coercive measures of a military nature, the sanctions represented international agreement that the treatment of the minority regime was illegal. No country, not even South Africa, had recognized it diplomatically.
- Rhodesia was denied access to any international conference, political or economic; and — even more significant — to the world money markets which are indispensable to its long-term survival.
- Sanctions and non-recognition prevented the Smith regime from consolidating its position, and kept it both economically and militarily vulnerable.

— Sanctions were one of the three main factors (the other two being guerrilla warfare and, lately, the independence of Mozambique) which forced the Smith regime to begin negotiations with the African nationalists.

On 3 March 1976, President Samora Machel of Mozambique announced the implementation of UN economic sanctions on Rhodesia by closing Rhodesia's lifelines to Beira and Maputo, by confiscating Rhodesian property and assets in Mozambique, and by putting Mozambique on a protective war footing against possible attacks from Rhodesia. Mozambique's decision threw the entire burden of Rhodesian international traffic onto South Africa. It coincided with the failure of what was probably the last peaceful effort at the settlement of the Rhodesian crisis, which had become known as 'the politics of détente'.

## 3. THE POLITICS OF DÉTENTE

'Détente' is described in the Oxford dictionary as the 'easing of strained relations between States'. Within the southern African context the word became known as a policy carried out by four OAU Member-States — Zambia, Tanzania, Botswana and Mozambique (later joined by Angola) — who, under the Organization's aegis, were exploring ways whereby the peaceful transfer of power to the African majority in Rhodesia could be achieved. The policy of 'détente' evolved from the contacts between the heads of these four States on the one hand and the South African Premier, Vorster, and the Rhodesian Premier, Ian Smith, on the other.[47]

Nyerere described the 'origins of détente' as follows:

'Independence in Mozambique appeared at first to achieve what the Lusaka Manifesto had failed to do. The Government of South Africa indicated a willingness to talk, on one subject, on the basis we had set out — that is on the basis of how, not whether, majority rule would come in Rhodesia. In accordance with the Lusaka Manifesto the governments of Tanzania, Zambia, and Botswana therefore accepted the responsibility of acting as intermediaries with the Rhodesian Nationalists, with Vorster accepting a similar function with the Smith regime. It is these discussions which gave rise to talk of a détente by South Africa, and our denial of détente.'[48]

Vorster saw in 'détente' the following prospects for South Africa:
— A constitutional solution in Rhodesia would relieve South Africa of its costly role as 'sanction-breaker' and allow it to withdraw its paramilitary forces, whose presence in Rhodesia was increasingly

an international embarrassment.

— In exchange for his 'goodwill' over Rhodesia, he might receive a guarantee from Mozambique that the rail links and harbours of Nacala, Beira and Maputo (Lourenco Marques) would remain open for South Africa and Rhodesia; that the Mozambique labour agreement concerning 82,000 Mozambique workers in South African gold mines would be maintained; that electrical power from the Cabora Bassa complex built in Mozambique would reach South Africa, and that Mozambique would keep the peace along the eastern borders with South Africa.

— He could 'buy time' to promote independence for South Africa's Bantustans and Namibia, and to convince his African neighbours of the advantages of the 'United Nations of Southern Africa' — which would mean 'vreede vooruitgang en ontwikkeling (peace, progress and development)' — with Pretoria as its political and economic centre. This, in his opinion, would pacify South Africa's critics at the UN and make it possible for him to argue even more stubbornly than before that South Africa's own internal affairs are nobody else's business: 'détente' would become a smoke screen for policies of apartheid and win it respectability both in and outside Africa.

— It might forestall a situation in which the white minority regime in Rhodesia would be forced to submit to the demands of African nationalists by military defeat of its forces at the hands of the Zimbabwe guerrillas. This would have disastrous consequences for the morale of the South African whites, a situation Vorster wished to avoid at any reasonable price.

The only price Vorster *was* prepared to pay, was to deliver Rhodesia to the conference table, but not to force it to accept *a priori* the condition of black majority rule. On this point he completely shared Ian Smith's view that this would never happen because of the disunity of the Rhodesian Africans. But as South Africans themselves reminded Vorster, there was a missing link in his grand design of 'détente' which nullified his efforts, at least in Africa. 'South Africa is ostracized not for her foreign policy', wrote the *Rand Daily Mail* on 25 October 1975, 'but for what she does internally. Domestic apartheid and discrimination offer a permanent affront to black people everywhere and the world is not willing to settle for a benign image marked for "export only". Since we must have peace in Southern Africa,' concluded the editorial, 'we must have a *real* change. It is still as simple as that.'

To Ian Smith, 'détente' was primarily a time-buying device helping him to ease the pressure of the mounting guerrilla warfare inside Rhodesia and to stave off the possibility of Mozambique joining the UN economic sanctions and allowing Zimbabwe liberation movements to operate from its territory. In agreeing to 'talk about talks' he was banking on the breakdown of the unity of the African National Council. He might then have the chance of making a deal with the kind of Rhodesian African leader who would accept that the postponement of the transfer of power to the African majority to the 'reasonably distant future' was inevitable.

There were many in Africa who saw 'détente' as a revival of the policy of 'dialogue'. Most critical were the liberation movements of South Africa (ANC, PCA, SWAPO), and the African National Council (ANC) of Rhodesia (which, since December 1974, included ZANU, ZAPU and FROLIZI).[49] Their suspicions were fed by the vigorous campaign launched by South Africa to have 'détente' linked with its efforts 'to improve apartheid'. Guinea, Algeria and Libya led the critics from within the OAU, amongst whom — rather surprisingly — were Lesotho and Kenya. The Guinean Ambassador to Western Europe, Seydiu Keita called 'détente' an attempt to demobilize the rest of the continent; and the Kenyan Foreign Minister, Dr. Waiyaki, told the Kenyan Parliament on 27 March 1975 that he opposed the idea of talking with South Africa 'unless and until the South African regime took concrete steps towards dialogue within the South African black majority.'

On Algeria's insistence, an extraordinary session of the Council of Ministers was convened at Dar-es-Salaam on 7 April 1975. The host to the conference, President Julius Nyerere, disarmed his critics in his opening speech to the Council, which set the tone of the meeting. He said:

'Your Conference will have succeeded if it leaves South Africa in no doubt at all that we are still ready to use peaceful means to achieve independence in Rhodesia and Namibia, but that if this is made impossible, we shall resume and intensify the armed struggle. It is important that both our friends and our enemies should know that we mean what we say.'[50]

In a bitter show-down with his opponents, the Zambian Foreign Minister Vernon Mwaanga succeeded in convincing the Council that Zambia's initiative, supported by Tanzania, Botswana and Mozambique, was a change of tactics but not strategy, and was carried out in full accord with the OAU's commitment to the liberation struggle. 'The initiative in the current exercise came from Prime Minister Vorster', said Vernon Mwaanga. 'The sole objective in our response was to liberate Zimbabwe, secure the independence of Namibia and demand the end of apartheid. This we have done.' In answer to those who accused Zambia of having dialogue with South Africa, he said: 'I state categorically, as I have said many times before, that Zambia and her friends have not been engaged in dialogue with South Africa. After all one can have dialogue only with a friend.' This was certainly not how the Foreign Minister of the Ivory Coast, Arsene Assouane Usher, saw it. He told the conference:

'My dear colleagues, the Ivory Coast has come to this special session because she is for dialogue between African States. We have found, not without incurring the displeasures of some of our colleagues, that dialogue which formally was considered to be 'sterile' now flourishes and has become a full bodied reality. Certainly, our Organizations can still pass anti-dialogue resolutions — and the farce will continue ... We regard the argument that Vorster is a two-headed monster — one head a saint with whom one can discuss Rhodesia and the other a demon with whom one cannot conduct dialogue on apartheid — as venomous and full of irony.'

The conference was then told about the concessions made by the white minority regime in Rhodesia with the assistance of South Africa, and heard a compliment paid to Prime Minister Vorster by Zambian Foreign Minister Mwaanga, who said:

'To this extent we would be less than honest if we did not acknowledge that Prime Minister Vorster regardless of our diametrically opposed positions on apartheid has honoured his word on the concrete issues we have dealt with under different circumstances. We know his limitations. We know our limitations too.'[51]

The Council of Ministers eventually adopted unanimously a declaration in which, in order to appease the critics of détente, clear distinction was drawn between the talks with South Africa on Rhodesia and Namibia and the talks on apartheid, the talks on the latter being declared as impermissible. After making the point that 'there is nothing for free Africa to talk about to the leaders of the apartheid regime in connection with their policies in South Africa', the 'Dar-es-Salaam Declaration on Southern Africa'* left doors open for negotiations on Rhodesia and Namibia subject to the following conditions:

'As long as the objective of majority rule before independence is not compromised, the OAU would support all efforts made by the Zimbabwe nationalists to win independence by peaceful means. This

*OAU Resolution ECM/St.15 (IX) 1975.

may mean the holding of a constitutional conference where the nationalist forces will negotiate with the Smith regime. If that takes place, the OAU has the duty to do everything possible to assist the success of such negotiations, in constant consultation with the nationalists until and unless the Zimbabwean nationalists themselves are convinced that talks with Smith have failed. In this event, the freedom fighters will have to intensify the armed struggle with the material, financial and diplomatic assistance of independent Africa.'

'Détente' as a policy towards South Africa was struck out from the African diplomatic dictionary as follows:

'Africans cannot and will never acquiesce in the perpetuation of colonial and/or racist oppression in their continent. That is why any talk of détente with the apartheid regime is such nonsense that it should be treated with the contempt it deserves. What the OAU demands is the dismantling of the institutions of oppression and repression against the non-white people by the racist minority. Otherwise, Vorster's outcries about détente can only have one meaning in so far as the situation within South Africa is concerned. And this is that free and independent Africa should co-exist with apartheid and thus acquiesce in the daily humiliation, degradation, oppression and repression of the African people in South Africa.'

The Dar-es-Salaam Declaration was endorsed by the 12th OAU Summit at Kampala in July 1975 in one of the most strongly-worded resolutions ever adopted on South Africa. The Resolution calls the Pretoria regime 'a product of colonial conquest now operating as a fully-fledged fascist power bent on perpetuating the ruthless domination of the indigenous people'. It rejects 'détente' as an attempt to 'legitimize' the oppression and exploitation of the South African people'.[52]

Certain positive aspects of 'detente' stand out quite clearly. It has radically changed the pattern of politics in southern Africa in the following ways:
— For the first time since UDI, the initiative on the settlement of the situation in Rhodesia passed from British into African hands. The plan for the transfer of power in Rhodesia passed from British into African hands. The plan for the transfer of power in Rhodesia to the African majority was not worked out in London but at Lusaka and Dar-es-Salaam. It was put to the British Foreign Secretary, James Callaghan, and to the US Secretary of State, Henry Kissinger, in August 1974 by the Zambian Foreign Minister, Vernon Mwaanga,

who asked them politely but firmly to keep out of the way. When Joshua Nkomo, Ndabaningi Sithole and Bishop Abel Muzorewa were secretly flown in a South African aeroplane to Lusaka on 1 November 1974 to confer with Presidents Nyerere,Kaunda, Seretse Khama and Samora Machel, the British Foreign Office only heard about it eight days later — and not from the Africans.

— With Ian Smith's agreement to negotiate a settlement in Rhodesia with Rhodesia's African nationalist leaders, some of whom had been kept ten years in detention, the Rhodesian problem entered its final and irreversible phase. The freeing of the nationalist leaders, to whom Smith used to refer as 'terrorists', constituted a humiliating political defeat of his policy of denying the legitimate representatives of Rhodesian Africans a part in shaping the fate of the country.

— For the first time in the history of white minority rule in southern Africa, African diplomacy forced a serious split between the white leaders of Rhodesia and South Africa. Ian Smith's intransigence was increasingly seen by Pretoria as a serious obstacle to South Africa's 'détente' policy, jeopardizing its hard-won concessions from Zambia and Mozambique about the 'peace on the eastern front'. Vorster's options on Rhodesia have been drastically reduced, and backing Smith has become a hopeless venture.

— The diplomacy of the Presidents of Tanzania, Zambia, Botswana and Mozambique, joined in 1976 by President Angostinho Neto of Angola, paved the way to the Geneva conference on Rhodesia which opened on 26 October 1976.

But it has also marked yet another step in the decline of the OAU's role as collective policy-maker over southern Africa. Since 1975 the OAU has left the issue of Zimbabwe to be handled solely by the front-line Presidents, who though assisted by the OAU Liberation Committee have acted quite independently and outside the OAU, reducing its role to a rubberstamp of their actions. This was true for example of the OAU attitude towards the Zimbabwe liberation movements. After shortlived unity under the ANC umbrella, it fell apart into several mutually hostile factions; and once the front-line Presidents had come to the conclusion that reunification of the ANC was impossible, and any efforts in that direction a complete waste of time, they threw their support behind the so-called 'Third Force'[53] — the guerrilla forces based largely in Mozambique, and known as the Zimbabwe People's Army (ZIPA). The OAU followed. At the 13th OAU Summit at Port Louis in July 1976, Muzorewa and Nkomo, leaders of the two main ANC factions, accused the OAU of imposing on them the military leadership of the guerrilla forces. But the OAU backed the front-line Presidents, endorsing the resolution adopted at the 26th Session of the Council of Ministers at

Addis Ababa in March 1976. This had hailed 'the valiant freedom fighters of the ANC of Zimbabwe who in spite of the differences within the leadership of the movement have united their ranks and intensified the armed struggle against the minority racist regime of Ian Smith', and had called upon the OAU Member-States to increase their assistance to the guerrilla forces in order 'to maintain and to uplift the tempo of the intensified armed struggle'.[54]

Nigeria set the example in recognizing the authority of the front-line Presidents when its Commissioner for External Affairs, Brigadier Joseph N. Garba, presented a cheque for $250,000 to the delegation of Mozambique rather than to the OAU Liberation Committee. He did so with an expression of deep regret that because of the bickering among the political leadership of Zimbabwe he had no choice but to make a presentation to another party. The monopoly of the front-line Presidents in determining policy over Rhodesia became even more pronounced when Dr Henry Kissinger entered the African scene in 1976.[55] The OAU was 'kept informed', but it was entirely excluded from Kissinger's negotiations with Presidents Nyerere and Kaunda — negotiations which produced the so-called 'Kissinger plan'[56] for majority rule in Rhodesia, accepted by Ian Smith in the dramatic broadcast of a 'surrender to the majority rule' on 24 September 1976.[57]

The OAU Summit at Port Louis was the first in OAU history to pass no direct resolution on Rhodesia, but it endorsed all the resolutions of the 26th Session of the Council of Ministers, including one on Zimbabwe.[58] This Resolution:

— reaffirmed the OAU's recognition of ANC as the sole and legitimate representative of the people of Zimbabwe;
— called upon the ANC to intensify the armed struggle for national liberation and majority rule; and
— invited OAU Member-States to render every moral, political and diplomatic support, and give material assistance to the just cause of national liberation of the people of Zimbabwe against the illegal and racist regime.

It bore a footnote explaining that 'this resolution was adopted on the recommendation of the 26th Ordinary Session of the Co-ordinating Committee for the Liberation of Africa', which indicates that the Council did not really wish to take up the issue at all.

The resolution also gave the green light to the Presidents of Botswana, Mozambique, Tanzania, Zambia and Angola to continue their 'efforts to ensure that the unity of the people and their organization, the ANC, is safeguarded', leaving it to their discretion to decide which of the ANC factions was to be regarded as the legitimate representative of the Zimbabwe people and thus entitled to the support

133

of the OAU. When the talks on Rhodesia's constitutional future opened in Geneva on 26 October[59] it was the sudden alliance between Joshua Nkomo and Robert Mugabe (the 'Patriotic Front') which won the backing of the front-line Presidents, and on their prompting also of the OAU. In fact, the proceedings of the Geneva Conference, which drifted into recess after seven weeks on 15 December 1976 and was never re-convened, and the post-conference diplomacy by its chairman Ivor Richard fully confirmed the virtual exclusion of the OAU from shaping the future of Zimbabwe.

The Conference, originally called to work out the mechanism for the transfer of power to the majority in Zimbabwe, ostensibly failed because of the disagreement on the date for the independence and on the length of the transitional period. The four black delegations led by Robert Mugabe (ZANU), Abel Muzorewa (ANC), Joshua Nkomo (ANC) and Ndabaningi Sithole (ZANU) were unanimous, though with varying emphasis that the interim phase should be no more than 12 months. They proposed 1st December 1977 as the date for independence. The Rhodesian Front delegation led by Piet van der Byl (after Ian Smith left because of 'lack of serious progress') called for a transitional period of 23 months with no specific date for independence mentioned. In between these two time scales, the British suggested a period of 15 months. However, the central point of divergence between the Africans on the one hand and the white Rhodesians and Britain on the other was over who should control the instruments of State power during the transitional phase of whatever length. Concurrently with the deepening split between the liberation movements and the Rhodesian Front grew also the gap within the liberation movements themselves.

Neither the Ivor Richard shuttle between the front-line capitals — Dar-es-Salaam, Gaberone, Lusaka and Maputo — and, after the Conference, to Pretoria and Salisbury, nor the similar exercise conducted in April 1977 by the British Foreign Secretary, Dr David Owen, brought about any positive results, nor did they narrow the differences between all parties concerned. And this is unlikely to be achieved by bringing in the United States as co-sponsor of a new conference, as Dr David Owen proposed.

Whatever emerges from the diplomatic activities which are still in full swing at the time of writing one thing has already become abundantly clear: the OAU has been left out from any avenues toward the independence of Zimbabwe.


## 4. PORTUGAL

When decolonization was discussed in 1963 at Addis Ababa by the

Summit Conference of Heads of State and Government of Independent African states, the largest colonial empire in Africa — indeed the largest left in the world — was that of Portugal. In Africa it consisted of Angola, Mozambique, Guinea-Bissau, Sao Tomé and Principé and the Cape Verde islands, embracing almost 13 million people and a territory of over 2 million square kilometres[60] Alone of the colonial powers, Portugal refused to consider granting independence to its overseas provinces, which it regarded as 'integral parts of Portugal' whose future was therefore not negotiable with any international authority. This was maintained by Portugal consistently at the UN from the time it joined that organization in 1955 to the military *coup* in 1974.[61]

The ruthless suppression of any attempt by the African populations of the Portuguese-African territories to claim the right to self-determination provoked armed rebellion, out of which grew a large-scale military confrontation between the liberation movements and the Portuguese colonial army. Armed uprisings broke out in Guinea-Bissau on 3 April 1961, in Angola on 4 February 1961 and in Mozambique on 25 September 1964. Portugal — a country with a GDP lower than that of many African countries —[62] could not bear the expense of the war in Africa, which was estimated in 1971 to have been over $400 million, representing 50 per cent of its annual budget. But the real power behind the Portuguese colonial wars in Africa which lasted thirteen years, was not Portugal itself but NATO, to which Portugal had been admitted in 1949.[63] The main reason for this was the strategic importance of all Portugal's African territories. Angola and Guinea-Bissau, between them controlling 1,816 kilometres of Atlantic coastline, were seen as an integral part of Atlantic defence and a base for eventual incursions to the centre of Africa. The Cape Verde islands held the key to the South Atlantic. And Mozambique constituted a buffer zone for South Africa while at the same time providing vital access to the sea for Rhodesia. At the same time, the economic potential of the Portuguese African possessions (notably Angola, which was rich in minerals and oil) represented vast raw-material resources for the industries of the NATO countries, so there was even more reason to give military support to Portugal, despite the growing disapproval of public opinion in the NATO countries themselves.

The 1963 Addis Ababa 'Resolution on Decolonization' recognized that Portugal was a pawn in a power play of its NATO allies. The OAU declared a diplomatic and economic boycott of Portugal similar to that applied against South Africa; but it saw that the ending of Portuguese colonialism in Africa rested primarily with the Western powers, in particular the United States and Great Britian. The resolution asked these powers to cease all direct and indirect support to Portugal, which was conducting what the OAU consistently held to be a 'real war of genocide'. The responsibility of the western powers for the Portuguese colonial wars was asserted in all resolutions passed by the OAU concerning the Portuguese territories. For example, the 'Resolution on Decolonization' adopted by the 1970 OAU Summit in Addis Ababa[64] stated that: 'the Portuguese regime is able to continue and intensify its colonial war of genocide because of the continuing massive assistance from NATO Member-States, especially the United States, West Germany, France and the United Kingdom.' It is not without interest that the express mention of the Western countries accused of collusion with Portugal was objected to by seventeen OAU Members[65] who were clearly concerned for their trade and financial relations with the powers in question.

OAU policy on Portugal between 1963 and 1974 largely followed the pattern of its policy on South Africa, Rhodesia and Namibia, which centered on the diplomatic offensive at the UN. There was however, one fundamental difference. The armed struggle in the Portuguese colonies exceeded all forms of resistance in Rhodesia, South Africa and Namibia; and the progress of the guerrilla warfare in Guineau-Bissau under the leadership of PAIGC, and in Mozambique under the leadership of FRELIMO, provided much-needed tangible proof of the success of the OAU decolonization policy. In return, OAU gave top priority to the support of PAIGC and FRELIMO. After the 1972 Rabat Summit, military and financial aid was doubled. By that time PAIGC was in control of most of Guinea-Bissau, with the exception of a small enclave on the coast around the capital which was being held by the Portuguese army at increasing cost. Similarly, by the end of 1973 the military operations of FRELIMO in Mozambique had extended into the Tete province, where a new front was opened at Guro, only 80 miles north of the Lourenço Marques, thus posing a threat to the completion of a multinational project of key importance to South Africa: Cabora Bassa.[66]

OAU support for the liberation movements in the Portuguese territories was further increased following the Portuguese attack on Guinea on 22 November 1970, which turned the relations between OAU Members and Portugal into a state of undeclared war. The invasion of 22 November was devised by General Antonio de Spinola, Commander-in-Chief of the Portuguese armed forces in Guinea-Bissau, and was executed by an invading force of 350-400 men, brought by sea to a point off Conakry by two troop transport ships supported by three or four smaller patrol-boats. The men in the invading force were equipped with infantry arms and divided into groups which were sent to attack strategic points: the army camp, the airport, the electric power station, the Presidential Palace (which was destroyed) and the headquarters of the PAIGC. The ships used to transport the force were

Portuguese; their crews were mostly white members of the Portuguese armed forces; and the invaders, who were commanded by Portuguese officers, were dissident Guineans and African troops of the Portuguese army trained in Bissau.[67]

The emergency session of the OAU Council of Ministers convened at Lagos on 9 December 1970 was a stormy affair where even such moderate members as Nigeria were calling for punitive military action against the Portuguese. The three main items on the agenda were:

— the means of helping Guinea to safeguard its sovereignty and integrity from any future attack;
— the means of protecting African States from any new foreign aggression; and
— the pursuit of the task of liberating those territories still under foreign domination, and measures to outlaw the use in Africa of mercenaries — who should be arrested and handed over to the country against which they were engaged.

It was agreed that an OAU special fund should be established to provide financial, military and technical assistance to Guinea, on the understanding that the States could also give bilateral aid, that the OAU should increase its aid to the liberation movements fighting against Portuguese colonialism, and that the OAU should take charge of co-ordinating co-operation between Member-States on all questions of defence and security.[68]

Following a report of the UN commission of inquiry, the Security Council adopted a resolution on 8 December 1970, with no votes against and four abstentions (the United States, France, Britain and Spain), 'strongly condemning the Portuguese Government for its invasion of Guinea', and demanding 'full compensation for the large losses in human life and goods caused by the armed attack'. The resolution also appealed to all other States to give moral and material help to Guinea to enable it to strengthen its independence and territorial integrity. It then demanded that all States should cease providing the Portuguese Government with military or material aid of any kind which could enable it to continue its acts of repression against the people of African territories under its control, or against independent countries.[69]

The other event which delivered a formidable blow to the Portuguese colonial policy was the massacre of the total population of the Wiriyamu village about 25 km south-east of Tete in Mozambique. According to the detailed account of the massacre by the Rev. Adrian Hastings in *The Times* (London) on 10 July 1973, 400 people were murdered, in most cases individually. Some were pushed into huts which were then set on fire or had grenades thrown into them. Many of the children were kicked to death, their heads used as footballs; some were hacked to death. The document published about the event included 130 names of which 67 were children. World reaction was reflected at the Special Meeting of the UN Decolonization Committee on 20 July 1973, at which the UN Secretary-General said that the report of Father Hastings 'aroused the conscience of mankind.'[70]

The Wiriyamu massacre destroyed the last remnants of credibility in Portugal's African policy which, in the words of Dr. Marcello Caetano, purported to be 'the enhancement of the land and the increased dignity of the inhabitants, a task that is being effected in a way of which we can be justly proud.'[71] Indignation over Wiriyamu and subsequent revelations of Portuguese brutality in the colonies led a significant increase in the volume of humanitarian aid from the governments, organizations and churches of Europe. When the OAU scored its first major victory against Portugal in Guinea-Bissau, which unilaterally declared independence on 24 September 1973, only Portugal's NATO allies and, surprisingly, the Scandinavian countries,[72] declined to recognize it. On 2 November 1973, seventy-seven UN members voted for the Resolution of the General Assembly entitled 'the illegal occupation by Portuguese military forces of certain sectors of the Republic of Guinea-Bissau and acts of aggression committed by them against the people of the Republic.'[73] Portugal dismissed the declaration of independence as a propaganda stunt, a view which was shared by her NATO allies. In anticipation of the veto by the United States, Britain and France at the Security Council, no resolution calling for the admission of Guinea-Bissau to the UN was submitted to the Council. However, Guinea-Bissau became a member of the Food and Agricultural Organization (FAO) and other UN specialized agencies.

The last chapter of the Portuguese colonial rule was written by the Portuguese themselves. In February 1974 General Antonio de Spinola, a key figure in the Portuguese military establishment, and the former Governor and Commander-in-Chief of Guinea-Bissau published a book called *Portugal and the Future,* in which he attacked the Portuguese war effort in Africa, asserting that the military activities in Mozambique, Angola and Guinea-Bissau were bound to result in the loss of Portugal's stand in Africa. Although most pessimistic about a continued war effort, Spinola did not suggest abandoning the Portuguese colonies; rather he suggested that a federation be formed in which Portugal and her territories would be on an equal footing. Spinola's book, which was widely read in Portugal, represented a set of views which had previously been suppressed in every quarter of Portuguese society. Spinola was dismissed, and this precipitated the army revolt which overthrew the Caetano government on 25 April 1974.

A proclamation issued by the 'Movement of the Armed Forces' (the group of officers who organized the *coup*) explained the reasons for the *coup d'état*. At the top of the list was the Caetano regime's failure, after thirteen years of fighting overseas, to establish a policy 'which would lead to peace between Portuguese of all races and creeds'. General Spinola became Portugal's new President and Mario Soares, leader of the Portuguese Socialist Party, returned from exile to become Foreign Minister. The relationship between Portugal and her African territories entered a new phase, which culminated in the granting of independence to all of them. The subsequent series of internal crises in Portugal, which began with the resignation of General Spinola from the Presidency and was followed by frequent changes of government, no longer had any effect on its former African possessions.

The OAU, at first sceptical about the intentions of the new Portuguese regime, went out of its way to express its appreciation of the new Portuguese African policy. At the OAU Summit in Mogadishu the Administrative Secretary-General, in his Report covering the period from June 1974 to February 1975, said 'Lisbon has not fulfilled the three conditions laid down by the Mogadishu summit conference, but has gone far beyond it'. After giving an account of the negotiations between Portugal and the liberation movements, he concluded: 'A sincere and well-deserved tribute should be paid here to the new Portuguese leaders who have made the necessary efforts and taken pains to understand the aspirations of the African peoples, who mainly desire to live in dignity and freedom.'[74]

Although in military terms the Portuguese colonial armies were not defeated to the point of capitulation (this came nearest in Guinea-Bissau, and quite near in Mozambique, but was still far off in Angola), there is no doubt that the military *coup* in Lisbon on 25 April 1974 would not have occurred when it did, had it not been for the loss of confidence in Portugal's African policy voiced in General Spinola's book.

The independence of Guinea-Bissau was recognized by the Portuguese government on 9 September 1974. It was followed by the independence of Mozambique on 25 June 1975, Cape Verde 5 July 1975, and Sao Tomé and Principé on 12 July 1975. The date of independence of Angola, 11 November 1975, was announced on 5 January 1975, following the negotiations between the Portuguese Government and all three Angolan liberation movements — MPLA, UNITA and FNLA. While the transfer of power in all other Portuguese territories was a smooth and orderly affair, Angola entered independence hopelessly torn apart by internal fighting between the same movements which had fought for its liberation. The conflict continued throughout 1975, and in October of that year it erupted into a full-scale war with all the ingredients of cold war politics. The crisis in

Angola was the main preoccupation of the OAU in 1975 and a cause for convening an extraordinary session of the OAU Summit.

The full story of the efforts of the OAU to reconcile liberation movements in Angola would exceed the scope of this book. Suffice it to say that it took nine years for the OAU Liberation Committee to persuade FNLA and MPLA to sign an agreement. At the OAU Summit in Rabat in June 1972, Agostinho Neto of MPLA and Holden Roberto of FNLA embraced each other in the assembly hall, applauded by the African Heads of State and Government; but the agreement was short-lived. Quite apart from the disputes between them, both FNLA and MPLA were plagued throughout the years by their own internal struggles. For example, in 1964 Dr Jonas Savimbi, who was later to found UNITA, parted company with FNLA dramatically at the OAU Cairo Summit, denouncing Holden Roberto as an imperialist agent. In 1974 army troops from Zaire had to quell a rebellion against Holden Roberto at an FNLA base near Kinshasa. MPLA's most severe crisis occurred in August 1974 when it split into three factions. Unity was restored through the efforts of Presidents Kaunda, Nyerere and Ngoubi meeting at Brazzaville. However, one of the leaders of the faction, Daniel Chipenda, later broke away, taking MPLA supporters with him, and joined the FNLA.

The dissension between the Angolan liberation movements became a crucial topic in the 1974 negotiations with the Portuguese Government over Angola's independence. The OAU Liberation Committee mobilized all available diplomatic resources and, assisted by the Heads of State of countries where the movements were based (Zaire, Tanzania, Zambia, Congo), succeeded in making the movements agree on negotiating jointly with the Portuguese Government at Penina on 5 January 1975. UNITA, so far denied OAU recognition, was hastily recognized for that purpose. The Penina Concordat, signed on 15 January, set Angola's independence day as 11 November. Until then, the country was to be ruled by a transitional government of appointees of both the Portuguese Government and MPLA, FNLA and UNITA, which were recognized as the 'only legitimate representatives of the Angolan people.'[75]

As events have demonstrated, the Penina Concordat was from the beginning a shaky experiment by a Portuguese Government desperate to find some governmental solution to the mounting crisis in Angola. But welding together three movements with great differences in ideology and rationale and supported by different African and non-African governments, with their main backing in different parts of the country and among different ethnic groups, proved impossible.

Within days of the investiture of the coalition government in Luanda on January 31, disputes broke out between the movements, coming to a head in vicious battles between their armed supporters which continued throughout most of 1975. From June 1975 onwards, UNITA was drawn into the conflict. In the course of the year more than ten peace and ceasefire agreements were signed and broken, including the agreements concluded under OAU auspices in Kinshasa, Mombasa and Alver.

The last conciliatory effort on the part of the OAU Liberation Committee prior to the OAU Summit at Kampala in July 1975 was the meeting between the leaders of MPLA, FNLA and UNITA at Nakuru (Kenya) in June 1975. There the most comprehensive and most promising of all agreements, the Nakuru Agreement, was signed in the presence of President Kenyatta.[76] The agreement reinforced hopes for peaceful transition to independence, but these were shattered by new armed hostilities which broke out on the eve of the Kampala Summit.

At the time of the Kampala Summit, the OAU still believed in a government of national unity — i.e. a coalition of MPLA, FNLA and UNITA, which would steer the country to independence — scheduled for 11 November 1975. OAU policy on Angola continued to be based on the Nakuru agreement despite its violation a few weeks after it was signed. A major setback to this policy was the refusal of the leaders of MPLA and FNLA to respond to the invitation extended to them by the Council of Ministers to come to Kampala. Only Dr Jonas Savimbi of UNITA turned up. He alone of the three leaders supported President Amin's call for a peace-keeping OAU force to be sent to Angola (seconded by the Congolese President Ngoubi) — something Agostinho Neto and Holden Roberto both rejected as impermissible interference in Angola's internal affairs.

Two resolutions on Angola were adopted at the Kampala Summit. The first, adopted by the Council of Ministers at their meeting, expressed regret at the violation of the previous agreements between the three movements, and urged them to end their hostilities. It also issued a warning that the situation in Angola was likely to divide Africa.[77] The resolution adopted by the Assembly of Heads of State and Government was much sharper in defining OAU's attitude to the liberation movements, and more specific in the demands it made on them. Going beyond 'regret', the Assembly 'deplored the bloody confrontations between the principal liberation movements and their non-respect for the agreements they signed.'[78] It issued the following directives: there should be an urgent appeal to the fighting parties to lay down their arms; Portugal should be requested to resume responsibilities for the maintenace of law and order in Angola until independence on 11 November 1975; a Fact-Finding Commission of

Inquiry and Conciliation should be established to depart for Angola immediately; and the OAU Defence Commission was requested to consider the possibility of creating and dispatching an OAU peace force to Angola.

Ironically, the only party which complied with the OAU policy on Angola was the colonial power, Portugal. Two weeks after the Kampala summit on 16 August, the acting Portuguese High Commissioner, General Ernesto Ferreira de Macedo announced that he was assuming full executive powers for the territory in the absence of any functioning government. The fighting in Angola continued and the chances of reconciliation became very slim.

No mention of foreign intervention in the Angolan conflict was made in either of the two OAU resolutions, despite the MPLA charge that regular units of the Zaire army were fighting with FNLA. As for Soviet supplies of arms to the MPLA,[79] these were regarded as having the approval of the OAU Liberation Committee which helped to secure them, while Chinese and American support for FNLA, channelled through Kinshasa, was part of the package of Zaire's assistance. President Mobutu's criticism of Portugal's alleged help to MPLA (at that time favoured by Lisbon) did get a little support, particularly after the sudden appearance of Louis Franque, President of the secessionist Front for the Liberation of Cabinda (FLEC) for which Zaire was held responsible. Although refused admittance to the OAU meetings, Louis Franque called a press conference on 1 August at which he declared Cabinda's independence. The document — 'Declaration solennelle à l'occasion de la proclamation de l'indépendence du Cabinda' — was circulated to all delegations with the consent of the OAU Chairman, President Amin, who also personally received Franque. Quickly realizing this to have been serious mistake, Amin retreated by endorsing the strong objections voiced against Cabinda's secession by all three Angolan movements. The significance of Franque's presence in Kampala was in its timing with Zaire's proposal, tabled at the Council of Ministers, calling for the 'self-determination of Cabinda'. This particular move increased the suspicion of Zaire's policy, which hung like a thick cloud over all sessions at which Angola was discussed.[80]

After the Kampala Summit, President Amin nominated nine members to a Fact-Finding Commission of Inquiry and Conciliation on Angola, which he himself chaired. He chose Somalia, Algeria, Burundi, Ghana, Kenya, Lesotho, Morocco, Niger and Upper Volta. The Commission, assisted by the OAU secretariat, made a ten-day tour of Angola. Its 'Report on the OAU Conciliation Commission on Angola' was discussed on 1 November 1975, at a special session of the OAU Bureau* which

*in which the current chairman deals with OAU problems between summit meetings.

MPLA, FNLA, and UNITA were invited to attend. The Bureau repeated the call for a government of national unity, for the integration of the military forces of the three liberation movements, and for the cessation of armed hostilities.

Completely oblivious to the realities of the conflict in Angola, which by that time had become a full-scale war with South Africa intervening on the side of UNITA-FNLA, and with massive Soviet arms supplies to the MPLA who had the support of 12,000 Cuban commandos, President Amin continued his diplomacy by convening a meeting of the OAU Defence Commission on 5 November. Apart from condemning South African aggression and expressing 'serious concern over the supply of arms to the warring Angolan nationalist movements', the Defence Commission set up an *ad hoc* advisory military committee, consisting of Egypt, Guinea, Kenya, Libya, Nigeria and Uganda, to help the current chairman and the Administrative Secretary-General of the OAU to maintain constant contacts with the Government of National Unity. The committee was to assess the need to despatch an OAU peace-keeping force to Angola; the need to despatch an African political military mission to help the Government of National Unity to set up a national army and an administrative structure; and the immediate needs of the independent State of Angola.

The point was, of course, that there was no Government of National Unity in Angola to which such assistance could be given.

On 10 January 1976 an extraordinary session of the Assembly of the Heads of State and Government — the first in OAU history — met in Addis Ababa. The policy on Angola, based on the premise that all three Angolan movements had an equally valid claim to share in the government of independent Angola, had collapsed for two reasons. First, the Angolan civil war was having international repercussions affecting inter-African, East-West and Sino-Soviet relations. The presence of white mercenaries supported by regular units of the South African armed forces, the engagement of 12,000-strong Cuban commando units, and the massive arms supplies by the Soviet Union had turned the conflict between the three Angolan movements into a full-scale war. Second, South Africa's heavy involvement on the side of the FNLA-UNITA coalition had not only stirred African hostility against Pretoria but had caused half the OAU Members to question whether FNLA and UNITA any longer had the right to be regarded as true national movements entitled to participate in an Angolan Government of National Unity.

In January 1976, South Africa was still keeping quiet about the size of its involvement in Angola, admitting only to the dispatch of a 'limited force' to protect the $180-million Cuene river hydro-electric and irrigation scheme under construction in Angola but destined primarily for use in Namibia. However, reports in the international (and South African) press were already giving a good idea of the true scale of South African intervention. *The Observer* of 11 January 1976 reported the presence of a 2,000-strong column of white mercenaries with logistic support from 3,000 South African troops. A third South African unit arrived in Angola in December 1975, comprising a battallion each of tanks and artillery.

In its own account of the intervention one year later (contained in a communiqué issued on 3 February 1977 by the Defence Headquarters in Pretoria, entitled 'Nature and extent of the South African Defence Forces' involvement in the Angolan conflict'), South Africa admitted that the first military assistance to the FNLA-UNITA coalition had been provided as early as 24 September 1975 at Silva Porto. In trying to play down the volume of its assistance (the numbers of the South African troops were witheld), the communiqué maintained that the help was given on a 'limited scale' only. However, after listing all South African victories in battles with MPLA and Cuban forces the statement concluded with a bold assertion that 'the allied FNLA-UNITA forces supported by South African forces could have conquered the whole of Angola, but Dr Savimbi insisted that he was only interested in controlling his traditional area because he was determined to reach a settlement with the MPLA to the advantage of Angola'.

In reality South African — FNLA-UNITA forces were defeated by the élite units of the Cuban army, the first contingent of which landed in Angola on 5 November 1975. In the course of an operation code-named 'Carlota', a total of 15,000 Cuban troops took part in the Angolan war. Equipped with heavy modern Soviet armaments, the supplies of which were poured into Angola at an unprecedented scale, the Cubans tipped the scale of war in favour of MPLA. By January 1976 MPLA had halted the advance of the South African and UNITA forces in the south. In the north MPLA captured FNLA headquarters at Carmona and pushed the FNLA forces back behind the Zaire frontiers.

The exposure of South African intervention damaged the case of FNLA and UNITA more than the discovery of arms supply from the United States. Even those African States which, because of their opposition to the Marxist-oriented MPLA were content to see American arms go quietly to the 'anti-communist' UNITA, were enraged when they learned that the South Africans were operating hundreds of miles inside Angola. Jonas Savimbi of UNITA, aware that this backlash was potentially fatal to his credibility, claimed that South Africa had 'stabbed him in the back'. The MPLA was now in an extremely strong position to repudiate any OAU policy of reconciliation by asking, as Dr

Agostinho Neto proceeded to do: 'How can we be expected to climb on to the same unity bandwagon with South Africa?' This was the line taken by Mozambique's President Machel, who opened the attack at the Addis Ababa Summit by demanding that MPLA should be recognized forthwith as the only legitimate government in Angola, and that the FNLA and UNITA should be treated as movements which had forfeited any right to be regarded as genuine nationalists. As chairman, President Amin of Uganda peremptorily rejected Machel's proposal.

Two draft resolutions were put before the OAU Summit. The first was sponsored by the following 12 countries: Botswana, Cameroon, Ivory Coast, Egypt, Gambia, Gabon, Upper Volta, Kenya, Liberia, Lesotho, Malawi, Morocco, Mauretania, Rwanda, Central African Republic, Senegal, Sierra Leone, Swaziland, Togo, Tunisia, Zaire and Zambia. The sponsors of the draft expressed serious concern about the situation in Angola, concern that its national unity and integrity had been jeopardized by foreign intervention and the internationalization of the conflict. They regarded any threat to the unity of Angola as a direct threat to the security and unity of Africa. Recognizing the need 'to preserve and consolidate African unity', and wishing to create 'conditions conducive to promoting peace, unity and reconciliation in Angola', they reaffirmed their determination to solve the Angolan problem within the framework of African unity. They 'unequivocally' condemned the intervention of South Africa as well as 'all forms of foreign intervention and intrusion in the internal affairs of Angola, whatever their motivation and origin'. In particular they 'vehemently condemned all recourse to mercenaries and any supply of arms to the parties of the conflict in Angola'.

The proposed the following measures:
— the immediate withdrawal of all African and non-African States and cessation of the arms supply;
— the termination of armed hostilities on a date to be agreed upon as soon as possible, and the freezing of troops in positions held at the time of the cease-fire;
— the immediate conclusion of an agreement by the leaders of the three movements to set up a Government of National Unity; and
— the establishment of an *ad hoc* Commission of Heads of State and Government for the implementation of these measures.

The other draft resolution (sponsored by Algeria, Benin, Burundi, Cape Verde, Comoros Island, Congo, Ghana, Guinea, Guinea-Bissau, Equatorial Guinea, Libya, Mauritius, Madagascar, Mali, Mozambique, Niger, Nigeria, Sao Tomé and Principé, Somalia, Sudan, Chad and Tanzania) put greatest emphasis and blame for the worsening of the situation in Angola on the 'aggression of fascist South Africa and its active collaborators' which endangered the security of independent States bordering Angola and Africa as a whole. It then singled out the MPLA as a movement which since 1956 had always been opposed to colonialism, and which continued to oppose by all means the invasion of Angolan territory by the regular troops of fascist South Africa, with the full connivance of local and foreign agents of imperialism.

On the basis of what the draft resolution described as 'incontrovertible evidence about the blatant interference of imperialist forces seeking to dictate to Africa a solution in keeping with their interests in Angola', the following measures were proposed:
— material and military assistance to the People's Republic of Angola, both through bilateral arrangements and collectively by the OAU;
— increased aid to liberation movements in Namibia, Zimbabwe and South Africa.

Contrary to the news reports from Addis Ababa about the meeting, the supporters of the MPLA did not call for the recognition of the People's Republic of Angola declared by the MPLA on 11 November 1975, but invited OAU Members to express their confidence in the MPLA's ability 'to create an atmosphere of reconciliation of all Angolans willing to work for the consolidation of national unity, territorial integrity'. The formulation clearly excluded the leadership of the FNLA and UNITA but left room for compromise with their followers.

In the view of the sponsors of the resolution, Angola under the MPLA constituted a reliable guarantee that the struggle for the total liberation of Southern Africa would go on. The condemnation of South African intervention was the only issue on which consensus was reached, but not unreservedly. Some states, such as the Central African Republic, Senegal, Ivory Coast and Zaire, insisted on the inclusion of 'other forces', meaning the Soviet Union and Cuba. This point was also pressed for by President Ford in his 'circular letter' sent to several African Heads of State before the meeting; but it achieved just the opposite. The Nigerian Foreign Ministry, in its reply of 6 January 1976, called Ford's letter an 'insult to the intelligence of African nations and scorn of the dignity of the black man'. The *Ethiopian Herald,* in its leader by Girmay Zewalde of 24 January 1976, joined the Nigerians by accusing the Western powers that 'the pinching and shouting by their biased communication media and through others in Africa, for the withdrawal of socialist countries from Angola is for their benefit, in that they will have an opportune time to slip through the back door'.[81]

Several more proposals circulated throughout the meeting, but none resolved the deadlock of 22:22, with Uganda (chairman of the OAU) and Ethiopia (host to the session) remaining neutral. By Monday, 12

146

January, it was already clear that the OAU would not reach any decision. The Monday session continued long into the night and ended on Tuesday, 13 January in the morning. All that was agreed upon was a one-sentence communiqué saying: 'After seriously considering the Angolan problem from January 10-13, the Assembly of the Heads of State and Government decided to adjourn and request the OAU bureau (office of the current Chairman of the OAU) to follow closely the Angolan problem'. President Amin read it out, banged his fist on the table and announced that the meeting was closed. None of the exhausted delegates raised his hand to demand that at least one more sentence should be added — condemnation of South African intervention — on which there had been a unanimous consensus throughout the session.

Many African delegations were disappointed by the inconclusive meeting, and some said so in public.[82] But it would be a mistake to regard the Extraordinary OAU Summit as a 'total failure' just because it did not pass any resolutions. The African leaders coming to Addis Ababa were surely well aware of the limitations of the OAU. It is not a supranational organization capable of imposing the views of a majority on a minority, still less of imposing them by punitive measures. Like the United Nations, the OAU can act effectively only when the great majority of its members are firmly agreed on a particular policy. Although no resolutions were passssed, the unanimous opposition of OAU Members to foreign intervention, despite the variety of emphasis on its East or West sources, clearly emerged as the most important consensus reached at the meeting. Its weight soon began to show:

— South Africa withdrew its forces from the Angolan territory, while the leader of UNITA, Jonas Savimbi, continued his efforts to dissociate himself from the South African connections.
— On 11 February 1976, less than a month after the OAU Summit, Angola was recognized by the majority of the OAU Members and admitted as 47th member of the OAU.
— The Security Council, which met at the request of Kenya on 31 March 1976 to consider the African charges against South Africa of aggression and interference into the domestic affairs of Angola, adopted Resolution 387 (1975), the operative paragraphs of which read as follows:

'The Security Council:
1. *condemns* South Africa's aggression against the People's Republic of Angola.
2. *demands* that South Africa scrupulously respect the independence, sovereignty and territorial integrity of the People's Republic of Angola.

3. *demands* also that South Africa desist from the utilization of the international territory of Namibia to mount provocative or aggressive acts against the People's Republic of Angola or any other neighbouring African state
4. *calls upon* the Government of South Africa to meet the just claims of the People's Republic of Angola for a full compensation for the damage and destruction inflicted on its state and for the restoration of the equipment and materials which its invading forces seized.'

Also Zaire and Zambia recognized the MPLA Government, though after a considerable delay: Zambia on 14 April 1976 and Zaire on 10 January 1977. But while the Angolan-Zambian relations gradually settled, those with Zaire remained strained. On 24 February 1977 President Angostinho Neto revealed the existence of 'Plan Cobra 77' — the invasion of Angola from seven bases in Zaire (near Kitana, Matadi, Kamuna, Songolo, Kinula, Kasango and Kipule). Zaire in turn accused Angola of abetting the invasion by some 5,000 guerrilla insurgents of the Congo National Liberation Front (FNLC) into Shaba in March 1977. Two months later, on 20 May 1977, it was Angola's turn. The Angolan Defence Ministry issued a communiqué charging Zaire with invading Cabinda province and colluding with South Africa, which had at the same time mounted an operation in Cunene Province in the South in which a squadron of helicopters attacked the Angolan Village Santa Clara.

The reported revival of the UNITA guerrillas in the southern part of Angola (believed to have been aided by South Africans), the continuing presence of the Cuban troops in Angola, and the increase in the military activities of SWAPO guerrilla forces operating from Angolan territory in Namibia, have added considerably to the tension in the south-west part of Africa, as have the internal developments in Namibia which are discussed below.

## 5. NAMIBIA

South Africa, Rhodesia and the Portuguese colonies were central issues in African diplomacy at the UN; but Namibia, which entered UN history under the name of the 'South-West Africa Case', featured most prominently of all. No other international legal issue has received more publicity than the South African mandate over that territory.[83] Of all cases considered by the International Court of Justice, no case has occupied more of its time or more space in its records.

The legal status of South West Africa derives from the Versailles Peace Treaty of 1918 which after its defeat in the First World War, placed the overseas possessions of Germany under so-called mandate.[84] The Mandate for South-West Africa was conferred upon the Union of South Africa by a resolution of the Council of the League of Nations on 17 December 1920. In accordance with Article 22 of the Covenant, South Africa was responsible for the administration of the territory under conditions which would guarantee freedom of conscience and religion, the prohibition of abuses such as the slave trade, arms traffic and liquor traffic, and the prevention of the establishment of fortifications or military and naval bases, and of military training of the natives for other than police purposes and defence of the territory. It is worth mentioning that a significant part was played in drafting Article 22 by the Prime Minister of the Union of South Africa, General Smuts. From the very outset of its Mandate for South-West Africa, the Union of South Africa on several occasions claimed sovereignty over the Mandated territory. But these attempts were resisted by the permanent mandate commission of the League of Nations.

The Charter of the United Nations, which came into force on 24 October 1945, had introduced the so-called international trusteeship system which, according to Article 77 of the Charter, applied *inter alia* to territories then held under mandate. At the first session of the General Assembly, the delegate of South Africa requested that the territory of South-West Africa be incorporated in the Union. He argued that the territory was sparsely inhabited and could not exist independently, and that the majority of the population wished it to be incorporated into the Union. The General Assembly did not agree with the proposed incorporation and recommended that South-West Africa be placed under the international trusteeship system inviting the Government of South Africa to propose a trusteeship agreement.[85]

South Africa adopted an attitude of defiance towards any UN efforts to bring South-West Africa under the international trusteeship system, and between 1950 and 1962 the International Court of Justice was asked three times to rule on several aspects of its legal status.[86] Liberia and Ethiopia, the only OAU Members to have belonged to the defunct League of Nations, instituted a case against South Africa on 4 November 1960. They asked the International Court to adjudge and declare *inter alia* that the Republic of South Africa had violated the Mandate for South-West Africa by failing to promote the material and moral well-being and social progress of the inhabitants of the territory and by practising in South-West Africa its policies of apartheid. To the astonishment of the general public the world over, as well as of most international lawyers, the Court, in its judgement of 16 July 1966, rejected by eight votes to seven (with the President casting a decisive

149

vote) the claims of Ethiopia and Liberia against South Africa, ruling that they had failed to establish any legal right or interests in the matter before the Court. In other words, they simply were not considered competent to institute the proceedings against South Africa.

In their dissenting opinions Judges Wellington Koo, Koretsky, Tanaka, Padilla-Nervo, Jessup, Forster and Mbanefo all exposed the weakness of the judgement. Judge Jessup, in his strongly-worded dissenting opinion, considered the judgement 'completely unfounded in law'. In his opinion, 'the Court was not legally justified in stopping at the threshold of the case, avoiding a decision on the fundamental question whether the policy and practice of apartheid in the mandated territory of South-West Africa is compatible with the discharge of the sacred trust confided to the Republic of South Africa as a mandatory'.[87]

The UN General Assembly adopted its own course of action. On 27 October 1966, by 114 votes to 2 (Portugal and South Africa) with three abstentions (France, Malawi and Great Britain), it adopted Resolution 2145 (XXX) terminating South Africa's mandate and bringing the territory under the direct administration and responsibility of the UN. The resolution was welcomed by the OAU, and the Council of Ministers at its 7th Session in Addis Ababa in October 1966 fully endorsed the UN action.[88] On 19 May 1967 the UN General Assembly created a UN Council for South-West Africa to administer the territory, and in the following year it renamed the territory Namibia. In 1974 it established the office of the UN High Commissioner for Namibia with Sean McBride as its first High Commissioner.

In order to strengthen its legal authority over the territory, the Security Council on 29 July 1970 approached the International Court of Justice for an opinion on the legal consequences of the continued presence of South Africa in Namibia. The Court, in its advisory opinion of 21 June 1971, stated that:

- the continued presence of South Africa in Namibia being illegal, South Africa was under obligation to withdraw its administration from Namibia immediately and thus put an end to its occupation of the territory; and that
- Member-States of the United Nations were under an obligation to recognize the illegality of South Africa's presence in Namibia and the invalidity of its acts on behalf of or concerning Namibia, and to refrain from any act and in particular from any dealing with the Government of South Africa, implying the recognition of the legality of, or lending support or assistance to, such presence and administrations.[89]

South Africa refused to implement the Court's ruling and, although changed in law, the new status of Namibia had no effect on its control over the territory. South Africa also ignored the demand by the African States, endorsed at the meeting of the Security Council in Addis Ababa in January-February 1972 that it should:

— end, immediately, repressive measures against the labourers of Namibia and abolish the system of labour which is in conflict with the Universal Declaration of Human Rights; and
— withdraw, immediately, its police and military forces as well as its civilian personnel from Namibia.[90]

The South African Government remained unmoved by the diplomatic efforts of the Secretary-General of the UN when he visited Pretoria in 1973 for talks on Namibia. On the contrary, it used the dialogue with the UN to neutralise the termination of the mandate and to consolidate its presence in Namibia. Africans saw this dialogue as giving encouragement to South Africa and called for the immediate severance of the South African contact. They contended that the only acceptable dialogue should be aimed at the transfer of power from South Africa to the Council for Namibia.

The Resolution on Namibia adopted at the OAU Summit at Addis Ababa in May 1973 called upon the Security Council 'to terminate the contacts of the UN Secretary-General with the South African racist authorities, as such exercise has proved ultimately to be detrimental to the interest of the people of Namibia and prejudicial to the early achievement of independence by the territory.'[91] The OAU request was met by the Resolution adopted by the UN General Assembly on 28 November 1973 asking for the termination of the contacts between the UN and the South African Government. The same resolution reaffirmed the legitimacy of the struggle of the people of Namibia against 'illegal occupation by South Africa', and recognized SWAPO (The South-West Africa People's Organization) as the authentic representative of the Namibian people.

The year 1973 also marked the peak of OAU dissatisfaction with the UN impotence over Namibia — which the UN has been supposed to administer until its independence. The OAU Administrative Secretary-General, in his report to the 10th OAU Summit in Addis Ababa in 1973, called Namibia a 'test of confidence of Africa in the United Nations'. He said:

'Every Head of State and Government of OAU has at one time or another affirmed our unflinching loyalty and hopes in the United Nations, as the sum total of the conscience of mankind and the guardian of the norms of justice and fairness in human society. But we are disappointed by the double standards in the United Nations. It went to war in Korea; it went to war in the Congo. If there is any challenge that ought justifiably to push the United Nations to the most extreme act in the defence of Justice, it is the defiance of this Organization by South Africa over Namibia. Namibia, which is a territory held in trust by the United Nations; Namibia, which is legally neither a colony nor a protectorate of South Africa, confirmed by verdict of the International Court at the Hague, this Namibia is allowed by the United Nations to continue to scream and bleed to death in the hands of apartheid South Africa.'[92]

The criticism by the Acting Vice-President of SWAPO, Muyongo, in his address to the UN Fourth Committee on 26 October 1973, was equally sharp:

'How are United Nations commitments being honoured? France, a permanent member of the Security Council, opened a new consulate in Namibia only two weeks ago. The Federal Republic of Germany, a new member of the Organization, has been allowed to join while stubbornly maintaining a consulate in Namibia. Moreover, the continuing economic and military aid by the United Kingdom, France, the United States, the Federal Republic of Germany and others, as well as the refusal of those countries to prohibit investments in Namibia and South Africa by their nationals and companies under their jurisdiction, continues to enable the regime of South Africa to maintain its illegal occupation of Namibia. Instead of stockpiling its resolutions, the United Nations should now sincerely begin to explore ways to implement all its oustanding commitments concerning Namibia.'[93]

The OAU diplomatic offensive against South Africa over Namibia entered a new stage with the negotiations of the four Presidents (Nyerere, Kaunda, Machel and Khama) with South Africa in 1974. The four Presidents demanded that South Africa recognize the territorial integrity and unity of Namibia as a nation and take necessary steps to transfer the powers in the territory to the people of Namibia with the assistance of the United Nations. On 13 December 1974 the Security Council adopted a resolution giving South Africa six months to do so.[94] One month later, on 17 January 1975, SWAPO issued a statement in Lusaka stating its conditions for talks with South Africa on the future of Namibia.[95] South Africa kept stalling the issue and ignored the warning addressed to it by the Dar-es-Salaam Declaration that 'in the absence of South Africa's willingness to terminate its illegal occupation of Namibia, the OAU must assist the national liberation movement of Namibia, SWAPO, to intensify the armed struggle in Namibia.'

The South African Government let the UN wait five and a half months before replying to the Security Council Resolution of 13 December 1974. When finally, on 20 May 1975, Premier Vorster stated his government's plans on Namibia in a speech at his constituency, Nigel, he dashed all hopes for the territory's early independence. His speech was nothing but a re-statement of old positions. To the UN demand to withdraw from Namibia he replied: 'We are not occupying the territory, we are there because the people of the territory want us to be there.' When he spoke of Namibia's future, he re-affirmed that this would be decided by the leaders of the various ethnic groups at a constitutional conference.

The South African government proceeded with the implementation of its blueprint for Namibia's independence by convening a constitutional conference at Windhoek in September 1975. The 156 delegates, drawn from eleven ethnic groups, approved a so-called 'Declaration of Intent' in which the all-white administration — in effect South Africa's agent to South-West Africa — committed itself to drawing up an independence constitution within three years.[97] The document was drafted by the only two white delegates attending the talks, Dirk Mudge and Eben Van Zijl of the white ruling National Party. SWAPO and the Namibia National Convention[98] were excluded from the talks. The constitutional Conference met again on 2 June 1976 at Turnhalle in Windhoek, and ended on 18 August by announcing an agreement that there would be a multinational provisional government leading to independence for Namibia on 31 December 1978.

The OAU Summit at Port Louis on 3 July condemned these talks as 'rubber-stamping the obnoxious policy of bantustans and so-called homelands'. SWAPO also rejected the Turnhalle agreement,[99] but this did not prevent South Africa from proceeding with its plans — which enjoyed the support of the Ford Administration.[100] The African response at the UN showed in a General Assembly resolution of 20 December 1976 which, for the first time, endorsed 'armed struggle' as a legitimate means of attaining Namibia's independence.

The final draft of the South African blueprint for the Constitution of Namibia was approved by the plenary session of the Turnhalle Constitutional Conference on 18 March 1977. It described the territory not as Namibia but as 'South West Africa' and as a 'Republican Democratic State which recognizes the principles of free enterprise and the unassailable right to possess grounds and goods . . .' Chapter 2 of the draft, providing for the protection of fundamental rights, gives assurances on the equality of all people before the law and lists all kinds of freedoms of movement, expression, religion and forming political parties, but it does not touch upon the South African discriminatory laws which remain valid. Political parties or groups with a 'Marxist-Leninist ideology' were prohibited as 'being enemies of the

153

State'. Moreover, the structure of the government under the Turnhalle constitution is based on the governments of eleven ethnic groups, that is Bantustans.

The exclusion of SWAPO from any say in shaping the constitutional future of Namibia, and the strong opposition voiced by the OAU against Turnhalle, began to worry even those African delegates who at first raised very few objections (such as the Herreros who began to protest). The white population too began to have their doubts about the viability of the Turnhalle Constitution, on which they were asked to vote in a referendum on 17 May 1977. Only half of the whites came to the polls. Those who did voted 'yes'. But by that time the constitution was already a non-starter. This was due to a surprise initiative on behalf of the five Security Council powers — USA, Britain, France, Canada and the Federal Republic of Germany. On 7 April 1977 the ambassadors of these countries met the South African Premier John Vorster in Cape Town and told him that the Turnhalle Constitution proposals were unacceptable and should be abandoned. Instead, they called for an 'internationally acceptable settlement to the Namibian problem consistent with the UN Security Council Resolution 385 of 30 January 1976', demanding the withdrawal of the South African police and army from Namibia and the holding of free national elections in the territory under UN supervision. They also demanded a repeal of South African discriminatory laws, the release of Namibian political prisoners, and the unrestricted participation of SWAPO in elections for an independent government. Namibia and Rhodesia dominated the UN-sponsored International Conference in Support of the Peoples of Zimbabwe and Namibia (held in Maputo on 16-18 May 1977), where the majority of 80 delegations both from African and non-African states reiterated demands for an arms embargo and economic sanctions against South Africa.

In an important speech on the first day of the conference President Samora Machel of Mozambique described the Western powers' efforts on Namibia as a positive factor which could contribute to the full implementation of the Security Council Resolution 385. However, he added that 'the West would fail if it was only trying to preserve its own interest there'.[101]

These Western interests in Namibia are motivated by a desire to secure access to Namibia's uranium wealth at Rössing, currently being mined by Rio Tinto Zinc. Its operations are conducted under the strict security and secrecy imposed by the South African Atomic Energy Act. The production which started in 1976 will reach in 1978 an output of 5,000 tons of uranium oxide ore, about one sixth of the total uranium output of the Western world. It is this fact which has prompted Western Germany, the country with particular interest in Namibian uranium,[102] to persuade the other Western powers to look for a solution which would sufficiently appease SWAPO for SWAPO to allow them to have their share in exploiting Namibia's mineral wealth (of which uranium is believed to be only a tip of an iceberg).

Neither the Maputo conference nor the meeting between the US Vice-President Walter Mondale and Premier John Vorster in Vienna on 20th May 1977 has made South Africa give up its Turnhalle Constitution plans. Moreover, as Vorster told Mondale, South Africa is also determined to keep the control over Walvis Bay, Namibia's only deep water port. Walvis Bay dominates the western approaches of the Cape sea routes and is regarded by NATO circles as the most important strategic port between Lobito and Cape Town. SWAPO, which denounced the Western powers' initiative and condemned the Vorster-Mondale talks, made it clear that Walvis Bay is an integral part of Namibia and as such not negotiable. The OAU Liberation Committee at its meeting in Luanda in June 1977 fully endorsed SWAPO's stand. South Africa's intransigence over Namibia, and the lack of determination on the part of the Western powers to *force* South Africa to accept the conditions for Namibia's independence laid down by the OAU and the UN, have created a situation in which the independence of Namibia is almost certain to be decided by the same means as that of Zimbabwe: by gun rather than by diplomacy.

# Chapter IX

# THE OAU AND AFRO-ARAB RELATIONS

When in May 1973 the Assembly of Heads of State and Government declared its intention to take political and economic measures against Israel on the grounds that Israel was 'threatening the security and unity of the African continent as a result of its continued aggression' and its refusal to evacuate the occupied Arab territories,[1] there were not many who thought that the African leaders would follow up their threat with action. Strongly-worded condemnations of Israel were not a novelty in OAU resolutions. So when a further twenty-one black African States broke off diplomatic relations with Israel after the outbreak of the new war between Israel and its two Arab neighbours, Egypt and Syria, in October 1973, the world public was astonished. Against the background of Israel's good relations with most Black African States and close friendship with countries like Ghana, Ivory Coast, Ethiopia and Kenya, and the presence, at the time of the break, of about 250 Israeli experts attached to projects in twenty-seven African countries, the sudden display of hostility towards Israel appeared to have been one of the most dramatic reversals in the foreign policy of the African States.

In reality, the change was neither sudden nor unexpected. The Arab members of the OAU had been pressing Africa for some time to take their side against Israel, and the campaign for an Afro-Arab alliance had begun long before the OAU was even founded. When the Casablanca group was founded in 1961, President Nasser of Egypt, who at that time dominated African politics, saw in it the first chance of some kind of alliance to challenge Israeli advances into Africa.

The success of Israel's African policy was largely due to its development aid. To explain their motives for helping Africa, the Israelis often quoted Theodor Herzl, the founder of Zionism, who had said that 'only the Negro race tragedy could be compared with the tragedy of the oppressed Jews'.[2] But this sense of common ground was not the only reason for Israel to be welcome in Africa: Israel had won Africa's respect for the success of its agricultural development in conditions similar to those of many African countries. Israel's development aid in Africa had, of course, strategic as well as humanitarian motives. Israel's ability to secure free navigation to the

Red Sea largely depended on its ability to win the friendship of nations along the coast of the Red Sea as far as the Indian Ocean. From a military point of view, a high priority was assigned to East African States because of their possible role in the Israeli-Egyptian conflict; and there were economic reasons for supporting the concentration of foreign aid on countries like Ghana, Nigeria and Zaire.[3]

By 1961, Israel was thus already recognized as a valuable partner by a number of newly-independent African States, including some of the Casablanca States themselves. For example, in Ghana the state shipping line 'Black Star' was run by the Israelis, who also directed the establishment and training of the 'Builders' Brigade', later transformed into Ghana's 'agricultural army'.[4] However, at the founding conference of the Casablanca group in January 1961, Nasser pleaded his case against Israel with great effect, comparable to that achieved by President Boumedienne twelve years later at the 10th Anniversary Summit of the OAU at Addis Ababa.

Nasser linked the problem of Palestine with the general theme of the defence of independence and security in Africa, which was entrusted in the Casablanca Charter to the 'Joint African High Command' proposed by Ghana. He argued that the establishment of Israel constituted a threat not only to the Arab States in the Middle East but to the whole of Africa:

'What was the aim of the imperialist powers in creating Israel? Their primary aim was to make it a spearhead for their advance and a base for their aggression. . . Where did the Franco-British troops come from at the time of the Suez affair? From Israel. For this Israel received $400 million as a recompense from the imperialist powers for using the country as a base for imperialist infiltration into Africa and Asia. . . Israel is at present granting aid in Africa, even though we know that she is not in a position to balance her budget from her own resources. That is because this country is acting as a go-between, between the colonial powers and the countries of Africa, passing on aid to them. Israel is the wolf which has got into the sheepfold.'[5]

He regarded Egypt as 'the gateway to the defence of the interests of North-East Africa', and felt himself responsible for defending it against the danger of becoming 'a highway for imperialist infiltration into the continent'. And he compared Egypt's responsibility with that of the independent black African countries for ensuring that Africa was not threatened by a similar danger emanating from South Africa.

Just how well Nasser's arguments went down with the leaders of the Casablanca States was amply shown by the wording of the Resolution on

Palestine, unanimously adopted at the meeting. The resolution:

> 'Notes with indignation that Israel has always taken the side of the imperialists each time an important position had to be taken concerning vital problems about Africa, notably Algeria, the Congo and the nuclear tests in Africa, and the Conference, therefore, denounces Israel as an instrument in the service of imperialism and neo-colonialism not only in the Middle East but also in Africa and Asia.
>
> Calls upon all the States of Africa and Asia to oppose this new policy which imperialism is carrying out to create bases for itself.'[6]

Although African members of the Casablanca group regarded the Resolution on Palestine simply as a gesture of support for Egypt's stand, which had little bearing on their policies at home, the anti-Israeli posture of the group was deeply resented by the Monrovia and Brazzaville States. So strong was their opposition to Arab efforts to make 'Palestine an African issue' that they made the dropping of the Palestine problem one of the conditions of their rapprochement with the Casablanca group. Accordingly, Nasser did not even mention it at the 1963 Addis Ababa Summit.

## 1. THE OAU PEACE INITIATIVE ON THE MIDDLE EAST CRISIS IN 1971

The view that the Middle East crisis was not truly an African problem (although it involves Egypt, a member of the OAU) still prevailed in 1967, when the majority of OAU Members rejected Somalia's call for an emergency OAU Summit to take a stand on the June war between Egypt and Israel. They maintained that the UN was the only appropriate authority to deal with the conflict. The Assembly of Heads of State and Government, meeting in Kinshasa in September 1967, chose to adopt a 'Declaration' rather than a resolution on the matter. The African leaders carefully avoided describing Israel as an aggressor, and simply expressed their concern at the grave situation prevailing in Egypt, an African country whose territory was partly occupied by a foreign power. They offered Egypt sympathy and a promise to work within the UN to secure the evacuation of its territory.[7]

The change in attitude within a mere four years can best be shown by a comparison of the wording of the OAU resolutions over that period. Only one year after the Assembly of Heads of State had devoted three non-committal paragraphs to the Egyptian plea for support against Israel, the resolution of 1968 was entitled 'Resolution on the aggression against the United Arab Republic',[8] and in it Egypt was called a 'victim of Zionism'. But except for a call for the immediate and unconditional withdrawal of foreign troops from all the Arab countries with occupied territory, the resolution was not specific on a pledge of 'active support' for Egypt. The following year, in the 'Resolution on the situation in the United Arab Republic',[9] the Assembly of Heads of State and Government endorsed the Security Council Resolution of 22 November 1967,[10] which it regarded as the basis on which the Middle East crisis should be solved. This stand was reaffirmed in the OAU resolution of 1970.[11] After that the OAU policy changed.

The 'Resolution on the continued aggression against U.A.R.', adopted in 1971,[12] constitutes a point of departure from the previous OAU policy of 'leaving the Middle East problem to the UN'. First of all, it was much more explicit in expressing the OAU's support for Egypt. Secondly, it used for the first time the words 'deploring Israel', criticizing Israel's defiance of the initiative of the Special Representative of the UN Secretary-General, the Swedish Amabassador Gunnar Jarring.* Thirdly, and most significantly, the OAU decided to take steps on its own. The current chairman of the Organization, President Ould Daddah of Mauritania, was asked 'to consult with the Heads of State and Government so that they may use their influence to ensure the full implementation of this resolution' — meaning the withdrawal of Israel from the occupied territories on the conditions specified by the Security Council Resolution 242. A Committee of Ten was formed, consisting of the Heads of State of Cameroun, Ethiopia, Ivory Coast, Kenya, Liberia, Mauritania, Nigeria, Senegal, Tanzania and Zaire (with the exception of Mauritania, all these countries maintained diplomatic relations with Israel); and a small subcommittee, composed of Presidents Ahidjo, Senghor and Mobotu and General Gowon, was given the task of assessing Egyptian and Israeli views.

The initiative for an OAU mission came from President Kaunda of Zambia, who had played host to the Summit Conference of the non-aligned countries held in Lusaka the previous year, in September 1970. Given the conclusions of that conference, which had given Egypt more outspoken support than the OAU had done, President Kaunda

---

* On 8 February 1971 Jarring had called for the re-opening of the indirect talks between Egypt and Israel, asking Israel to commit itself to withdrawal from the occupied territories. Israel refused.

saw in this peace-move on the Middle East an opportunity of increasing Africa's prestige among the non-aligned countries. The general motive was a genuine concern to bring about peace and security in the Middle East, since whatever happened there would affect Africa and the entire world. Zambia also sought to reassert its impartiality. It has supported the Arab position since the Six-Day War, in the UN and in Third World forums; but at the same time it has kept up friendly bilateral relations with Israel, and has benefited from Israeli technical assistance, especially for co-operatives.

Opinion as to the objectives of the mission varied substantially. The OAU Secretary-General, Diallo Telli, held that it was essential to find a solution to the Middle East crisis, particularly because the UN effort had failed. In his view the Committee of Ten had to resolve whether the African countries would fight side by side with the Arab countries to push Israel out of the occupied territories, and whether the OAU would give material aid to the Arabs. President Ould Daddah, because of his position as Chairman of the OAU Assembly, was more concerned with OAU prestige; he felt that the Committee should first gather information and then present considered and concrete proposals for a practicable solution. A third approach was chosen by President Senghor, the head of the subcommittee of four, who stressed that the mission's aim was to help bring peace to the Middle East. Its members simply wanted to see the two sides opening a dialogue and furthering the application of the Security Council Resolution. They had no intention of taking the place of the great powers or the UN.

Both Egypt and Israel were sympathetic towards the mission, although sceptical as to what it could achieve. The Israelis hoped that the OAU mission would result in a modification of the pro-Egyptian positions previously adopted by the OAU, and that the mission could be used as a platform for a new approach in negotiations. Egypt insisted on regarding the task of the OAU mission as not to mediate but to seek ways and means of implementing the Security Council Resolution 242. Moreover, it was keen to make use of Israel's negative response to the Jarring initiative of 8 February to intensify Israel's international isolation. Egypt hoped that Israel's economic and political interests in Africa would be put in jeopardy by its rebuff of the principle of 'non-acquisition of territory by war'.[13]

Egypt's assessment of African sensitivity on the question of territorial integrity proved to be correct. Despite the variety of opinions held by different members of the Committee of Ten, all agreed on the priority to be given to the following provisions of Resolution 242:
- respect for the sovereignty, territorial integrity and political independence of every State in the area;
- guarantee of territorial inviolability; and

— the need to work for a just, lasting and secure peace.

The OAU emphasis on these principles can be explained not only by reference to Article III (3) of the OAU Charter, which made the same stipulations, but also, and above all, because of the thought that South Africa might be their Israel, launching a 'preventive military action' against one of its neighbours, and occupying its territory.[14]

The OAU peace plan submitted to the Prime Minister Golda Meir and President Sadat by President Senghor on 21 November 1971 was never made public; but according to UN and OAU sources it contained the following recommendations:

— the resumption of negotiations under Jarring's auspices;
— agreement on the opening of the Suez Canal, and the stationing, on the eastern bank of the Canal, of UN forces between the Egyptian and Israeli lines;
— acceptance of such boundaries as will be determined by the peace agreement;
— the creation of demilitarized zones and the presence of an international peace force at some strategic points under UN auspices and guarantees;
— the inclusion in the peace agreement of terms of withdrawal from the occupied territories; and
— the stationing of international forces at Sharm el Sheikh in order to guarantee freedom of navigation to all ships passing through the Strait of Tiran.

The OAU mission was unable to find a compromise between the Egyptian demand for immediate withdrawal and the Israeli insistence upon negotiations without preconditions. It met with willingness on both sides to proceed with the Jarring negotiations, but could not overcome the impasse over the *terms* for its continuation.[15] At the OAU Summit at Rabat, the current Chairman of the OAU, President Ould Daddah of Mauritania, attributed the mission's failure to Israel, which 'strongly rejected any peace settlement and was even more strongly opposed to anything that might lead to the withdrawal of its forces from occupied territories'. Faced with a lobby of Arab, and some militant African, States, the Assembly of Heads of State and Government opted for unanimity. This produced a resolution strongly condemning Israel. Significantly, this resolution was moved by the Ivory Coast, perhaps the most pro-Israeli of African States.[16]

There were other indications at Rabat of growing Arab influence in OAU affairs. The outgoing chairman, President Ould Daddah, was succeeded by another Arab leader, King Hassan II of Morocco, who had been host to the Summit. And the Palestinian Liberation Organization (PLO) was granted the status of observer, with the right to attend the OAU meetings.

## 2. AFRO-ARAB UNITY AT THE 1973 OAU SUMMIT

The emergence of an African-Arab alliance in 1973 was attributed to the following factors:

— Disappointment over Israel's refusal to comply with the Security Council Resolution 242 of 22 November 1967, which had demanded its withdrawal from the Arab territories occupied in the 1967 war: the OAU held Israel responsible for the failure of its mediation in the Middle East conflict in 1971.

— The assaults by Pretoria and Jerusalem against neighbouring States because of their support for the African and Arab freedom fighters; and the growing African concern about the military and economic collaboration between South Africa and Israel — each considering itself as a besieged State whose policies should therefore always be based on military and strategic superiority.[17]

— The growing co-operation between the PLO, the ANC of Zimbabwe, the African National Congress of South Africa and SWAPO.

— The growing relationship between the OAU and the Arab League.

— The disillusion of Africa with the attitude of Western powers and their policies of supporting the white minority regimes in Southern Africa; and the Arab offer of military assistance to finish the decolonization of Africa.[18]

— And, last but not least, the skill of Arab diplomacy within the OAU, spearheaded by President Boumedienne of Algeria who played a key role in convincing black Africa that Israel was a threat to the peace and security of Africa, and that Egypt's struggle for the recovery of its territory occupied by Israel could be equated with the struggle to liberate Southern Africa from white supremacy.

One of the most remarkable aspects of the Afro-Arab alliance was the fact that it was forged as a 'political pact' long before a number of European countries became converted by the 'oil weapon' from Israeli support to friendship with the Arabs. There is no evidence either that the Arabs ever mentioned the possibility of using the 'oil weapon' against African countries or that the African countries threw their support behind the Arabs with financial benefit in mind. But the diplomatic victory by the Arabs in Addis Ababa was particularly striking in that it was achieved despite a serious dispute between Libya and Ethiopia. A few weeks before the OAU Summit in May 1973 the Libyan leader, President Gaddafi, urged all African leaders to boycott the meeting unless the venue was changed to Cairo and unless Ethiopia agreed immediately to sever its relations with Israel. He accused Ethiopia of supporting Israel and called on all African States to 'define their attitudes to the Zionist enemy and co-ordinate them with the Libyan views'. Colonel Gaddafi followed up his message by sending a delegation to Kenya, Somalia, Tanzania, Uganda and Zambia to win support for his proposal.

To retrieve the situation, Emperor Haile Selassie paid a secret visit to Egypt on 12 May 1973 to seek the support of President Sadat and to persuade him to attend the conference. In his reply to Gaddafi's accusation, the Emperor pointed out that Ethiopia had consistently supported all UN resolutions on the Middle East and had shown solidarity with the Arab States in supporting OAU and UN resolutions calling for Israel's withdrawal from all occupied territories. He maintained that Ethiopia's relations with Israel had in no way affected its position where basic principles of international law and justice had been at stake in the Middle East. Ethiopia also sent delegations to a number of African States to enlist support against Libya.[19] As a result, far from there being a boycott of the anniversary celebrations, every member of the OAU, including Libya, sent a delegation. The session of the Council of Ministers was opened on 17 May and was followed by the meeting of the Assembly of Heads of State and Government on 27 May 1973. Twenty-one Heads of State and four Heads of Government attended the conference, and in addition, there were sixteen high-ranking representatives of other countries.

But Libya did not give up its campaign against Ethiopia. At the closing session of the Council of Ministers of the OAU on 24 May 1973, the leader of the Libyan delegation, Abauzeid Durda, reopened the dispute. He accused Ethiopia of maintaining United States military bases on its territory and described Ethiopia as an instrument of the enemies of Africa, collaborating with American and Israeli spies. He also charged Ethiopia with active support of Israel's collusion with Portugal and South Africa in fighting the African liberation movements.[20] The Ethiopian Foreign Minister, Menassie Haile, in an emotional reply, accused Libya of harbouring rebels against other African governments, including Ethiopia, and described this as a gross violation of the OAU Charter. The Libyan motion to move the OAU headquarters from Addis Ababa had scant support, even among the Arabs, who were rather embarrassed by Libyan attacks against Ethiopia and did not spare efforts to hush up the whole affair and prevent it flaring up again at the meeting of the Assembly.

The meeting of the Assembly brought the Arabs great diplomatic triumph. There the Arab cause was presented by President Boumedienne of Algeria, with a detachment that won the support of all the African leaders present. Choosing his words carefully, President Boumedienne compared the occupation of the Arab lands by the Israelis with the occupation of Rhodesia and South Africa by the white settlers. He said: 'Africa cannot adopt one attitude towards colonialism in Southern Africa and a completely different one towards Zionist colonization in North Africa'. He pointed out that, since the 1967 war, Israel had occupied the Sinai peninsula right up to the Suez Canal, which was nearly one-third of the total area of Egypt. Despite UN pressure and OAU diplomatic initiatives, Israel would not withdraw from the occupied territories. The Algerian leader described the situation as an insult to the continent: a foreign power illegally occupying a piece of African soil. From this point of view, Israel was committing aggression similar to that of the white settlers in Rhodesia, the Portuguese in Angola, Mozambique and Guinea-Bissau, and the South Africans in Namibia.

The tough resolution unanimously adopted by the Assembly of Heads of State and Government on 29 May 1973,[21] stated that respect for the inalienable rights of the Palestinian people was an essential element of any just and equitable solution of the Middle East problem. But it omitted the guarantee of the sovereignty, territorial integrity and political independence of Israel embodied in Security Council Resolution 242. The strongest paragraph of the OAU resolution was the warning to Israel that its refusal to evacuate the Arab territories constituted an act of aggression threatening the security and unity of the African continent, which might lead OAU Member-States to take, individually or collectively, political and economic measures against it.

When on 6 October of the same year a new war in the Middle East broke out, the OAU members carried out their pledge. Within the period from October to 13 November 1973, twenty-one African States broke off their diplomatic relations with Israel. And when an emergency session of the Council of Ministers was convened at Addis Ababa on 19 November 1973 to consider the Algerian proposal 'Consideration of the current Middle East situation with particular reference to its effects in Africa', forty-two OAU Members, that is all but four (Malawi, Lesotho, Swaziland and Botswana), severed diplomatic relations with Israel. The Declaration of policy on the international situation adopted at the meeting[22] formally sealed the Afro-Arab alliance forged at the 1973 summit. It states:

'The African countries which have worked continuously for peace and the removal of the causes of tension realize that, despite the progress made towards a détente between the great powers, their peoples are still directly faced with colonialism, racial discrimination and apartheid, aggression, foreign occupation and domination, neo-colonialism, imperialism and Zionism.'

This is elaborated as follows:

'The struggle of the African countries and the action taken by the

164

Organization of African Unity reflect the profound aspirations of the peoples of the continent to justice, freedom and progress. Their aim is to free themselves from colonialism everywhere, to eliminate apartheid and Zionism, to safeguard their own identities and personalities, to recover and enhance their cultural heritage and to assert, in every way, "authenticity", and finally, consolidate their national independence by rejecting all forms of foreign domination, interference and pressure.

In pursuance of this policy, the Council of Ministers underlines the need for the African countries to undertake firm and concerted action so as to contribute to the settlement of disputes affecting the Third World, at grips with the power politics of imperialism, colonialism and Zionism. The Middle East is once again the scene of a war provoked by Israel's expansionist policy of aggression against the Arab countries.'

This broad statement of a new African-Arab policy endorsed by the OAU was summed up in the resolution on the Middle East.[23] The measures listed in the resolution included the following:

— severance of relations with Israel until it withdraws from all the occupied Arab territories;
— recognition of the legitimacy of the struggle of the Palestinian people to restore their national rights by all means available to them;
— strengthening of individual and collective measures further to isolate Israel in the political, economic and cultural fields until a just and lasting solution to the Middle East problem is found;
— recommendation that all African States should take all possible measures to put an end to Israel's defiance of the international community.

After completely endorsing the Arab position on the Middle East, the black African members of the OAU then demanded that an oil embargo applied to Israel should be immediately applied also against South Africa, Portugal and Rhodesia. They also asked for better terms over oil supplies to African countries which had been severely hit by increased prices and by the shortage of oil products (the import of which was suspended on account of the embargo imposed on their Western exporters).[24] The African demands were met by a resolution appealing to oil-producing Arab countries, as well as to Iran, 'to extend the oil embargo to South Africa, Portugal and Southern Rhodesia until they comply with the UN General Assembly and Security Council Resolutions on decolonization'. The resolution also provided for the establishment of a special committee charged with maintaining liaison with the Arab League to supervise the oil embargo and ensure that its operations do not harm African States. It consists of Botswana,

Cameroon, Ghana, Mali, Tanzania, Sudan and Zaire (and became known as the Committee of Seven).

The Tanzanian *Daily News* of 23 November 1973 commented on the event as follows:

'During the recent war in the Middle East in which the Arab peoples were fighting to recover their lost territories, African States demonstrated their solidarity by severing relations with Israel and censuring Israel's Western supporters. There is no question of a *quid pro quo*. For ultimately the struggles of the downtrodden, underdeveloped and exploited are one. This common struggle is against imperialism and its worldwide puppets. And in this common struggle, the victims of imperialism, colonialism and neo-colonialism must identify with each other and support each other materially and in spirit.'

A week after the Addis Ababa emergency session, a Conference of Arab Kings and Presidents held in Algiers responded to the OAU resolution by deciding that all diplomatic, consular, economic, cultural and other relations with South Africa, Portugal and Rhodesia should be severed by those Arab States which had not yet done so and that a strict Arab oil embargo be imposed on the three countries. The same resolution decided to render every assistance politically and materially to the African liberation movements. President Boumedienne of Algeria, in his address to the Conference, called the African-Arab solidarity a turning point in Africa's history:

'The time has come to consolidate African-Arab solidarity in other spheres, of mutual co-operation between the political, economic and technical institutions of OAU and the Arab League. Such co-operation representing the human and material resources of the Arab and African countries, will constitute a formidable force in international relations capable of playing a decisive role in the service of justice and freedom in the whole world.'[25]

The Arab Summit also resolved to establish an 'Arab Bank for Industrial and Agricultural Development of Africa', with an initial capital of $231 million. The following year another institution, called a 'Special Fund for Africa', was established to assist African oil imports and to develop Africa's own oil resources.[26]

## 3. THE CRUMBLING OF THE AFRO-ARAB ALLIANCE

However, apart from the funds made available to Africa by the Special

Arab Fund, which were rather small compared with what these States paid for their oil imports, the principal beneficiaries of Arab development aid (provided both on a multilateral and on a bilateral basis) were the Muslim African States.[27] Africa's initial enthusiasm soon gave way to growing concern at the effects of the rising price of oil. Oil is the predominant source of energy of almost every African country, Ghana relying on it for 80 per cent of its energy requirements and Tanzania for 95 per cent — in marked contrast to North America and Western Europe which can get by with greater reliance on coal. Furthermore, as development brings in its wake increased transport needs, industrialization and urbanization, so the demand for energy in most African countries is rising rapidly. In fact, each percentage point rise in Gross National Product in these countries brings about a 2 per cent rise in energy use, compared to less than 1 per cent in the advanced industrial countries. The fivefold rise in oil prices has therefore dealt a devastating blow to the development plans of these countries even though, in absolute terms, Africa's crude oil consumption of 47 million tons in 1974, about 1.7 per cent of the world total, is extremely small.[28]

The most seriously affected were those States which neither produce oil nor have their own refineries, namely Botswana, Burundi, Cameroon, Chad, Benin, Gambia, Malawi, Mali, Mauritania, Mauritius, Niger, Lesotho, Somalia, Swaziland, Uganda, Upper Volta and Togo. In addition, eight of these States are land-locked and thus entirely dependent on transit facilities granted by their neighbours. Although their consumption of oil is only about 10 million tons per annum, the increased oil prices cost them an additional $180 million in 1974. The cost of oil imports to thirty African countries, i.e. all those without enough oil of their own, rose from $500 million in 1973 to $1,300 million in 1974. Although this amount is small compared with that paid by the industrialized nations, the increase is a heavy additional burden for their already strained economies.[29]

This is not all. The industrialized countries have also added the increased costs of fuel to the prices of their exports of manufactured and industrial goods. Furthermore, the costs of fertilizers, pesticides and other chemical by-products from petroleum have increased even more sharply than the cost of fuel oil. This has hit countries dependent on agricultural production with a special severity. And all this has coincided with world-wide food shortages and soaring food prices. The non-oil-producing countries of Africa have not been compensated by obtaining higher prices for their own exports. These prices have dropped, and in some cases very rapidly, from the levels they achieved in 1973 (levels which in any case did no more than restore the trading relationships of the Third World countries to the industrialized countries existing in the early 1950s).

Oil prices and the consequences for the independent African States were the main topic at the Cairo meeting of the OAU Committee of Seven with representatives of the ten Arab oil-producing countries in January 1974. The Africans were assured of all the oil they needed, but their request for preferential prices was rejected on three counts: first, a dual price policy could be abused by the international oil companies which still handle all the distribution of oil in Africa; second, the price of oil is fixed by the Organization of Oil Exporting Countries (OPEC) and cannot be changed unilaterally by only some of its members; and third, a two-tier price would give rise to a black market, since cheap oil would undoubtedly be re-exported before long.

The African Oil Conference which took place in Tripoli, Libya, on 2-12 February 1974, also failed to solve the problem of oil prices. The meeting was held under the joint auspices of the OAU and the Economic Commission of Africa (ECA). The ECA Executive Secretary, Dr Robert Gardiner, called for a plan to export oil from the African producing States directly to their neighbours instead of shipping it first to Europe and re-importing it at much higher prices. The Conference ended with a recommendation for setting up an African oil organization, and with a series of recommendations concerning an oil industry in Africa, and the exploration, refining and utilisation of oil. These recommendations, although important in the long term for the African economy, were not measures calculated to yield immediate results, and the Africans did not hide their disappointment. A commentator of the Nigerian Broadcasting Service in Kaduna, in a broadcast on 11 February 1974 about the Third World need for Arab aid, bitterly remarked that 'Paradoxically, the developing countries, who are in solidarity with the Arabs, the major world oil-producers, are the worst casualties of their own oil weapon'.

The extent of African disappointment was reflected in a proposal made by Zambia and Ghana at the OAU Council of Ministers meeting at Mogadishu in June 1974, to dissolve the Committee of Seven because of the failure of its negotiations with the Arab oil-producing countries. Faced by the criticism of the black African countries, intensified in a showdown over the election of the new OAU Administrative Secretary-General, the Arab countries averted the dissolution of the Committee of Seven by supporting the proposal that the $200 million promised to be the starting capital of the Special Arab Fund for Africa should be deposited with the African Development Bank. The Arab delegations pointed out that the Arab fund should not be regarded as 'a reward' for African support of the Arab stand on Israel, but should be seen as part of a genuine effort at economic co-operation.[30] The Africans agreed, but they let it be known that professions of

168

brotherhood and solidarity should not end at the OAU rostrum.

## 4. AFRO-ARAB ALLIANCE AT THE 1975 KAMPALA SUMMIT

The 12th OAU Summit at Kampala was attended by the Heads of State of six of the eight African members of the Arab League (Egypt, Libya, Sudan, Algeria, Somalia and Mauritania — the other two being Morocco and Tunisia), and also by Yasser Arafat, leader of the Palestinian Liberation Organization (PLO). Despite protest by some African delegations, Arafat was accorded the status of a Head of State. This strong Arab presence was a clear indication that the Arab members of the OAU expected the Organization to endorse a call for the expulsion of Israel from the UN made at the Islamic Summit in Jeddah two weeks earlier. The five African countries (Ghana, Sierra Leone, Senegal and Liberia, led by Zaire) which opposed the move took full advantage of the embitterment on the part of most of the black African delegates over the Afro-Arab co-operation. Hilary Ng'wengo, editor-in-chief of an influential Kenyan magazine *The Weekly Review*, in the issue of 4 August 1974 summed up the African discontent as follows:

'It is about time a more reciprocal relationship was set up. Arab spokesmen have often pointed out that the only support they have asked from Africa is moral support not material support. They have not asked Africans to send armies to the Middle East or money to help the Palestinians. This is, of course, true, but African moral support for the Arab cause seems to have gone unappreciated. In the great tactical move adopted by Arab oil exporters in 1973 to embargo oil supplies to Western nations and quadruple the price of oil, little or no account whatsoever was taken of this African moral support. Admittedly Arab nations set up funds of one kind or another to assist African nations badly hit by the oil price hikes, but it does not take much imagination to discover that these funds bear little relation to the magnitude of the devastation wrought by the oil exporters' moves upon the economies of African countries. The irony of the situation is that in the critical twelve months following the devastating price increases, African nations received more emergency financial assistance from the Western nations, who are supposedly enemies of Africa, than from Arab States whose coffers were bursting at the seams with their new-found wealth.

From a moral and ideological point of view, Africa may have no choice but to support the Palestinian cause and the general effort of the Arab people to regain their rightful place in the world community. But Africa must eschew empty rhetoric in her relations with her Arab friends.'

After a heated debate the Council of Ministers submitted to the Assembly a Resolution 'on the Middle East and Occupied Arab Territories',[31] asking the OAU members to co-operate with the Arab countries in order to deprive Israel of its membership of the United Nations as long as it refuses to withdraw from the occupied Arab territories and recognize the full national rights of the Palestinian people to their homeland. But the Assembly of Heads of State and Government chose to adopt two separate resolutions on the Middle East problem. The first was an amended draft of the resolution submitted by the Council. The strong language of condemnation of Israel was offset by comparatively soft measures proposed. The first measure is a suggestion that '... owing to Israel's continued aggression against Arab countries and the Palestinian people, *it is time to apply the sanctions stipulated by the Charter of the UN against Israel.*'[32] The second resolution — 'on the Question of Palestine'[33] — is more strongly worded. It calls the Palestinian question 'the root cause of the struggle against the Zionist enemy', but all that it says about Israel's membership in the UN is that '... the continuation of the membership of Israel in the United Nations contradicts the principles and Charter of the United Nations and encourages Israel to ignore United Nations resolutions and to collude with various racist, expansionist and aggressive regimes'. The resolution also recommends that 'the OAU Liberation Committee and the Palestine Liberation Organization should jointly lay down a strategy aiming at liberating Palestine, considering that the cause of Palestine is an African cause'. Zaire voted against both resolutions; Sierra Leone, Senegal and Liberia registered their reservations; while Ghana joined them in making reservations on the second resolution.

The move for expulsion was spearheaded by President Gaddafi of Libya, while Egypt pressed for suspension. But even this milder form of sanction was deemed too harsh by moderates within the African ranks. The disagreement over the expulsion of Israel from the UN influenced the African vote on the resolution on 'Elimination of all forms of racial discrimination' at the 13th Session of the UN General Assembly in November 1975. The resolution equating Zionism with racism was put to a roll-call vote on 10 November 1975. Four African States voted against (Ivory Coast, Liberia, Malawi and Central African Republic) and twelve abstained (Ghana, Kenya, Lesotho, Mauritius, Sierra Leone, Togo, Upper Volta, Zaire, Zambia, Botswana, Ethiopia and Gabon).

## 5. AFRO-ARAB CO-OPERATION IN 1976

Afro-Arab relations took a turn for the better in 1976 because of the following developments:

— *The increase in the economic and military co-operation between Israel and South Africa*

Connections between Israel and South Africa[34] emphasized by the visit of the South African Premier John Vorster to Israel in April 1976. The rise in the volume of trade between them, and the suspicion that Israel takes part in the South African nuclear programme and supplies it with its combat KFIR planes, has been given great publicity in the African press. This has brought many 'disillusioned' African States back to firm support of the Arab cause.

— *The smoother flow of Arab money into the African economies and the intensification of the institutional co-operation between the OAU and the Arab League*

One of the principal channels for Afro-Arab economic co-operation became the Arab Bank for African Economic Development (BADEA — an abbreviation of its French name *La Banque arabe pour le développement économique en Afrique*). Within a year it had granted $124,5 million in loans and raised its capital from $231 million in 1973 to $500 million in 1976.[35] In April 1976 a special session of the OAU Council of Ministers met with twenty-one Members of the Arab League and representatives of the African Development Bank (ADB) and BADEA, in Dakar. It adopted the 'Dakar declaration and action programme', which outlines the principles of mutual co-operation. The OAU Summit at Port Louis in July 1976 authorized the OAU Secretary-General to undertake consultations with the Secretary-General of the Arab League with the aim of holding an Afro-Arab Summit.

— *The Entebbe raid by the Israeli commandos on 28 June 1976*

Special commando units of the Israeli army flew 3,000 miles from Israel to Uganda to free 108 hostages of Jewish origin held at Entebbe airport by the members of the Popular Front for the Liberation of Palestine, who had hi-jacked an Air France airbus en route from Athens to Paris. They were given refuge and protection by President Idi Amin of Uganda, who joined them in negotiating the release of Palestinian prisoners in Israel, Switzerland, West Germany and Kenya in exchange for hostages. The Israelis then stormed Entebbe airport, freed the hostages, killed their guards (including a number of Ugandan soldiers), destroyed parked Ugandan MIG fighters and departed after completing a mission of science-fiction proportions which flabbergasted the whole world.

While many of the African leaders were privately delighted by the swift release of the hostages and by Amin's humiliation, their feelings soon gave way to profound shock at what they described as 'the rape of Africa'. The resolution adopted by the 13th OAU Summit at Port

Louis, which was in session when the raid took place, speaks for itself:

'The Assembly of Heads of State and Government. . .

*Deeply alarmed* about Israeli aggression on Uganda which constitutes a threat to international peace and security;

*Considering* that an aggression against one OAU Member State, is aggression against all Member States requiring collective measures to repel it;

*Believing* that such aggression results from the policy of co-operation between Israel and South Africa which aims at threatening the independence and territorial integrity of all African and Arab States and undermining the aim of Africa to liberate the territories which are still under colonialism and racist domination in the Southern part of Africa,

1. *Strongly condemns* the Israeli aggression against the sovereignty and territorial integrity of Uganda; the deliberate killing and injuring of people and wanton destruction of property; and the thwarting of the humanitarian efforts by the President of Uganda to have the hostages released;

2. *Calls* for an immediate meeting of the United Nations Security Council with a view to taking all appropriate measures against Israel, including measures under Chapter 7 of the United Nations Charter.'

In public pronouncements African leaders focused on the illegality of the operation, but the real indignation stemmed from the shocking revelation of Africa's military impotence. There was resentment at the ease with which the mission was accomplished, resentment at the fact that the Israelis crossed into the heart of Africa apparently undetected, and underlying fears that the Israelis had set a precedent that could be imitated by South Africa. But, as the Nigerian writer Peter Enahoro summed it up in *Africa* of August 1976:

`. . . deepest of all was the resentment for the embarrassment which many Africans felt Israel had inflicted on the Black man as a whole at the critical juncture of the liberation struggle and in the atmosphere of racial conflicts which wraps the world at this moment. It was Uganda that was disgraced but as many Africans saw it, Uganda is African and thus the humiliation belonged to the entire African race. This racial hurt continues to dominate the attitude of most Africans towards the whole episode even now.'

## 6. THE AFRO-ARAB SUMMIT IN CAIRO (MARCH 7-10, 1977)

The search for new forms of Afro-Arab co-operation had been the task of a Committee consisting of 24 African and Arab countries (Mali,

Mauritania, Sierra Leone, Sudan, Tanzania, Zaire, Somalia, Senegal, Ghana, Cameroon, Botswana, Burundi, Egypt, Iraq, Lebanon, Saudi Arabia, United Arab Emirates, Tunisia, Syria, Palestine Liberation Organization, Morocco, Libya and Kuwait) set up by the joint meeting of the Council of Foreign Ministers of the Arab League and the OAU held in Dakar in April 1976. At its meeting in Lusaka in January 1977 the Committee prepared the agenda for the Afro-Arab Summit which took place from 7 to 10 March 1977. Among the papers submitted to the conference was an appeal made by the OAU urging greater Arab assistance to African countries seriously affected by the oil price rises and world inflation. The OAU argued that the Arab offer of a $450 million loan fund to meet the costs of high oil prices was insufficient as it represented only 25 per cent of the total annual increases. The OAU paper expressed fear that unless some stern measures were taken to alleviate the situation the economies of some non oil-producing countries would collapse.

The Arab response to the African plea surpassed all expectations. At the opening meeting of the Afro-Arab Summit in Cairo on 7 January 1977, Prince Saud Al-Feisal of Saudi Arabia reacted to African criticism by pledging $1 billion in economic aid to the black African countries. Following Saudi Arabia's lead the Kuwaiti Foreign Minister, Sheik Sabah Al Ahmed, pledged $240 million over the next five years to finance African development projects. In addition Kuwait promised to increase its contribution to the Arab Fund for African Economic Development by $20 million. Emir of Qatar and Sheik Zayed Ben Nahyane of the United Arab Emirates announced that they would make a total of $216 million available to African countries. Each also pledged $1 million to African liberation movements. The total promised Arab aid at the Afro-Arab Summit approached $1.5 billion — indeed a startling figure.

The Summit also approved a programme of action on Afro-Arab co-operation, the main points of which are as follows:
— respect for the sovereignty, territorial integrity and political independence of all States;
— equality of all States;
— permanent sovereignty of States and peoples over their natural resources;
— non-aggression, and inadmissibility of occupying or annexing territories by force;
— non-interference in the internal affairs of other States;
— the safeguarding of mutual interests on the basis of reciprocity and equality;
— peaceful settlement of differences and disputes in a spirit of tolerance;

— joint struggle against domination, racism and exploitation in all their forms to safeguard work, peace and security.

The document also expressed an undertaking on the part of the Arab and African countries to develop their relations in political, diplomatic, economic, financial, cultural, scientific, technical and information fields. This was further specified by the following commitments:

— joint support for African and Arab causes at the United Nations and other international organizations and conferences;
— political, material and moral support to African and Arab liberation movements recognized both by the OAU and the Arab League;
— establishment of diplomatic representation between all members of the OAU and the League, and promotion of the contacts between their respective political and social institutions;
— expanding co-operation in trade, mining, industry, agriculture and animal husbandry, energy and water resources, transport, communications and financial affairs, such as bilateral long-term loans and joint participation in international financial consortia for the financing of joint projects in Africa and the Arab world.

In conclusion the Afro-Arab Summit called on the OAU and the Arab League to co-operate with the African Development Bank, the Arab Bank for Economic Development in Africa and other specialized institutions in the search for an adequate formula for closer economic, financial and technical co-operation, in particular through the setting up of Afro-Arab financial institutions and the drawing up of an Afro-Arab Agreement governing investments. The Committee on Afro-Arab co-operation was asked to see to the implementation of the programme of action and the fulfillment of the promises made at the Summit.

The Arab pledge greatly impressed the Africans and their appreciation was echoed on the front pages of all African papers. However, while commending the seriousness of the Arab offer the Africans also had made it clear that they wished to reserve their final judgement until the first results would show.


## 7. WHAT FUTURE FOR AFRO-ARAB CO-OPERATION?

Oil prices are not the only sources of division. The Libyan-Egyptian disputes, Sudanese support for the Eritrean Liberation Front against Ethiopia, Arab backing of President Amin of Uganda against Tanzania and Zambia, and most recently the Arab support of President Mobutu during the armed conflict in Shaba province, Zaire (March-April 1977), have contributed considerably to the erosion of the alliance. The Moroccan intervention in Zaire backed by Egypt and Sudan produced a strong reaction, particularly in Nigeria where anti-Arab sentiments had been simmering for some time. Dr. Bolaji Akinyemi, Director-General of the influential Nigerian Institute of International Affairs, in an interview published by the *Daily Times* of Lagos on 16 April, sharply criticized Morocco, Sudan and Egypt for trying to 'arrogate the right to be the guardians of the African soul'. 'Who gave them the mandate?', asked Dr Akinyemi, '... the time has come to ask what are the Arabs up to in Africa.' Three weeks later Chief J. E. Adetoro, former Federal Commissioner for Health, Agriculture and National Resources, in a letter to the *Daily Times* of Lagos on 10 May 1977, went much further and called for the re-establishment of diplomatic relations between Nigeria and Israel. He called the severance of Nigeria's relations with Israel in 1973 'an unfortunate step which has not done Nigeria any good. We have lost the enormous diplomatic value of its national effort to play the role of an honest broker.' However, the spirit of co-operation has not been lost entirely. Arabs and Africans both realize that there is a definite bond between them. They share a common history of colonial domination and are linked by geopolitical factors: 'the present Arab-African co-operation is the natural thing and Arab investors should look increasingly towards the African countries'.[36]

An obvious solution to the problem — to divert part of the Arab funds invested in Western countries into development projects in Africa — is difficult to implement. Arab funds are administered by Western-educated and pro-Western bankers who traditionally seek secure investment in European, American and Japanese markets, rather than in the Third World.[37] There are other constraints which prevent a radical alteration of the investment policies of Arab countries namely their dependence on technology, industrial supplies and foodstuffs from the West. More significantly, some of them depend on the Western powers for the purchase of arms. Arms need spares, and this gives the supplier a powerful influence with the purchaser. Nevertheless, a radical change in investment policy is needed in order to strengthen the Afro-Arab alliance. Gifts are insufficient. 'Invest in Africa, not in the Western industrial countries' is an appeal made frequently by African economists.

Whatever the obstacles to Afro-Arab economic co-operation, they have to be surmounted. The Arabs can hardly afford to desert independent Africa. By failing to honour Afro-Arab solidarity, they would not only lose African political support against Israel but they would also forfeit their claim to participate in the development of the world. Once the Arab industrialization programmes are completed and the dependence on Western technology is over, the time will come when the Arab States will be in search of the raw materials to sustain their industries. Only Africa will be in a position to supply them.

# Chapter X

# THE OAU AND ECONOMIC CO-OPERATION IN AFRICA

A book about the OAU would not be complete without mentioning, at least briefly, the role of the organization in the economic development of Africa and in inter-African economic co-operation. Unfortunately, there is not much to tell. Compared with the progress made by the OAU on decolonization, and with the success of its international campaign against apartheid, its performance in the economic field has been disappointing.

The small place occupied by economic problems in OAU affairs contrasts sharply with Africa's position as potentially one of the richest continents in the world, with mineral and natural resources which even now have not been fully explored. But it is also surprising, given the express statement in the Preamble of the Charter of the OAU's responsibility for the economic development of Africa. The economic co-operation between the members of the OAU was also given prominence in the purposes of the Charter listed in Article II, which includes a duty on the part of OAU members (1) to co-ordinate and intensify their co-operation and efforts to achieve a better life for the peoples of Africa; (2) to promote international co-operation, having due regard to the Charter of the United Nations; and (3) to co-operate in the fields of transport, communications, health, sanitation and nutrition, as well as science and technology.

Here it should be recalled that the majority of the founding fathers of the OAU sincerely believed in 1963 that African unity could be achieved only through economic co-operation. Sir Abubakar Tafewa Balewa, for example, the Prime Minister of Nigeria, talked of 'practical steps in economic, scientific and cultural co-operation'. At that time much confidence was placed on regional economic groupings, which President Nyerere of Tanzania called the 'stepping stones towards African unity'. 'I should like to lay special emphasis on the importance of economic co-operation as an approach to African unity', said the President of Gabon, Mr Leon Mba; and he expressed the hope that 'Realism and efficiency will prevail over passion and precipitance'. President Nkrumah's suggestion that African unity might best be reached politically, through a Continental Government of Africa, was rejected as unrealistic.

Time has shown that while the 'political kingdom' envisaged by Kwame Nkrumah is still very far away, the economic unity of Africa is no closer. The fact that the OAU has turned into a political organization which has survived only because of the unanimous stand of its members on decolonization and apartheid, indicates that economic unity could only be achieved by the broadening of this unity into a true political alliance — and not vice versa. This point was proved in 1977 by the collapse of the East African Economic Community, generally regarded as the most successful regional economic organization of Africa.[1]

However, it would be unfair to criticize the OAU for its failure to bring about a substantial improvement in Africa's economic situation without mentioning two obstacles which stood in the way of inter-African co-operation when the OAU was established. The major one was the state of the African economy; the other the rivalry between the OAU and the UN Economic Commission for Africa, ECA.[2] A vast number of books have been written on the constraints on the economic development of Africa, and this is not the place to examine them in detail. The major economic difficulties faced by the OAU at the time of its birth can be summed up as follows:
— the slow growth of gross domestic product (GDP),
— single-commodity economies,
— the small size of African economies,
— the backwardness of African agriculture,
— the low degree of industrialization,
— the lack of inter-African infrastructure,
— the economic dependence on ex-colonial powers as well as other industrialized Western countries.[3]


## 1. THE RELATIONSHIP BETWEEN THE OAU AND THE ECONOMIC COMMISSION FOR AFRICA

When the OAU came into existence in 1963, the Economic Commission for Africa (ECA), was already an established economic institution. The Report of the Fifth Session of the ECA, held at Kinshasa in February-March 1963 — i.e. two months before the Addis Ababa Conference in May of the same year — gives a good idea of its achievements.[4] They included the setting up of the African Institute for Economic Development and Planning at Dakar in 1962 and the plans for founding the African Development Bank.[5] The ECA's programme and list of priorities included an integrated approach to problems of economic and social development based on studies dealing with the trends of living, health, education, labour, community development and social welfare. Great emphasis was put on economic surveys, reviews and analyses of current economic trends in Africa, which were subsequently published in a series of ECA publications. Among these were compilations and studies of industrial statistics, inter-African trade, African mineral resources, surface and ground waters, transit and transportation problems, land reform, agricultural marketing boards, soil erosion and programmes for professional training. The ECA's attitude towards the OAU was, at first, most sympathetic. At its 5th meeting in Kinshasa in February 1963, the ECA extended good wishes to the forthcoming Addis Ababa Conference.[6] The ECA also demonstrated its willingness to co-operate with the OAU by submitting to the Conference a paper entitled 'Approaches to African economic integration: towards co-operation in economic planning and an African Common Market'.[7]

The Provisional Secretariat of the OAU (set up after the Addis Ababa Conference in May 1963), understaffed and struggling with its own organizational problems, was no match for the ECA, set up and led by an experienced administrator, Dr Robert Gardiner of Ghana, who assumed the post of Executive Secretary in 1962. Staffed with highly-paid UN economic experts, the ECA was in an incomparably better position to take initiatives on African economic problems, and indeed took full advantage of this. The ECA's monopoly in dealing with African economic problems is quite clear if we read the OAU resolutions adopted in the course of its first four years; only three touched economic issues.[8]

Gradually, the OAU began to feel uneasy about the superiority of the ECA in handling African economic policy. An agreement between the OAU and the ECA, signed on 16 December 1965 between the OAU Administrative Secretary and the UN General Secretary, did not alter the relationship between the two organizations. The co-operation was to be carried out 'within their respective spheres of responsibility', implying that African economic problems were really none of the OAU's business.[9]

When the OAU Economic and Social Commission was asked at its first meeting in Cairo in 1964 to submit to OAU Members its findings on matters such as the establishment of a common external tariff, the protection of emergent African industries, the formulation of a raw material price stabilization fund, the co-ordination of inter-African transport systems or else recommendations for the reconstruction of inter-African trade, the answers were provided by the ECA. Considering the scarcity of expert personnel in most OAU countries, and the fact that for the most part the delegates at meetings of the OAU specialized Commissions and those at the various meetings of the ECA were the same people, it is not surprising that the resulting duplication of effort

was resolved by 'leaving it to the ECA'.

Soon the competition between the two organizations turned into direct rivalry, intensified by the difference in personality between their respective heads. The Executive Secretary of the ECA, Dr Robert Gardiner — a smooth diplomatic negotiator from Ghana, with a moderate political outlook and access to the economic hierarchies of the Western countries — tried to keep the ECA out of political controversies, whether African or non-African. The OAU chief, Diallo Telli (a Guinean radical socialist, deeply committed to the decolonization of Africa), was fighting colonialism and neo-colonialism fiercely on all fronts. He had little understanding for Dr Gardiner's 'soft' approach towards the West, and strongly resented all ECA attempts to divorce African economic problems from their political context. He relentlessly tried to impress upon OAU Members the need to bring the ECA under the political control of the OAU. An example of his efforts was a resolution adopted by the Council of Ministers in 1965 calling for a more detailed study of the relationship between the ECA and OAU.[10] The study was not forthcoming, but Diallo Telli did not give up. He submitted to the meeting of the Council of Ministers in Addis Ababa in March 1967 a detailed report on African economic co-operation, and demanded action.[11] The Council expressed its thanks for the report, but not until the OAU Summit at Kinshasa in September that year did the OAU make a decisive move towards assuming responsibility for the shaping of economic policy in Africa.

The OAU's sudden attention to Africa's economic problems was of course mainly due to the turbulent political situation in Africa (the outbreak of the civil war in Nigeria, and the series of military *coups*): concentration on economic problems was a way out of political malaise. The deterioration of the national economies of most OAU Members added a further incentive. The Kinshasa OAU Summit was the first occasion in four years when economic issues featured prominently on the agenda; more than half the resolutions prepared by the Council of Ministers for endorsement by the Summit dealt with economic and social problems. These included a resolution on matters until then regarded as the exclusive domain of the ECA, such as industrialization, intra-African co-operation, regional economic groupings, African civil aviation, telecommunication, and road and maritime transport. But most significant was the resolution on intra-African co-operation,[12] which endorsed Diallo Telli's views by recognizing the indissoluble link between politics and economics in the attempts by OAU Members to terminate their dependence on developed countries. The resolution expressed concern at the lack of organized trade-flows on a continental scale in Africa (a problem under constant ECA consideration), which, as the resolution put it, 'drastically impedes the expansion of the

economies of the African countries'. A remedy for the situation was sought in the establishment of an African common market and the development of regional economic groupings. The Administrative Secretary-General was asked to study the matter and report to the Council. Until then the ECA, while repeatedly recognizing the necessity to establish an African common market, had believed that such a common market could not be established until numerous detailed arrangements regarding customs, different monetary systems, finance, transport, legislation and other relevant matters had been made.[13]

In 1967 the Council of Ministers set up a plenary committee (Committee 'C') within the Council, which considered reports on various aspects of economic and social development submitted to the Council by the Administrative Secretary-General. In this way the OAU Secretariat managed to sustain the interest of the Council of Ministers in economic and social affairs. It provided each of its sessions with so-called 'economic balance sheets', on the basis of which recommendations could be made on guidelines for the OAU's policy on economic development.

The preoccupation of the OAU with economic matters continued into 1968, when the OAU General Secretariat paid great attention to the preparations for the second UN Trade and Development Conference (UNCTAD II). The most important event in this respect was the meeting of thirty-one African countries in Algiers on 7-15 October 1967, where they adopted the 'African Declaration of Algiers'; this was endorsed by the ministerial meeting of the non-aligned countries which also met at Algiers, and was submitted to UNCTAD II (held at New Delhi, 1 February-29 March 1968).[14] The OAU Summit meeting held at Algiers in September 1968 made a further step towards strengthening the OAU's role in African economic development by recognizing that 'the economic integration of the African continent constitutes an essential prerequisite for the realization of the aspirations of the OAU'.[15]

But the 'decisive' political victory over the ECA was won on its own ground — at the UN in 1969. The 'African group' at the UN, composed of the heads of African missions, grew into a new force, whose influence was reflected in the more resolute stand taken by the UN General Assembly on colonialism and the apartheid policy of South Africa, as well as on UN economic policy (centred at the UN Social and Economic Council). The Africans were asking for a more decisive say in the formulation of UN economic policy on Africa. They demanded that the ECA be compelled to take OAU opinion into consideration in all its plans and projects. The word used was 'co-operation'; but the essence was that the OAU was to become a partner, with the political (and thus the stronger) voice.

The acceptance of the primary responsibility of the OAU for co-operation between African States under the terms of Article II of the OAU Charter was recognized by the ECA at its 9th Session held in February 1969 in Addis Ababa. In a resolution on 'Relations with the Organization of African Unity',[16] the deference of the ECA to the authority of the OAU was specified as follows:

— African ministers and senior officials working within the framework of the ECA and the OAU Economic and Social Commission should be 'constantly guided by decisions of the Assembly of Heads of State and Government of the OAU in economic and social matters'; and

— reports on the activities of the ECA should be presented regularly for the consideration of the Assembly of Heads of State and Government of OAU, 'in order that the Commission might enjoy the necessary political support'.

The secretaries of the ECA and the OAU were also asked 'to pursue all forms of desired co-operation in the interest of the development of Africa'.

The Administrative Secretary-General, in his report covering the period February-September 1970,[17] welcomed this as an achievement of the 'determination of the African leaders to keep the initiative and maintain control over any activity carried out in Africa for the sake of Africa', and as 'an additional guarantee to the African peoples that ECA's activities will be integrated more harmoniously than in the past into the work of OAU'. In the same report he called on the Assembly of Heads of State and Government to rectify the omission in the OAU Charter of clear guidelines determining OAU's responsibilities in economic and social matters. This was done by a resolution adopted by the OAU Summit at Addis Ababa in August 1970.[18]

The ECA adjusted itself to the new situation with remarkable ease. Dr Robert Gardiner preferred to view the new arrangement as one which would bring increased benefits to Africa. He also expressed confidence that the ECA would be able to prove itself better equipped than the OAU to deal with African economic problems. Indeed, while most of the economic programmes, projects and conferences were carried out under joint OAU/ECA sponsorship, it was the latter which did most of the work. However, while the element of competition never really disappeared from the relationship between the two organizations, their mutual co-operation has since considerably improved.

The first meeting of the Conference of Ministers of the Economic Commission for Africa,[19] at Tunis in February 1971, launched 'Africa's strategy for development in the 1970s',[20] which was based on the programme of priorities adopted by the OAU Summit in 1970. It required African countries to:

- develop agriculture-based programmes;
- increase export and export earning in order to reduce excessive dependence upon foreign economies for development financing;
- develop better and more co-ordinated trade promotion organizations and programmes;
- promote labour-intensive industries using local raw materials, wherever they can be competitive in the world market;
- promote industrial and agricultural research and ensure practical application of results;
- realign the educational and training systems with the needs and demands of a progressively developing economy and society; and
- formulate population policies commensurate with the national growth potential.[21]

An emphasis was put on the mutual co-operation among seventy-five African intergovernmental economic organizations.[22]

Perhaps the most important example of OAU-ECA co-operation was the 'Declaration on Co-operation, Development and Economic Independence' adopted by the African ministerial conference on trade development and monetary problems, organized jointly by the OAU, the ECA and the African Development Bank at Abidjan on 13 May 1973. It stipulates, *inter alia*, Africa's demand for the 'New International Economic Order'. Unfortunately, however, not even the joint efforts of the OAU and the ECA in the economic field have been enough to make their projects work, and most of them remain embodied in resolutions, reports and recommendations which the OAU Members have failed to implement partly because of lack of funds and manpower, and partly through lack of political will. The co-operation between the OAU and the ECA has made some progress — that is, if progress can be measured by the number of conferences held in Africa under their joint auspices. But the ideological divisions between OAU Members have made close co-operation between capitalist and socialist oriented economies virtually impossible. The economic relations between Tanzania and Kenya illustrate the point.


## 2. THE OAU AND THE NEW INTERNATIONAL ECONOMIC ORDER

The call for a New International Economic Order came from the 6th Special Session of the UN General Assembly which adopted two resolutions on 1 May 1974[23] laying down the principles of a new relationship between the rich and poor countries. The first resolution is called 'Declaration on the Establishment of a New International Economic Order' and the other 'Programme of Action'. Later the same year the General Assembly at its 29th Session adopted the 'Charter of Economic Rights and Duties of States',[24] which attempted to establish norms governing international economic relations and to promote the New International Economic Order. This was the result of a ten-year-long initiative by 'Group 77', an association of Third World countries which made its first appearance at the 18th Session of the UN General Assembly in 1963.[25] Although 'Group 77' has never been formally constituted, it has developed into a permanent consulting organ of the developing countries at the UN. Its number had increased to ninety by 1976, and its efforts were complementary to the policies formulated at the meetings of the non-aligned countries. The membership of 'Group 77' and that of the non-aligned conferences is identical, but 'Group 77' deals exclusively with economic issues while the non-aligned meetings cover a wide range of political problems.

The main credit for the initiative in searching for a new relationship between the developed and developing countries goes to Algeria. Since October 1967 when the 'African Declaration of Algiers' was adopted there, the Algerian capital has been the scene of several important meetings of a similar character. In September 1973 it hosted the 4th Summit Conference of non-aligned countries, where the Algerian delegation introduced a document entitled 'The Third World Countries and the Energy Crisis'.[26] Algeria drew attention to the changing relationship with industrialized countries, now that the latter were increasingly dependent on the energy and the raw material resources of the Third World. 'We are at present witnessing a basic reversal in the relative positions of the markets for raw materials and the sources supplying such materials,' stated the Algerian document; and it called this reversal 'a new phenomenon in the economic relations between poor and rich countries'.

What the Algerians were trying to show was that the Third World, of which Africa is the richest part, has in its energy and raw material resources a formidable lever to use against the industrial nations and that the time had come to use it. Indeed, a few weeks later the Non-Aligned Summit and the countries associated with the Organization of Petroleum Exporting Countries (OPEC)[27] held the Western industrialized countries to ransom. The oil weapon — a combination of oil price increases and the imposition of an embargo on its delivery — was used primarily to exert pressure on the Western supporters of Israel to alter their policy on the Arab-Israeli conflict which erupted in the October 1973 war. However, its disastrous effects on the economies of the Western world proved the correctness of the Algerian thesis. The price of crude oil, which in October 1973 stood at $1.25 per barrel, had jumped to $11.50 by 1976.

The call for a new pattern of international economic relations was at last taken seriously, and ways and means of achieving this became a topic of a number of international conferences and meetings. At the UN level the most important meetings were the two special sessions of the General Assembly in 1974. At the 6th Special Session (9 April-2 May) the above-mentioned Declaration and the Programme of Action on the Establishment of a New International Economic Order were adopted. The 7th Special Session (convened from 1 to 12 September, to discuss 'Development and International Co-operation') adopted a resolution dealing with international trade, the transfer of real resources for financing the development of developing countries, international monetary reforms, science and technology, industrialization, food and agriculture, co-operation among developing countries and the restructuring of the economic and social sections of the UN.[28]

The New International Economic Order, the essence of which was simply 'full and complete emancipation of developing countries', was also discussed at a conference of 110 developing countries in Dakar in February 1975,[29] at the Fifth Ministerial Conference of Non-Aligned Countries in Lima in August 1975[30] and at the Second General Conference of the United Nations Industrial Development Organization (UNIDO) in March 1975.[31] Although members of the OAU actively participated in all these conferences, the Organization's role was marginal. It restricted itself to the support of African initiative led by the ECA and of the ECA's 'African plan for the Implementation of the Programme of Action on the Establishment of a New International Economic Order', adopted at the Third Conference of Ministers of the ECA in Nairobi in February 1975.[32]

The best example of the OAU's attitude is its resolution on the New International Economic Order submitted by the Council of Ministers to the OAU Summit in Kampala in July 1975.[33] It states that 'the responsibility for their development rests on the African countries themselves', and yet it shifts the responsibility to the UN and the non-aligned countries. The OAU's decision to convene a meeting of experts of the OAU, the ECA, the African Development Bank and the Institute for Development and Planning, to formulate an African position at the forthcoming meetings dealing with the New International Economic Order, can hardly be called an 'adequate OAU initiative'. When the 20th Commonwealth Conference of thirty-three countries, held in Kingston in April 1975, agreed to the six commitments set out later in a report called *Towards a New International Economic Order*, this was due more to British initiative than to the African Commonwealth members.[34] Africa's greatest achievement so far in its struggle to establish a juster economic relationship with industrialized countries was the signing of the Lomé Convention on 28 February 1975 between forty-six African, Caribbean and Pacific countries and the nine countries of the EEC after eighteen months of tough negotiations. The Lomé Convention represents a major concession obtained by Africa from the European community,[35] although there is much that is still on paper only.

At the 7th Special Session of the UN General Assembly, African delegates showed awareness of the acute economic problems facing their continent and put forward a number of constructive proposals.[36] At the same time it became apparent that Africa still lacked the kind of economic unity needed for effective participation in shaping the economic future of the continent. In the negotiations between the industrialized countries, Africa became a mere appendage of OPEC, hoping to benefit from OPEC's successes; this continues to be the case despite the efforts of Algeria to broaden the base of negotiations beyond the issue of energy resources which the United States, West Germany and other industrialized countries (except France) have wished to single out.[37] As on many previous occasions, Algeria assumed the role of spokesman for Africa at the Paris International Conference on Economic Co-operation held in December 1975. Called the 'North-South Dialogue',[38] the conference revealed that the gulf of differences between the developing and industrial countries had not narrowed but widened.

To make matters worse, the mutual distrust which characterizes the present relationship between rich and poor nations has slowly been creeping into the ranks of the Third World. A number of African countries are beginning to have second thoughts on whether their interests are best served by countries belonging to such an exclusive club as OPEC. It is also common knowledge that Algeria's initiative in OPEC is being blocked by countries like Iran — South Africa's largest supplier of oil, which has been deaf to African pleas to impose a blockade on the white minority regimes in southern Africa — and Saudi Arabia, whose interests (especially financial ones) are closer to those of the United States than to those of Africa. The conspicuous silence of Nigeria and Gabon, the only black African OPEC members, has increased the doubts about OPEC's attitude towards the need to alleviate the burden of African oil importers.

Most African countries find themselves between two crushing pressures: one originating in the high oil prices and the other in the inflation in the industrialized world, which is now being steadily imported into their own economies. President Nyerere of Tanzania, in his address to the Royal Commonwealth Society in London in November 1975, put it like this:

'Rich countries do not only increase the price of a tractor to the extent of the extra oil costs directly involved in producing it. They also make the new price compensate the workers and the owners for the higher oil prices involved in producing the goods which they want to consume. For the workers in wealthy countries get "cost of living" increases to prevent their standard of living from falling. And the owners seek to arrange that their profits should not go down in real terms. Both these costs are covered by additions to the price of the goods they sell. As a result we do not only pay from our poverty for the extra wealth acquired from us by the oil producers. We also compensate the people in the wealthy countries for any loss which they experienced through a transfer of wealth from their economies to the oil producers.'


## 3. THE NEW OAU INITIATIVE ON ECONOMIC PROBLEMS

To provide Africa with economic leadership was regarded by many as one of the most important tasks of the OAU in its second decade. Until 1977 it has been a task which the OAU has not even considered seriously. In this respect, the 11th Extraordinary Session of the Council of Ministers, held from 6 to 10 December in Kinshasa and devoted to the economic problems of Africa, constitutes the most serious breakthrough in the OAU's economic policy. The meeting was attended by all OAU Members with only Angola, Mauritius, Seychelles, Malawi and Malagasy absent. The tone of the meeting was set by the host to the conference, President Mobutu Sese Seko, who had for some time been pressing for an OAU Summit on the economic problems of Africa.[39] He put before the ministers the following proposals:

'I propose to you the setting up of the African economic community. I know that such a proposition seems rash, even Utopian, but frankly, I believe in it, and I believe in it so much that if the conference asked me, I would go all around Africa to convince each of my colleagues.

At certain ministerial meetings, this problem has been discussed and they have preferred to consign it to oblivion, by asking the Secretariat of the OAU to study its opportuneness and viability. I say to you that in my opinion, that must all come from the will of the heads of state and government themselves, because if we have to wait for the opportune moment for such an economic grouping, we shall wait a very long time.

Note the example of Europe and the Rome Treaty and the progress towards integration at the Lomé Convention negotiations at which there was one European delegate and 46 African ones. The EEC began with the setting up of the European Coal and Steel

Community.

I think that it would also be more realistic for us to begin by the setting up of the African energy commission. It would be enough to refer to the recommendations of the second African meeting on energy held at Accra in Ghana this year, from 7 to 19 November 1976. Such an initiative seems to me to be justifiable from several points of view, first of all because energy is the driving force of any economic and social development, and the present crisis accentuates the vital importance of this.

Another suggestion which I would like to make to this conference is the institutionalization of the conference of ministers responsible for economy, finance, planning and trade, and there also, in order to avoid our getting tangled up in a forest of resolutions, we would need to set up an African planning institute, so that all the national planning of each African state would relate to the general plan for the continent. This would tend to promote and speed up the creation of regional common markets, embryos of the great continental common market structures.

This planning organization must be joined to a logistics body, which would be a data bank. In fact, today when we need economic and social information about African states we need to consult statistical institutes of the developed countries. We should harmonize the introduction of computers in Africa. At present the whole of independent Africa possesses only 60 computers, and two thirds are concentrated in just five countries.'[40]

Mobutu also impressed the Ministers by giving them his word of honour 'that the hydroelectric power we produce at Inga will be made available to Africa'. He said:

'In fact, if we had directed the national high-tension network leading from Inga to Shaba which is 1,800 km long to the west instead, it would have reached Lagos, because the distance from Kinshasa to Lubumbashi is exactly equal to that from Kinshasa to Lagos. It is note-worthy that a nuclear power station is to be built in Nigeria of 1,000 MW and is to cost no less than 500,000,000 dollars while the line from Inga to Lagos would be cheaper, allowing also for tapping off in the People's Republic of Congo, in the Gabon Republic, and in the United Republic of Cameroon, and with the advantage of an extremely important quantity of energy, because Inga alone represents 14 per cent of the world's hydroelectric potential.'

The Council took up the lead from Zaire's President and set up several committees to consider the ways and means of implementing his suggestions. The meeting did not adopt any document but decided to put before the next OAU Summit (held in July 1977 in Libreville, Gabon) proposals for an African Common Market to be created gradually within a period of 15 years and based on regional integration. The Summit was also asked to consider establishing an African Payment Union, an African Energy Commission and an African Data Bank, and making the conferences of African ministers of economy, finance, planning, industry and trade permanent institutions of the OAU which would meet annually.

## 4. OAU SUPPORT FOR ECOWAS

While economic co-operation on a continental scale has continued to elude Africa, the OAU has thrown its support behind the regional economic groupings — of which the Economic Community of West African States (ECOWAS) has made the most encouraging progress.[40] The treaty establishing ECOWAS was signed on 4 November 1976 at Lomé by the Heads of fifteen States — Ivory Coast, Senegal, Niger, Guinea Bissau, Mauretania, Liberia, Sierra Leone, Benin, Upper Volta, Togo, Nigeria, Mali, Ghana, Gambia and Guinea.

It was agreed that the economic co-operation between the members of ECOWAS should proceed through the following stages:
— the elimination of all customs duties or other import or export taxes between Member-States;
— the abolition of quantitative and administrative restrictions on trade between Member-States (to be carried out gradually within ten years);
— the establishment of a joint customs tariff and a joint trade policy, to cover relations with non-members (the process to be completed within 15 years);
— the elimination of all barriers to the free circulation of people, services and capital between Member-States: citizens of Member-States to be regarded as citizens of the Community (therefore not requiring visas or residence permits when travelling to other Member-States) and to be able to work and carry on business in all countries of the Community; and
— the harmonizing of agricultural policies and encouragement of joint projects between Member-States, notably in marketing research and agro-industrial projects.
The OAU Secretary-General William Eteki, who attended the ECOWAS Summit, called it a right step in the right direction at the right time. He pledged the OAU's support for working on the expansion of similar structures in all parts of Africa in the 'Pan-African economic unity'

capable of 'liberating Africa from its foreign bases and its outside economic and cultural domination, and of bringing about a new international order'.


## 5. THE UNDOING OF ILLUSIONS

The economic encounters between African countries and the club of rich Western industrialized nations during 1976 and 1977 have seriously shaken Africa's faith in a New International Economic Order.

The meagre results of the UNCTAD IV in Nairobi in June 1976, the growing discontent of the 46 countries of Africa, the Caribbean and the Pacific (ACP) with the Lomé Convention, and the collapse of the UNCTAD Common Fund Conference in Geneva in March 1977,[41] showed quite clearly both that the industrialized countries had not yet changed their economic policies (based on pursuing their own interests at the expense of their weaker partners) and that they were unlikely to do so at all.

The declaration of the seven leading Western nations (USA, Canada, France, West Germany, Italy, Canada and Britain), whose leaders met in London on 8-9 May 1977, promised the Third World a 'continuing dialogue' and 'a successful conclusion of the North-South Dialogue' in Paris; but this vague guarantee has not been followed up by action. Described by the OAU Secretary-General as a 'shipwreck', the North-South Dialogue was finally sunk by the Ministerial Meeting held in Paris on 30 May — 1 June 1977. The concessions offered by the industrialized countries to their Third World partners were aptly described by Melvyn Westlake of the London *Times* as 'crumbs from the rich north's table'.[43]

The ECA Secretary-General, Dr Adebayo Adedeji of Nigeria (who succeeded Dr Gardiner in 1976), when addressing the ECA annual meeting held on 24 February — 4 March 1977 in Kinshasa, described the economic situation in Africa as 'alarming'. According to ECA figures, between 1960 and 1975 per capita annual income had grown in only nine countries while in fourteen it had dropped below $100. The external economic position had also been weakened by Africa's indebtedness, which grew from $7,000 million to a staggering $28,000 million during those fifteen years. Servicing those debts took up more than one fifth of Africa's total exports. Prices for African export commodities, even after they were raised, could not keep up with the constant growth of the price of manufactured goods imported from the industrialized countries. As a result the trade terms of Africa had worsened by almost 15 per cent in the period 1973-1975.

These developments have served as a reminder to the OAU that Africa cannot expect a solution of her economic problems through a New International Economic Order which died before even coming into existence. Despite its enormous economic potential, the attainment of 'economic independence' for the African continent will be an arduous task calling for drastic reforms in both the internal and external economic policies of African States.

So far the priority of national interests over those of Africa as a whole has been the main African weakness both in the relations between independent African States and in their relations with the industrialized countries. The success of the new OAU initiative will depend on whether the African leaders recognize the need for changes in the concept of national economic development, and decide to gear it towards continental co-operation. After fourteen years of the OAU, the real struggle for the liberation of the continent of Africa from economic domination by outside powers has hardly begun.

# Notes

The OAU resolutions, both of the Council of Ministers (referred to below as CM/Res.) and of the Assembly of Heads of State and Government (AHG/Res.), as well as declarations (CM/St.) and resolutions adopted at the Extraordinary Sessions of the Council (ECM/Res.), have been released by the OAU Secretariat in mimeographed form only for use primarily by OAU delegations. Although they are sent on request to friendly governmental and non-governmental institutions in and outside Africa, a complete set is rarely to be found outside the OAU. Since 1971 the most important OAU resolutions have been reproduced in the document section of the *African Contemporary Record* (ACR), ed. Colin Legum (London: Rex Collings).

## Chapter One

1. The name 'Casablanca group' was used to describe the participants at a conference at Casablanca convened on 3 January 1961 by Kind Mohammed V of Morocco and attended by representatives from Egypt, Libya, Ghana, Guinea, Mali, Morocco and the Algerian Provisional Government. Nigeria, Tunisia, Ethiopia, Liberia, Sudan, Togo and Gambia were invited but declined to attend. Of the Asian participants at the Bandung Conference, India, Ceylon and Indonesia were invited but only Ceylon sent an observer. The French-speaking States which had earlier formed the so-called Brazzaville Twelve were not invited. The most important result of the Casablanca Conference was the adoption of the 'African Charter of Casablanca'. It affirmed the determination of its signatories 'to promote the triumph of liberty all over Africa and to achieve its unity'. For the full text of the Charter see Louis B. Sohn (ed.), *Basic Documents of African Regional Organizations,* (New York: Oceana Publications, 1971), Vol. 1, p. 42.

2. The Monrovia group owes its name to the Monrovia Conference, held during 8-12 May 1961, and attended by delegations from twenty African States. The States represented were: Cameroon, Chad, Central African Republic, Congo (Brazzaville), Dahomey (Benin), Ethiopia, Gabon, Ivory Coast, Liberia, Malagasy Republic, Mauritania, Niger, Nigeria, Senegal, Sierra Leone, Somalia, Togo, Tunisia and Upper Volta. Of the Casablanca group, only Libya accepted the invitation. Sudan withdrew its acceptance because it objected to the presence of a Mauritanian delegation. Congo (Zaire) was not invited because of the unsettled situation in that State. The participants agreed on the following five principles which were later embodied in the 'Lagos Charter':
— absolute equality and sovereignty of African States;
— each African State to have the right to exist and no State to try to annex another;
— voluntary union of one State with another;
— non-interference in the affairs of other African States;
— no dissident elements from one State to be harboured by another state.
For the text of the Charter see Louis B. Sohn, op.cit., p. 55.

The Monrovia Conference was followed by a conference in Lagos which took place in January 1962. The conference reaffirmed the principles set out at Monrovia and approved the Draft Charter of the African and Malagasy States. The Charter was submitted to all governments for ratification and was finally adopted on 20 December 1962. The original signatories of the Lagos 'Charter of the Organization of African and Malagasy States' were Cameroon, Central African Republic, Chad, Congo (Brazzaville), Dahomey (Benin), Ethiopia, Gabon, Ivory Coast, Liberia, Mauritania, Niger, Senegal, Togo, Upper Volta, Nigeria, Sierra Leone and Congo (Zaire).

3. The Brazzaville Twelve was formed in October 1960 at Abidjan (Ivory Coast) at a meeting of Heads of State of former French colonies — Senegal, Mauritania, Ivory Coast, Upper Volta, Niger, Dahomey (Benin), Chad, Gabon, the Central African Republic, Congo (Brazzaville), Malagasy Republic and Cameroon. The meeting was initiated by President Houphouet-Boigny of the Ivory Coast, who wanted the French-speaking African States to mediate in the Algerian conflict without alienating France. No Arab State in North Africa attended the meeting; Togo declined the invitation and Guinea strongly denounced it. President Tsiranana of Malagasy Republic did not come to Abidjan but later joined the group and attended the Brazzaville meeting.

The meeting at Brazzaville, which gave the group its name, was held in December 1960 with twelve Heads of State in attendance (hence Brazzaville Twelve). They shared a desire to remain on the best of terms with the *'ancienne mère patrie'*, France, they strongly opposed any kind of communist presence in Africa, and they sided with France in the Franco-Algerian conflict. They also agreed to become a permanent association (Union Africaine et Malgache), the Charter of which was subsequently signed in Tananarive (Malagasy) on 12 September 1961. For a detailed analysis of UAM see Albert Tévoédjrè, *Pan Africanism in Action* (Harvard University: Occasional papers in international affairs, No. 11, 1965).

4. During the early hours of Sunday, 13 January 1963, a *coup d'état* was carried out in the Republic of Togo, in the course of which President Olympio was assassinated. Ghana was suspected of having initiated the coup because of its strained relations with Togo over the harbouring of Ghanaian political refugees. The event also gave rise to the question of recognition of a regime brought about by a *coup détat* (Discussed in Chapter VII.)

5. The Bandung Conference was jointly convened by Burma, Ceylon, Indonesia, India, and Pakistan for the period 18-24 April 1955. In addition to the sponsors it was attended by representatives from the following countries: Afghanistan, Cambodia, People's Republic of China, Egypt, Ethiopia, Gold Coast (now Ghana), Iran, Iraq, Jordan, Laos, Lebanon, Liberia, Libya, Nepal, Philippines, Saudi Arabia, Sudan, Syria, Thailand, Turkey, North Vietnam, South Vietnam, and Yemen.

Among other issues, the Conference considered problems 'affecting national sovereignty, racialism and colonialism'. For an assessment of the Conference see A. Appadorai, *The Bandung Conference* (New Delhi, Indian Council of World Affairs, 1955), and G. McTurnan Kahin, *The Asian-African Conference.* (Ithaca, New York: Cornell University Press, 1955).

6. The Atlantic Charter is a joint declaration of the British Prime Minister Winston Churchill and the United States President F. D. Roosevelt signed on 11 August 1941. For the full text of the Atlantic Charter, see R. B. Russel, *A History of the United Nations Charter* (Washington: The Brookings Institution, 1958), p. 975.

7. *Time* magazine of 20 May, 1963 wrote: 'Osagyefo would be peddling his pet scheme for a bicameral all-African parliament and other similar quickie approaches to a unified Africa. No one was likely to buy Nkrumah's schemes, however, for it has long been obvious to all of Africa that it was basically Nkrumah that Nkrumah wants to promote.'

8. Rumours about contact between the draftsmen of the OAU Charter and an Organization of American States expert, Ambassador Manuel Trucco of Chile, were reported in *Newsweek* in April 1963. This caused consternation among Ghanaian and other African politicians, who regarded with suspicion the growing interest of the United States in African affairs. In an article headed 'An American Torpedo for Addis Ababa', the columnist of *The Ghanaian Times*, H. M. Basner, wrote: 'Short of war, earthquake or famine, we can think of no greater disaster for Africa than an organization on the lines of the charter of the Organization of American States. Of all instruments which have served to maintain the Latin American Continent in disunity and peonage under USA neo-colonialism, the Charter of the OAS takes foremost place.' *Ghanaian Times*, 20 April, 1963, p. 2.

9. When France granted independence to Mauritania on 28 November 1960, Morocco strongly protested and claimed Mauritania as historically Moroccan territory. Some of Mauritania's 600,000 people, mainly Moors, sought unity with Morocco; but its first independent government preferred membership of the French community, and formed alliances with the ex-French African republics to the south. The dispute over Mauritania embittered Franco-Moroccan relations, already strained by the Algerian war. Moroccans resented French plans to exploit the iron ore deposits near Fort Gouraud, and they also claimed Tindouf, the iron ore field in the Algerian Sahara.

10. See Volume 1 of the *Proceedings of the Summit Conference of the Heads of State and Government held at Addis Ababa in May 1963*, published by the Provisional Secretariat at Addis Ababa, from which this and all subsequent statements by Heads of State and Government are quoted.

11. The difficulty of meeting this obligation is inferred in the resolution of the Second Session of the Council of Ministers held in Lagos in February 1964, which adopted a resolution on African Non-Alignment. The resolution dilutes considerably the principle of non-alignment as stated at the Addis Ababa Summit. In particular it deletes any express reference to the necessity for removing military bases from African soil. It merely recommends 'the removal of commitments, as soon as possible, which would militate against a consistent policy of non-alignment'.

12. The Committee was asked to submit to the Member-States its findings on the following matters:
— a free trade area between the various African countries;
— the establishment of a common external tariff to protect the emergent industries, and the formation of a raw material price stabilization fund;
— the restructuring of international trade;
— the means of developing trade among African countries by the organization of African trade fairs and exhibitions, and by granting transport and transit facilities;
— the co-ordination of transport and the establishment of road, air and maritime enterprises;
— the establishment of an African Payments and Clearing Union;
— the freeing of national currencies from all non-technical external attachments and the establishment of a Pan-African monetary zone;
— ways and means of co-ordinating national development plans.

13. The Commission for Technical Co-operation in Africa South of the Sahara (CTCA) was established by an international agreement dated 18 January 1954, which became operative on 30 May 1958. The original members were the four colonial powers — the United Kingdom, France, Belgium and Portugal — together with South Africa and the Federation of Rhodesia and Nyasaland. Later, most of the independent African countries joined in their own initiative. In 1962 the

Commission expelled South Africa and Portugal.

14. The resolutions envisaged the following programmes with a view to raising social standards and strengthening inter-African co-operation:
- the exchange of social and labour legislation;
- the establishment of an African Youth Organization,
- the organization of an African Scouts Union and an annual continental jamboree;
- the organization of an annual African Games;
- the organization of vocational training courses for African workers;
- the establishment of an African Trade Union;
- the establishment of an Institute of African Studies within the African University proposed by Ethiopia;
- programmes in the major African languages in the broadcasts of the independent African states, and the exchage of radio and television programmes.

The resolution on Health, Sanitation and Nutrition charged the Committee 'to conduct extensive studies on health problems facing the continent', 'to lay down detailed programmes with a view to raising health standards among the peoples', and to strengthen inter-African co-operation through:
- the exchange of information about endemic and epidemic diseases and the means of controlling them.
- the exchange of doctors and nurses;
- reciprocal scholarships for medical students, and the establishment of training courses in health, sanitation and nutrition.

15. *Ghanaian Times,* 30 May 1963, p. 2.


### Chapter Two

1. T. O. Elias, 'The Charter of the OAU', *The American Journal of International Law,* No. 69 (Washington DC, 1965), p. 24.

2. The great respect of Africa's leaders for the UN is expressed by a direct reference to the UN Charter: '. . . persuaded that the Charter of the United Nations and the Universal Declaration of Human Rights, to the principles of which we reaffirm our adherence, provided a solid foundation for peaceful and positive co-operation among States . . .' The relations between the OAU and the UN are examined in B. Andemicael, *The OAU and the UN: relations between the Organization of African Unity and the United Nations* (New York: Africana Publishing Co., 1977).

The opening paragraph of the Preamble echoes the 'Declaration to the Colonial Peoples', adopted at the Fifth Pan-African Congress at Manchester in 1945, which begins: 'We affirm the right of all people to control their own destiny', and continues by recalling the Universal Declaration of Human Rights: '. . . freedom, equality, justice and dignity are essential objectives for the achievement of the legitimate aspirations of the African peoples. . .'

The Declaration adopted in 1958 by the Accra Conference of Independent African States stipulates the determination 'to safeguard and consolidate the hard-won independence as well as the sovereignty and territorial integrity of our States, and to fight against neo-colonialism in all its forms.'

3. For example, during 1971 the OAU Administrative Secretary-General, Diallo Telli, in his message to mark the eight anniversary of the OAU recalled that 'Since it was established, the Organization of African Unity's prime and urgent objective has been the total liberation of our continent from all forms of foreign

occupation, oppression and exploitation . . .' Diallo Telli, 'The Organization of African Unity in Historical Perspective', *African Forum,* Vol. 1, No. 3 (1965).

The Summit Conference at Addis Ababa in 1973 confirmed its 'Solemn Declaration on Policy', that the colonial and racial domination of the continent is the greatest challenge to African unity. President Kenyatta of Kenya, in his message to the Summit emphasised 'the sacred and inescapable duty to remove the last vestiges of colonialism from African soil, and recalled Nkrumah's thesis by saying that 'unless each and every part of Africa is free and independent, both in political and economic terms, our independence remains incomplete and meaningless.'

Doudan Thiam, Minister of Foreign Affairs of Senegal, in his book *The Foreign Policy of African States* (New York, Praeger, 1965), also makes it clear that '. . . decolonization is undoubtedly the subject which commands the greatest measure of unity between the various African countries.'

4. CM/Res. 272 (XIX).

5. The legitimacy of the struggle of the colonial peoples to exercise their right to self-determination and independence by all necessary means at their disposal has been recognized also by the General Assembly of the UN in a Declaration adopted by the General Assembly on 23 October 1970, to mark the 25th anniversary of the UN. It was subsequently reiterated by a number of General Assembly resolutions, e.g. Resolution 2908 (XXVII) adopted on 2 November 1972.

6. For example, the principle of sovereign equality of the OAU Members echoes Article 2 (1) of the UN Charter which states that the Organization is based on the principle of sovereign equality of all its members. The principle of non-interference reflects the provision of Article 2(7) of the UN Charter. Respect for sovereignty, as required by principle 3 of the OAU Charter, is a paraphrase of Article 1(2) of the UN Charter which states the intention to develop friendly relations among nations based on respect for the principle of equal rights and self-determination of peoples. . .'.

The fourth principle of the OAU Charter, about the peaceful settlement of disputes, corresponds to the provision of the UN Charter: 'All members settle their international disputes by peaceful means in such a manner that international peace and justice are not endangered. . .' The OAU Charter defines 'peaceful means' applicable within the framework of the OAU by enumerating 'negotiation, mediation, conciliation or arbitration'. It omits any reference to the judical means for the settlement of disputes, namely the International Court of Justice.

7. See the speech by President Tito of Yugoslavia at the 1973 Conference at Algiers, reproduced in the document quoted in *The Review of International Affairs,* (No. 564, Belgrade, 5 October, 1973), which also contains speeches made by other participating heads of state and government. The texts of the documents adopted by the Conference are reproduced in No. 563 of 20 September, 1973. It also includes the following statement made by President of Libya, Muammar Gaddafi, describing his policy on non-alignment: 'Most of us are friends of the Soviet Union and I am a friend of the Soviet Union. But the Soviet Union as great power would be stupid not to seek zones of influence in its struggle against the United States. It is forced to become an imperialist power like the United States because circumstances demand it. . . My country has liquidated the military bases which were located in it and has forbidden the entry of the Soviet naval ships into its harbours. The result is that our own position did not please the Soviet Union, Nevertheless, I cannot permit this for either the Soviets or the Americans. In this way I have performed non-alignment.'

The documents of the fifth Conference of Heads of State and Government of

Non-Aligned Countries (held in Colombo, 16-19 August, 1976) are reproduced in *The Review of International Affairs* (No. 634, Belgrade, 5 September, 1976).

8. Associate membership was requested by liberation movements in a joint memorandum submitted at the Addis Ababa Conference: 'We urge sincerely that in this summit conference we be accorded a status commensurate to our position as brothers and comrades of the other African freedom fighters who have already won their independence. We request that the opportunity be given to us to participate in and address the summit conference as associate members.'

9. Modern international law makes no distinction between 'adhesion' and 'accession'. It is true that, some fifty years ago, some authors regarded 'adhesion' as being merely a 'partial' acceptance of rights and duties arising out of an international treaty, while 'accession' was regarded as the proper term to be used for joining an international treaty as a whole. However, the Committee of Experts on the Codification of International Law, functioning within the framework of the League of Nations, already maintained in its report of 24 March 1927 that current international practice does not recognize this theoretical difference and usually takes no notice of it. Accession is 'an act whereby a State having a legitimate interest in the subject matter of an open multilateral convention, which it did not sign and ratify, expresses by a formal manifestation of its will (corresponding to the analogical will of the other parties to the convention) its acceptance of rights and obligations arising from the convention.' V. Pĕchota, *International Multilateral Treaties and Accession Thereto* (Czechoslovak Academy of Sciences, Prague, 1955), pp 50-1.

10. CM/Res. 419(XXV).

11. CM/St. 5(XVII). The 'Question of Dialogue' refers to the issue about whether or not the independent African States should enter into dialogue with the South African Government and, by establishing their presence in South Africa through diplomatic and trade representations and visits, try to 'erode apartheid from within'. See also Chapter XI.

## Chapter Three

1. The Rules of Procedure of the Assembly of Heads of State and Government were adopted at the meeting of the Assembly held in Cairo in July 1964 (AHG/3).

2. Yashpal Tandon calls the consensus 'Collective good' and an elusive and immeasurable commodity at that. ('The Organization of African Unity. A Forum for African International Relations', *The Round Table*, London, April 1972).

3. Quoted in 'OAU Perspective' (Third Regular Assembly 1966), Addis Ababa, Ministry of Information, 1966, p. 35.

4. The difference between Malawi and the OAU on apartheid is about the means that should be used for its eradication. On no occasion has President Banda ever condoned apartheid. He believes, however, that it can be eroded from within by the intensification of contacts between Africa and South Africa, which will eventually lead to a change of heart by the Nationalist Party.

5. This was the position adopted by the Somali Republic and Morocco in relation to the Resolution of the OAU Summit Conference held in Cairo in July 1964, which affirmed the validity of all existing fontiers.

6. The Rules of Procedure of the Council of Ministers were adopted at its first session held in Dakar on 2-11 August 1963, and were published by the Provisional Secretariat in Addis Ababa.

7. Article XVII states the obligations of the Secretariat staff and the

Member-States:

(1) In the performance of their duties, the Administrative Secretary-General and the staff shall not seek or receive instructions from any government or from any other authority external to the Organization. They shall refrain from any action which might reflect on their position as international officials responsible only to the Organization.

(2) Each member of the Organization undertakes to respect the exclusive character of the responsibilities of the Administrative Secretary-General and the Staff and not to seek to influence them in discharge of their responsibilities.

8. In practice, the Adminstrative Secretary-General does not submit annual reports. Instead, his reports cover the periods between the meetings of the OAU Council of Ministers and those of the Assembly of Heads of State and Government.

9. The decision of the Council of Ministers is quoted by the Administrative Secretary-General in this report (CM 330, Pt II, p. 4). In the same report the Council's decision is challenged as folows: 'It is easy to imagine the disruption which political appointments, with the inevitable allegiances they entail, could cause in the smooth functioning of the General Secretariat of a young organization like ours. In the overriding interest of OAU, The General Secretariat wishes to appeal to the Council of Ministers to consider possible and practical improvements in the present staff rules and regulations, but to avoid any upheaval that would threaten to disorganize, paralyse and even undermine the very foundations of this effectively working OAU organ, the General Secretariat.'

10. Nzo Ekangaki, in his exclusive interview for Africa (London, August 1974).

11. H. R. Amonoo, 'The Organization of African Unity: Its Defects and Solutions', *Pan-Africanist Review,* Vol. 1, No. 1 (Accra, 1964), p. 38.

12. The compliance of Member-States has always been a problem for the Administrative Secretary-General. In 1968, for example, when the report on arrears was made public for the first time, probably to add the pressure of public opinion to that of the Secretariat, only half the members had paid their contributions in full. The situation has not improved since. In 1976 *The New Nigerian* of 27 February brought out a critical editorial on the subject. At that time only eight out of 47 OAU Members had fully paid their dues. 'The OAU's financial position can only improve,' wrote *The New Nigerian,* 'when member countries make up their mind to honour their political — and consequently financial — commitments. By paying lip service to the organization and refusing to pay dues, member nations are making non-sense of the whole organization.'

13. A detailed account of the OAU-LONRHO deal constitutes Chapter 10 (*The Commanding Heights*) of the book 'LONRHO — Portrait of a multinational', by Cronjé, Ling and Cronjé (London: J. Friedmann, 1976).

14. Resolution on the Activities of the African group at the UN 233 (XV) 1970.

15. A detailed review of the first two years' activities of the Bureau is contained in the Repot of the Administrative Secretary-General covering the period June 1974 to February 1975 (CM 613, Pt II, pp. 36-37), In this Report the Administrative Secretary-General deplored the 'self-centred' attitude of the Lagos Secretariat, and called for measures to improve coordination and supervision by Addis Ababa.

16. In UN practice, specialized commissions or committees operate within the framework of the UN and are subject to the overall responsibility of that organization, whereas the Specialized Agencies are virtually autonomous organizations operating under separate constitutions. The International Atomic Energy Agency is an example of the latter.

17. For details see Chapter X.

18. The Health, Sanitation and Nutrition Commission held its first meeting at Alexandria in January 1964. It recommended, *inter alia,* the establishment of a Public Health Division within the OAU Secretariat, and a Bureau of Documentation and Information on public health matters to co-ordinate statistics, health legislation and the education of medical personnel.

19. The Educational and Cultural Commission met at Kinshasa in January 1964. It resolved to create an Inter-African News Agency charged with 'collecting and disseminating fruitful, objective and impartial news about Africa to the African and world press, radio and television. Another project considered by the Commission was a proposal for an institute of African studies to form part of a pan-African university.

20. The first meeting of the Scientific, Technical and Research Commission was held in Algiers in February 1964. The Commission drew up plans for the training and exchange of scientific, technical and research personnel and for the effective utilization of the results of research. It also proposed to conduct scientific surveys of the natural resources of the continent.

21. For a critical appraisal of the UN technical assistance to Africa see Yashpal Tandon, *Technical Assistance Administration in East Africa.* (Uppsala: The Dag Hammarskjöld Foundation, 1973).

22. The Legal Commission was composed of lawyers from Egypt, Ethiopia, Guinea, Nigeria, Senegal, Sudan, Tanzania, Tunisia and Zambia. The mandate of the Commission was given in 1971 in connection with the drafting of the Declaration on the Activities of the Mercenaries in Africa (adopted by the 1971 OAU Summit), and was subsequently extended to include review of inter-African legal co-operation. The OAU Declaration on the Law of the Sea and the Draft Convention on Extradition are other examples of its work.

23. So far, three conferences of African Ministers of Commerce and Industry have been held. The first in Addis Ababa in May 1971, the second in Cairo in December 1973 and the third in Nairobi in December 1975. The last two were also sponsored by the United Nations Industrial Development Organization (UNIDO). African Trade Ministers have already held four conferences, the last one in Algiers in November 1975.

24. At the meeting of the experts of the Casablanca States in Accra in April 1961, three months after the adoption of the Casablanca Charter, an agreement was reached on a common defence policy, and the following organs of the Joint African High Command were set up: a Supreme Council composed of the chiefs-of-staff of Member-States, and a permanent Military Staff Committee consisting of a chief appointed by the Supreme Council, with staff officers and other personnel from all Member-States. This Committee would be the Executive Organ of Command and would be located in permanent headquarters (later agreed to be situated in Accra).

25. President Nkrumah saw that it was impossible for one African State to afford a fully-integrated defence force. The most that any one country could do was to contribute that element which its strategic position and technical facilities made possible. He was proposing this sort of planning even before the OAU was established and before an agreement was reached on any form of African union government. For example, he argued the establishment of a Joint African High Command in his address to the 'Nationalist Conference of African Freedom Fighters' held at Winneba in June 1962. The speech was published in *Bulletin on African Affairs,* Vol. 2, No. 113 (Accra, 1962).

26. Doc.AHG/3, of 13 July 1964. The proposal was listed as agenda-item No. II of the Assembly, but no resolution was passed on the matter — at least it

does not appear in the list of resolutions released by the OAU Secretariat.

27. ECM/Res. 14 (VI). The Council also appealed to Member-States 'to make military or other contributions to meet any emergency that may arise in member-states which are neighbours of Southern Rhodesia'.

28. *Daily Express,* London, 10 November 1965.

29. Report of the Administrative Secretary-General covering the period from February to September 1970. Doc. CM/330.

30. ECM/Res. 17 (VII).

31. No official OAU documents were released on the matter. The quoted text appeared in *Africa Research Bulletin,* Vol. 8, No. 12, (London, January 1972), p. 1204, with reference to Agence France Presse.

32. According to the 1976 Yearbook of the Stockholm International Peace Research Institute (SIPRI) on World Armaments and Disarments, major arms transfers to Sub-Saharan Africa more than doubled between 1974 and 1975, the leading purchasing nations being Ethiopia, Ghana, Nigeria, Tanzania, Uganda and Zaire.

33. CM/Res. 426 (XXV).

34. See Peter Enahoro, 'East Africa: Arms Race', *Africa* (London, August 1975). For more details on the arms build-up in Africa, and East Africa in particular, see the 1977 SIPRI Yearbook.

## Chapter Four

1. During the author's visit to the Committee's Headquarters in Dar-es-Salaam in August 1974, the Deputy Executive Secretary for Defence, Ahmed Sidky, firmly refuted the allegation that the Committee is engaged in arms deals. He said that during the previous two years the Committee had not purchased a single gun or round of ammunition. The purchase of arms is made by the liberation movements directly, with the money supplied by the Committee; the committee may on occasion be asked for technical advice.

2. For a detailed study see Yassin El Ayouty, 'Legitimization of National Liberation: the United Nations and Southern Africa' (New York, IMAS, 1973). The 'Recommendations of Special Measures to be adopted on decolonization and the struggle against apartheid and racial discrimination' endorsed by the OAU Summit at Rabat in 1972 confirmed the OAU position on the issues by stating that any retaliation by Portugal, South Africa and Rhodesia against the States providing support for the guerrillas would be regarded as 'acts constituting aggression against the whole of Africa'.

3. The following liberation movements were recognized by the OAU and granted the right of participation in the meetings of the Liberation Committee and the Council of Ministers:
— The African Party for the Independence of Guinea-Bissau and the Cape Verde Islands — PAIGC
— The Liberation Front of Mozambique — FRELIMO
— The People's Movement for the Liberation of Angola — MPLA
— The National Liberation Front of Angola — FNLA (GRAE)
— The National Union for the Total Independence of Angola — UNITA
— South West Africa People's Organization — SWAPO
— African National Council (Zimbabwe), comprising two movements previously recognized by the OAU, namely the Zimbabwe African People's Union (ZAPU) and the Zimbabwe African National Union (ZANU); and the Front for the Liberation of Zimbabwe (FROLIZI), which was not accorded

199

recognition before — ANC. (Since 1976 the OAU Liberation Committee has thrown its support behind the 'Patriotic Front' of J. Nkomo and R. Mugabe.)
— The National Front for the Liberation of Somali Coast — FLSC
— The Djibouti Liberation Movement — LMD. (In 1977, recognition was extended also to the Front for the Liberation of the Somali Coast — FLCS — the People's Liberation Movement — MPL — and the National Unity for Independence — (UNI.)
— The African National Congress of South Africa — ANC
— The Pan-African National Congress of Azania (African name for South Africa) — PAC
— The Movement for the Liberation of Săo Tomé and Principé — MLST
— The Movement for the Liberation of the Comoro Islands — FLCS
— The Seychelles Peoples United Party — SPUP

For details about the OAU Liberation Committee and the liberation movements see E. M. Dube, 'Relations Between Liberation Movements and OAU', in N. M. Shamuyarira (ed.), *Essays on the Liberation of Southern Africa* (Dar-es-Salaam: Tanzania Publishing House, 1971)and R. Gibson *African Liberation Movements* (London: Oxford University Press, 1972).

4. *Daily News* Dar-es-Salaam, 20 January 1977.

5. The Tanzanian paper *The Nationalist* made the following comment on the impact of Tshombe's accession to power on the Liberation Committee: 'It is absurd to think how the Congo government headed by Moise Tshombe could have effectively played its proper role in supporting freedom fighters in Angola when Mr. Tshombe has been known all along to be hob-nobbing with the Portuguese authorities in Angola during and after the Katanga seceesion.' *The Nationalist* (Dar-es-Salaam, 23 October 1963), p. 4.

6. At this meeting, the Ghanaian delegate had tried to pacify his colleagues by assuring them that '*Spark* is not the mouthpiece of the Ghana Government'. While condemning the newspaper, which was founded by President Nkrumah, he tried to console the delegates by saying: 'A sister-paper of *Spark* has described some of us as black-coated intellectual friends of Western diplomacy. Perhaps this is why some of us are changing our ties these days, I do not know. . .'

The disapproval of Ghana's criticism came out in the Committee's report: 'Delegates expressed surprise at the unjustified attacks made by Ghana on the activities of the Co-ordinating Committee for Liberation of Africa.' The Council of Ministers then assured the Committee of Nine of its full confidence and expressed its satisfaction to the Committee for the work it had done and also its appreciation to the Government of Tanzania for the facilities it had provided for the Committee.

7. Title accorded to President Nkrumah in Ghana, meaning 'Redeemer'. In Tanzania, President Nyerere is called 'Mwalimu', meaning 'Teacher'.

8. CM/Res. 154 (XI).

9. CM/175 (XII). In its 'Recommendations concerning the coordinating Committee for the Liberation of Africa', the *ad hoc* Committee was asked to study distribution of means of struggle, storage of war equipment and improvement of transit facilities.

10. *Africa Research Bulletin*, Vol. 9, No. 6 (London, July 1972), p. 2945.

11. The following were the resolutions on various problems of decolonization adopted by the Rabat Summit:
— Resolution on Zimbabwe (CM/Res. 267 [XIX]);
— Resolution on Portuguese colonies (CM/Res. 268 [XIX]);
— Resolution on Namibia (CM/Res. 269 [XIX]); and
— Recommendations on Special Measures to be adopted on decolonization and

the struggle against apartheid and racial discrimination (CM/Res. 272 [XIX] ).

12. The Tanzanian position paper on 'African Strategy in Southern Africa', submitted to the 9th Extraordinary Session of the OAU Council of Ministers in Dar-es-Salaam in April 1975, stipulated the OAU position very clearly as follows: 'Africa has always acknowledged that the real struggle must be conducted and led by the peoples directly concerned. While they are able to campaign peacefully for their freedom, the prime function of Africa has been, and is, to give moral and diplomatic support to their struggle. But when peaceful campaigning becomes impossible, then OAU and its Member-States have the responsibility to give assistance in military training, in transit for arms and in providing a rear base, with hospitals, stores, etc.' *Daily News,* Dar-es-Salaam, 10 April 1975.

13. For details of the proceedings of the OAU Liberation Committee and the Declaration, see Africa Research Bulletin, Vol. 10, No. 1 (January 1973), pp. 2714-15.

14. The Special Committee which drew up the strategy proposed the following immediate allocations: PAIGC, 25 per cent; FRELIMO, 25 per cent; FNLA, 20 per cent; SWAPO, 10 per cent; ANC and PAC, 5 per cent; other liberation movements, 5 per cent. At the November 1974 meeting of the Committee in Dar-es-Salaam it was revealed that £2 million had been provided for the liberation movements for the period from June to October 1974 in addition to £864,000 allocated previously. The FNLA and MPLA had each been allocated £115,000, the contribution to FRELIMO was increased from £245,000 to £800,000, and PAIGC was promised a sum of £1 million as a contribution to its first independence budget. During the Dar-es-Salaam meeting, Libya donated £250,000 to SWAPO, ZANU and ZAPU in addition to its annual contribution to the Special Fund.

15. See Z. Cervenka, 'Romania's Year in Africa', *Africa Contemporary Record,* 1972-73, Colin Legum (ed.) (London 1973), pp. A95-A101.

16. The Mombasa Agreement is a joint declaration of principles on the territorial integrity, national unity and economic situation of Angola signed on 5 January 1975 by the leaders of FNLA, MPLA and UNITA at Mombasa under the chairmanship of President Kenyatta. For the text, see Africa Contemporary Record 1975-76, ed. Colin Legum (London: Rex Collings), p. C78.

## Chapter Five

1. The only attempt to make use of the Commission was in 1967, to settle a dispute between Guinea and Ghana concerning the detention of several Guinean officials in retaliation for the arrest by Guinea of some Ivory Coast citizens suspected of involvement in a plot to kidnap the deposed President of Ghana, Kwame Nkrumah, then living in Guinea. But little could be done by the Commission because one of its vice-presidents, Dr Daniels, was detained by the military regime.

2. The Emperor said in his address to the opening session of the Commission in Addis Ababa in 1967: 'This Commission occupies a special place in the Charter of OAU as one of its four principal institutions. There is nothing that is closer to our hearts than the work with which it is entrusted in the peaceful settlement of disputes; it is a task of great significance, for without conditions of security and peace, none of the objectives and aspirations enshrined in the Charter can be realized.'

3. Article 19 of the OAU Charter states: 'Member-States pledge to settle all disputes among themselves by peaceful means and to this end decide to establish a

Commission of Mediation, Conciliation and Arbitration, the composition of which and conditions of service shall be defined in a separate Protocol to be approved by the Assembly of Heads of State and Government. The said Protocol shall be regarded as forming an integral part of the present Charter.'

4. Arbitration differs from conciliation in two important aspects. The arbitration tribunal is a court which bases its conclusions on rules of international law, and these conclusions are binding upon the parties. Their consent to the arbitration is required — either in general terms, in advance of the emergence of any concrete dispute, or *ad hoc* after its emergence. It is possible for the parties to permit the tribunal to decide *ex aequo et bono*, i.e. as it sees reasonable and just; but if such permission is not given — which is unusual — the tribunal must base its judgement exclusively on legal rules.

5. Justice M. A. Odesanya in his paper, 'Reflections on the Pacific Settlement of Inter-State Disputes in Africa', given at the Third Annual Conference of the Nigerian Society of International Law held in Lagos in March 1971. The papers, edited by Dr. T. O. Elias, were published in 1972 by Ethiope Publishing Co., Benin City.

6. 'Any misunderstandings which arise among brotherly members of this organization must be essentially considered a family affair in which no foreign hand can be allowed to play any role whatsoever.' *Africa Research Bulletin* (Exeter, December 1963), p. 1.

7. For example, the resolution on the Algerian-Moroccan dispute refers to the need to settle all differences between African States by peaceful means and strictly within an African framework (ECM/Res. 1 [I] ). The Resolution on the Congo says that the Congo problem would find its best solution within the framework of the OAU (ECM/Res. 7 [IV] ). The Resolution on Nigeria appeals to all governments and international organizations to desist from any measure likely to jeopardize the efforts of the OAU in finding an African solution to the Nigerian crisis (AHG/Res. 58 [VI] ).

8. See B. Andemicael, *Peaceful Settlement among African States: Roles of the United Nations and the Organization of African Unity* (New York, 1972), p. 46.

9. For a recent review of boundary disputes, see Saadia Touval, *The Boundary Politics of Independent Africa* (Cambridge, Mass., 1972); see also *African Boundary Problems,* Carl Gösta Widstrand (ed.), (Uppsala, 1968), and Hanspeter F. Strauch, 'L'OAU et les conflits frontaliers', *Revue française d'études politiques africaines,* No. 22 (1967), pp. 59-81. No. 80 of the same *Revue* (August 1972) contains articles by Y. Person ('Les frontières africaines'), H. Deschamps ('Les frontières de la Sénégambie') and J. Woronoff ('Différents frontaliers en Afrique'). No. 121 (January 1976) has a special section devoted to the boundary problems of Togo and the status of Cabinda.

10. For the details and map, see *African Research Bulletin*, Vol. 13, No. 2 (Exeter, pp. 3919-3920. For the Kenyan reaction see *The Weekly Review*, Nairobi, 23 February and 1 March.

11. For an excellent analysis of the background to the dispute over the Sahara, the plight of POLISARIO and the policies of Algeria, Morocco and Mauritania, see a publication by the German-African-Arab Bureau (Bonn: Progress Dritte Welt, March 1976), entitled 'Demokratische Arabische Republik Sahara — Befreiungskampf und internationali Einflüsse'.

12. Saadia Touval, 'The Sources of the Status Quo and Irredentist Policies', *African Boundary Problems (op. cit.),* p. 81.

13. AHG/Res. 16 (I).

14. The agreement was signed in Nairobi by President Jomo Kenyatta and Emperor Haile Selassie during the latter's visit to Kenya on 8-10 June 1970. A

joint communiqué said that the two leaders were convinced that the signature of the treaty 'represented a triumph for the cause of good neighbourliness, harmony, and understanding between neighbouring States'. They were confident that 'secure and recognized borders helped to foster friendship and co-operation between sovereign States with common borders', and that the agreement was 'concrete fulfilment of the principles of friendly relations and co-operation enshrined in the OAU Charter'. *African Research Bulletin* Vol. 7, No. 6 (Exeter, July 1970), p. 1775.

15. For a comprehensive study of the African refugee problem see H. C. Brooks (ed.) and Y. El Ayouty, *Refugees South of the Sahara: An African Dilemma* (Westport, Conn., 1970), and Jan Woronoff, 'L'organisation de l'unité africaine et le probléme des réfugiés', *Revue française d'etudes politiques africaines*, No. 93 (Paris, 1973). For a recent, very informative book with an excellent bibliography on the problem of refugees, see Issa Ben Yacine Diallo, *Les réfugiés en Afrique: De la conception à l'application d'un instrument juridique de protection* (Vienna: Wilhelm Braumüller Universitäts-Verlagsbuchhandlung, 1974).

16. AHG/Res. 26/II

17. For the text of the Convention see *Refugees South of the Sahara (op cit.)*, pp. 271-78.

18. OCAM was established on 13 February 1965 at Nouakchott by thirteen African States, as a successor to a shortlived organization called Union Africain et Malgache de Co-opération Economique (UAMCE). The founding members of OCAM were Cameroon, Central African Republic, Chad, Congo, Dahomey (now Benin), Gabon, Ivory Coast, Malagasy, Mauritania, Niger, Senegal, Togo and Upper Volta. For more details about OCAM's relations with the OAU see ' Z. Cervenka, *The Organization of African Unity and Its Charter* (London: Ch. Hurst, 1969), Chapter 7 (The Regional and Political Groups and their Compatibility with the Charter of the OAU).

19. ECM/Res. 9/(V), 13 June 1965.

20. UN General Assembly Resolution 2131 (XX) of 21 December 1965.

21. See 'Tension Among Certain West African States 1965-67', in A. Andemicael, *op.cit.*, pp. 39-44. For a detailed analysis of the Ghana-Ivory Coast relationship, see Jan Woronoff, *West African Wager: Houphouet versus Nkrumah*, (Metuchen, N. J., 1972).

22. Quoted in *Africa Research Bulletin*, Vol. 3, No. 3 (London, April 1966), p. 484.

23. Ibid.

24. See Claude E. Welch, 'The OAU and International Recognition: Lessons from Uganda', Y. El Ayouty (ed.), *The Organization of African Unity After Ten Years* (New York, 1975).

25. The letter described the execution, torture and atrocities which, according to ex-President Obote, had assumed the proportions of genocide. The detailed description of the events in Uganda included macabre accounts of orgies in which Ugandan soldiers allegedly cut off parts of the bodies of the victims, roasted the human flesh, and fed the starving victims on their own flesh until they died.

26. The agreement provided for the following measures:
— Uganda accepts responsibility for the deaths of twenty-four Tanzanians in Uganda and agrees to pay compensation;
— both parties undertake not to use their territories for subversion against the other;
— Tanzania undertakes that Dr Obote will not interfere in the internal affairs of Uganda;

— Uganda will not demand the eviction of Dr Obote from Tanzania.

27. For the full text of the statement see *Daily News,* Dar es Salaam, 26 July 1975.

## Chapter Six

1. Within the context of this chapter the previous name of Zaire — The Congo (Leopoldville) — is used, as this is how Zaire was referred to in the UN and OAU documents and writings at the time of the crisis. Similarly, the old names of Zaire's cities: Leopoldville (Kinshasa), Stanleyville (Kisangani) and Albertville (Kalemie). Katanga province was re-named Shaba.

2. Kwame Nkrumah, *Challenge of the Congo* (London, 1967).

3. Under the rule of King Leopold II the Congo's population, more than that of any other African country, was ravaged by the slave trade, and declined by 3 million. During the slave trade some 15 million Congolese were shipped across the Atlantic, of whom 10 million died *en route* from ill treatment. King Leopold did not supress slavery but merely changed its nature. He made forced labour more profitable than the slave trade. By the time of his death in 1908, the stock value of his personal stake in the Congo stood at about 60 million Belgian francs. The state of the Congo was pitiful when he took it over, but it was even more so when he had finished with it. In his book *The Agony of the Congo,* Ritchie Calder has estimated that in the twenty-three years of Leopold's personal rule, 5-8 million Congolese were killed by his security forces and agents engaged in the collection of rubber and ivory. When it is remembered that in 1960, when the Congo became independent, its population was around 13 million, the extent of Leopold's tyranny and inhumanity can be realized. See also E. D. Morel, *Red Rubber: the Story of the Rubber Slave Trade of the Congo* (1906), quoted in Nkrumah, *op.cit.* Public outcry against King Leopold's rule in the Congo reached such a height that on 18 October 1908 Belgium assumed control over the territory by changing its status from a private estate of the king into a colony. Economic conditions improved, but the pattern of political oppression remained unchanged. Throughout its colonial rule, Belgium applied a system of political emasculation in the hope that it would be impossible for African nationalists to fight for emancipation.

4. Nkrumah's book about the Congo, quoted above, is probably the best analysis of the events from the African point of view, the more so it was written by a man who greatly influenced the Congo's policies. For an account of the crisis see also an excellent book by Colin Legum, *The Congo Disaster* (London: Penguin Books, 1962). For the UN role, see Conor Cruise O'Brien's book, *To Katanga and Back* (London: Hutchinson, 1962). (Conor Cruise O'Brien was for a time in charge of UN operations in the Congo.)

5. Antoine Gizenga, the political successor to Patrice Lumumba, was first deputy in a government headed by Cyrille Adoula, formed under UN pressure at Lovanium on 2 August 1961. However, the government soon fell apart due to disagreements between Adoula and Gizenga. The latter then announced the establishment of his own government in Stanleyville on 12 December 1961. On 20 January 1962, he was arrested and detained until July 1964.

6. This is claimed by Nkrumah, *op.cit.,* p. 119.

7. George W. Shepherd, Jr., *Nonaligned Black Africa* (Lexington, Mass., 1970), p. 42.

8. ECM/Res. 5 (III).

9. Quoted by Catharine Hoskyns, *Case Studies in African Diplomacy: I. The*

*Organization of African Unity and the Congo Crisis 1964-65* (Dar-es-Salaam: Oxford University Press, 1969), p. 24.

10. Ibid., p. 25.

11. The OAU press release of 10 September 1964 states that the Secretary of State assured the Commission 'of the desire of the United States Government to co-operate with the Commission in every appropriate way in carrying out the mission entrusted to it by the OAU'.

12. Conference Document NAC 11/Heads/5, 9 October 1964.

13. *Simba* means in Swahili 'lion'.

14. Mike Hoare, *Mercenary* (London, 1968) pp. 130-31.

15. See the articles by Paul Semonin quoted by Catharine Hoskyns, *op.cit.,* pp. 42-53.

16. Tshombe's letter to Ambassador Dogley of 21 November 1964 (reproduced in Catharine Hoskyns, *op.cit.,* pp. 35—6), states: 'The Government of the Democratic Republic of the Congo has accordingly decided to authorize the Belgian Government to send an adequate rescue force to carry out the humanitarian task of evacuating the civilians held as hostages by the rebels and to authorize the American Government to furnish necessary transport for this humanitarian mission.'

17. Conor Cruise O'Brien, 'Mercy and Mercenaries', *The Observer*, London, 6 December, 1964. President Nasser of Egypt wrote to President Nkrumah on 3 December calling the invasion 'strong evidence that the colonial powers will not hesitate to resort to armed force and aggression in order to maintain their policy of robbing Africa of her natural resources' (Kwame Nkrumah, *op.cit.,* p.265).

18. The sponsors of the Resolution were: Afghanistan, Algeria, Burundi, Cambodia, Central African Republic, Congo (Brazzaville), Dahomey (Benin), Ethiopia, Ghana, Guinea, Indonesia, Kenya, Malawi, Mali, Mauritania, Somalia, Sudan, Tanzania, Uganda, the United Arab Republic (Egypt), Yugoslavia and Zambia.

19. UN Document S/6076.

20. ECM/Res. 7 (IV).

21. AHG/Res. 49 (IV).

## Chapter Seven

1. Military operations, peace efforts and the role of the Great Powers and the relief organizations are also described in the author's book on the conflict: Z. Cervenka, *The History of the Nigerian War 1967-70* (Frankfurt: Bernard Graefe, 1971; and Ibadan: Oniboje Press, 1972). An excellent documentary of the conflict has been provided in A. H. M. Kirk-Greene, *Crisis and Conflict in Nigeria: A Documentary Sourcebook 1966-70*, 2 vols (London: Oxford University Press, 1971). Perhaps the best account of the war is that by John de St Jorre, *The Nigerian Civil War* (London: Hodder & Stoughton, 1972). For guidance regarding books on the Nigerian War and its background see Ch. Agoutu, *Nigerian Civil War 1967-70: An Annotated Bibliography* (Boston, Mass., 1973).

2. *Le Monde* of October 17 1968, in an article called 'Des armes seraient acheminées chaque nuit du Gabon au Biafra', reported on the delivery of arms of French and German manufacture by mercenary pilots from Libreville to Biafra. France, however, consistently denied giving any military assistance to the Ojukwu regime.

3. President de Gaulle said at a press conference in Paris in the first week of September 1968 that French recognition could not be excluded in the future. In

his own words, 'France in this affair has assisted to the extent of her possibilities. She has not taken the step of recognition of the Biafran Republic, because she thinks that the gestation of Africa is above all a matter for the Africans . . . This means that for France the decision which has not been taken cannot be excluded in the future.' *West Africa,* 14 September 1968, p. 1036.

4. The word 'genocide' has often been used in relation to Nigeria's war, with little appreciation of its meaning. According to the Geneva Convention on the Prevention and Punishment of Genocide of 1948, acts of genocide are those committed with intent to destroy, in whole or in part, a national, ethnic, racial or religious group, to cause serious bodily or mental harm to members of the group, deliberately to inflict on the group conditions of life calculated to bring about its total or partial destruction, to impose measures intended to prevent births within the group, or forcibly to transfer children of one group to another. For the text of the Convention, see *American Journal of International Law,* 45 (1951).

5. In his welcoming address, General Gowon stated the terms on which he was prepared to listen to the mission. He said: '. . . We have always insisted that our friends are only those who are firmly committed to the maintenance of the territorial integrity and unity of Nigeria. Our true friends are those who publicly and genuinely condemn the attempted secession by the few who have imposed their will on the former Eastern Region of Nigeria. The Kinshasha Resolution of the OAU Summit on the Nigerian situation proves that all African States are true friends of Nigeria. I wish to take this opportunity to express formally our appreciation of the brotherly spirit of the OAU Summit in recognizing the need for Nigeria to be preserved as one country. It is in the interest of all Africa that Nigeria remains one political and economic entity. The OAU has rightly seen our problem as a purely domestic affair and, in accordance with the OAU resolution, your mission is not here to mediate.' Press release by the Federal Republic of Nigeria, 23 November 1967.

6. *Africa Research Bulletin*, Vol. 5, No. 7, p. 1122.

7. ibid.

8. In an article in *The Observer* (London) on 26 April 1968, entitled 'Why we recognized Biafra', Nyerere stated: 'Unity can only be based on the general consent of the people involved. The people must feel that this State, or this Union is theirs and they must be willing to have their quarrels in that context . . . We in this country believe that unity is vital for the future of Africa. But it must be a unity which serves the people and which is freely determined upon by the people . . . it seemed to us that by refusing to recognize the existence of Biafra we were tacitly supporting a war against the people of Eastern Nigeria — and a war conducted in the name of unity. We could not continue doing this any longer.'

9. President Houphouet-Boigny, in his declaration on the recognition of Biafra on 9 May, said: 'Unity is the fruit of the common will to live together; it should not be imposed by force by one group upon another. If we are all in agreement in OAU in recognizing the imperious necessity of unity, unity as the ideal framework for the full development of the African man, we also admit that it should not become his grave. We say yes to unity in peace, unity in love and through brotherhood. Unity is for the living and not for the dead.' The statement was reproduced in *Afrique Express,* Brussels, 25 May 1968, p. 7.

10. AHG/Res. 51 (IV), 1967.

11. *West Africa,* London, 21 September 1968, p. 1091.

12. U Thant called on the OAU to bring about a settlement, and warned that the continuance of the crisis would endanger African unity. He said that the Nigerian conflict had already 'created difficulties in relations between African States, and its continuation is bound to affect badly-needed co-operation and unity among

African countries'. He referred to the 1967 OAU Summit Resolution — which had pledged faith in the Nigerian Federal Government and recognized Nigeria's territorial integrity — and expressed his firm belief 'that the OAU should be the most appropriate instrument for the promotion of peace in Nigeria'.

13. Logically, the policy of non-recognition implies a refusal to admit the validity of change. Whether the change is legal or not is another matter: hence the emphasis on the term 'policy', which should not be confused with law. A secession from an existing State — although constitutionally a breach of the law and therefore, from the point of view of the parent-State, illegal, and an internal matter at that — is not contrary to international law. Some experts go even further and maintain that it is the duty of States to recognize a new State which has come into existence as a result of secession. 'Although rebellion is treason in the eyes of municipal law, it results — when followed by the establishment of an effective government wielding power over the entity of national territory, with a reasonable prospect of permanency and with the consent or the acquiescence of the people — in a duty of other States to recognize the change and to treat the new government as representing the State in the international sphere'. Lauterpacht, *Recognition in International Law* (1974), p. 409.

The OAU's resolute opposition to any kind of secession has been the main reason for Africa's lack of interest in the struggle of the Eritrean people for self-determination and independent existence. For details, see Z. Červenka, 'Eritrea: struggle for self-determination or secession?', in *Afrika Spectrum,* vol. 12, no. 1 (Hamburg, 1977).

14. AHG/Res. 58 (VI), 1969.

15. G. O. Ojukwu, *Biafra: Selected Speeches with Journal of Events* (New York: Harper and Row, 1969).

16. The Agency was acting as a public relations office for the Biafran Government.

17. The whereabouts of Colonel Ojukwu were not known until 24 January 1970, when it was announced that he had been granted asylum in the Ivory Coast, on condition that he would not engage in political activity. He still lives there.

18. A pamphlet published by the Federal Government of Nigeria in 1970, entitled *Victory for Unity.*

19. The number of States within the Nigerian Federation has since risen to 19. Seven new States were created on 3 February 1976. See the speech by General M. Muhammed of 3 February, explaining the reasons for the change, reproduced in full in *The Nigerian Observer,* 4 February 1976.


Chapter Eight

1. For recent facts about apartheid see Julian R. Friedman, 'Basic Facts on the Republic of South Africa and the Policy of Apartheid', in *Unit on Apartheid,* No. 20/74, August 1974, published by the Department of Political and Security Council Affairs of the United Nations. For a detailed list of writings on apartheid see *Unit on Apartheid,* No. 10/74, May 1974.

2. General Assembly Resolution 1976 (XVII) of 6 November 1962.

3. The resolution adopted by the Assembly of Heads of State and Government called on all African States to boycott South African goods and end the supply of minerals and other raw materials to South Africa. It then requested the co-operation of the major trading partners of South Africa in the boycott and established a body within the OAU Secretariat entrusted *inter alia* with the following functions (AHG/Res. 7 [I] ):

(a) to plan co-ordination of sanctions against South Africa among the Member States, and to ensure the strictest implementation of all relevant resolutions of the OAU.

(b) to harmonize co-operation with friendly States with a view to implementing an effective boycott of South Africa.

(c) to collect and disseminate information about governmental and private financial, economic and commercial institutions, which trade with South Africa.

(d) to promote, in co-operation with other international bodies, the campaign for international economic sanctions against South Africa by all appropriate means, in particular by countering the propaganda and pressures of the South African Government.'

4. At the request of the African States the Security Council met on 7 August 1963 to discus a joint draft resolution submitted by Ghana, Morocco and the Philippines. It asked the Security Council to call 'upon all States to cease forthwith the sale and shipment of arms, ammunition of all types and military vehicles to South Africa, to boycott any South African goods and to refrain from exporting to South Africa any strategic materials of direct military significance.' The delegation of the United States opposed the second part of the resolution; and with the support of Great Britain, France, China (then still the Taiwan regime) and Brazil, the call for boycott of South African goods was struck out. The Security Council's resolution S/5386 of 7 August 1963 imposed an embargo on the exports of arms to South Africa with Great Britain and France abstaining.

5. On 25 October 1974 three African members of the Security Council (Cameroon, Kenya and Mauretania) introduced a resolution calling for the immediate expulsion of South Africa on the grounds that apartheid is contrary to the principles and purposes of the UN Charter, and because South Africa refuses to withdraw its forces from Namibia and supports the illegal regime in Rhodesia. In explaining their veto the Western Powers stated that, unless South Africa showed some willingness to change its racially discriminatory policies and abide by UN resolutions on Namibia, it could not necessarily count on their veto in the future.

6. The Resolution on South Africa (CM/Res 428 [XXV]) also expressed grave concern that France, the United States, the Federal Republic of Germany and the United Kingdom 'in their anti-African role as allies of the Pretoria regime have stepped up their activities designed at increasing the repressive and aggressive potential of the Pretoria regime'.

7. The conference also said that 'arguments that vital economic interests are at stake' were 'highly exaggerated'. For the proceedings of the conference see Ronald Segal (ed.), *Sanctions against South Africa* (London: Penguin Books, 1964).

8. Resolution on Sanctions against South Africa, CM/Res. 485.

9. CM/Res 102 (IX), September 1967.

10. As explained earlier in Chapter II (Section 5), the OAU Charter does not provide for the expulsion of its members. It is not without interest that Zambia, the sharpest critic of Malawi at the Kinshasa meeting, had a 'dialogue' of its own with South Africa. It consisted of an exchange of letters between President Kaunda and South African Premier Vorster during 1968. They were primarily concerned with Rhodesia. In January 1971 after President Kaunda's return from the Commonwealth Conference in Singapore where he, together with President Nyerere of Tanzania, played a leading part in the storm of criticism of the British decision to resume arms supplies to South Africa, Vorster threatened to expose Dr Kaunda as a 'double-talker'. When Kaunda remained calm, Vorster made their

correspondence public on 21 April 1971 in the House of Assembly. He quoted parts of the letters and showered President Kaunda with insults. If his purpose was to destroy the credibility of Kaunda in Africa, the final effect, despite the initial shock, was the reverse. Dr Kaunda replied by publishing the correspondence in full, and thus exposing Vorster's misrepresentation of the facts. For an account of the Zambian-South African contacts see Douglas G. Anglin, 'Zambia and Southern African détente', *International Journal* (Ottawa: Canadian Institute of International Affairs), Vol. XXX, No. 3, 1975. The full text of all the letters between President Kaunda and Premier Vorster was released by the Zambian Government of 23 April 1971 in a publication entitled *'Dear Mr Vorster . . .'*

11. The intransigence of the Western powers arises not only from their business and financial interests in South Africa but also from strategic considerations, made the more pressing by the closure of the Suez Canal between 1967 and 1975 and the presence of the Soviet Navy in the Indian Ocean. While the Suez Canal was closed, the sea-route around the Cape of Good Hope assumed a vital importance to the West, both for oil supplies and for Western military strategy in the Indian Ocean. The October War in 1973 between Israel, Syria and Egypt, and the ensuing Arab oil boycott against the United States, Western Europe and South Africa, suddenly highlighted the strategic importance of the Cape route. Before the oil crisis in 1973, the total monthly volume of oil shipped around the Cape amounted to some 20 million tons, of which about 90 per cent was destined for European ports. About 20,000 ships a year call at the Cape, and another 14,000 pass without calling. The large supertankers carrying up to 350,000 dwt. will still have to use the Cape Route, as the Canal is limited to ships in the 60,000-dwt. class at most.

The possibility that the 'vacuum' in the Indian Ocean might be filled by the Soviet Union after Britain's withdrawal from east of Suez was expressed, for example, by the South African Admiral H. H. Biermann as follows: 'Communist penetration into the Southern Hemisphere, and the threats that this portends, have caused the Southern Hemisphere, and particularly the Indian Ocean, to emerge dramatically from a position of relative obscurity and to assume a conspicuous position in the East-West power struggle. The focal point in this changed perspective is occupied by Southern Africa – and the Republic of South Africa.' (Quoted by Signe Landgren in *Southern Africa: the Escalation of a Conflict*, Stockholm, SIPRI, 1975). For more details on the military strategy in Southern Africa see also J. E. Spence, *The Political and Military Framework* (London: Africa Publication Trust, 1975). For a study of the US financial interests in Southern Africa, see Barbara Rogers, *White Wealth and Black Poverty: American Investment in Southern Africa* (Westport, Conn.: Greenwood Press, 1976).

12. Of all Western powers, West Germany has emerged as the most important ally of South Africa in Europe and as a friend most ready to offer the South African policy of 'détente' a helping hand. Since 1951 the volume of West German exports to South Africa has increased twenty-sevenfold, and in 1974 it stood at £620 million; West Germany has become South Africa's biggest trading partner. South African exports to West Germany increased only eleven times, the deficit being made up by loans, half of which are funded by banks. In 1974, the government and private companies in South Africa owed West Germany almost £400 million. At the same time Western Germany has stepped up its contributions to the military potential of South Africa. See B. Rogers and Z. Červenka, *The Nuclear Axis: secret collaboration between West Germany and South Africa* (London: J. Friedmann, 1977).

13. *Apartheid and racial discrimination in the Republic of South Africa:* CM/Res. 66 (V).

14. *Resolution on apartheid and racial discrimination,* adopted by the Council of Ministers at its 10th session, Addis Ababa, February 1968. CM/Res. 142 (X).

15. Ever since the establishment of the OAU the statehood of the Republic of South Africa has been in doubt. While none of the OAU resolutions on South Africa have questioned it in so many words, the OAU Members were unanimous in their opinion that South Africa was not eligible for OAU membership. The Lusaka Manifesto's concession that South Africa is an independent State albeit one with deplorable racists policies was the first OAU pronouncement on the issue. It has been vigorously challenged by the Pan-Africanist Congress of Azania (PAC), which submitted to the OAU Summit at Kampala in 1975 a document stating that South Africa's political status is 'that of a semi-colonial country owned by the imperialist consortium of her investors and trading partners who own more than 80 per cent of South African property in company with the white bourgeoisie of which the government is a significant part.' African National Congress of South Africa (ANC) also questioned the legal status of South Africa, and joined PAC in pressing the OAU to take a stand on the issue. The Resolution adopted by the OAU Summit at Port Louis, Mauritius in July 1976 resolved the matter by adopting the 'Resolution on the international status of racist South Africa' (CM/Res 500 [XXVII] ) and setting up a Commission of African Legal experts to review this question and present a report to the next meeting of the Council of Ministers. It is very unlikely, however, that the OAU will endorse the views of PAC and ANC and reverse its recognition of South Africa as an independent State.

16. President Houphouet-Boigny's statement on Dialogue appeared in *Jeune Afrique,* Paris, 17 November 1970. However, the word 'Dialogue' came into use in this connection in 1969 when Foreign Minister, Dr Hilgard Müller, told the UN: 'South Africa's dialogue with other African States will grow in the future, despite the Republic's policy of separate development.'

17. *Le Monde,* Paris, 7 November 1970.

18. President Maga of Dahomey (Benin) at the meeting of the Entente Council in Ougadougou, quoted by Colin Legum, *op cit.,* n. 18.

19. Peter Enahoro, 'Dialogue', *Africa* (London, 1971), No. 2 (July), p. 15.

20. Press Release by the Federal Ministry of Information, No. 466, 12 May 1971.

21. Speaking at a banquet given for him by President Kenyatta, General Gowon said: '. . . It will be a great betrayal if we only pay lip-service to the cause of liberation of the people of South Africa, or if we assume that we can restore their dignity by bargaining on economic or other selfish grounds with their oppressors. . . Nigeria will not be a party to any dialogue with those whose only aim is to divide our ranks and subjugate our brothers, forever, in servitude and degradation. . .' (ibid).

22. CM/St. 5 (XVII), 1971.

23. The text of the Mogadishu Declaration was published as UN Document UN/93 (137) of 23 February 1972.

24. See Ruth Weiss, 'South Africa: The Grand Economic Design', *Africa Contemporary Record,* 1970-71, Colin Legum (ed.), (London: Rex Collings 1971), pp. A11-A17.

25. Resolution on South Africa (CM/Res. 299 [XXI]).The OAU initiated the holding, jointly with the United Nations, of an international conference of experts on colonialism and apartheid in Southern Africa in Oslo on 9-14 April 1973. The agenda of the Oslo Conference included an assessment of the situation

in the various fields of action on decolonization and apartheid. For the conference proceedings see Olav Stokke and C.-G. Widstrand (eds), *Southern Africa (UN-OAU Conference, 9-14 April 1973)*, 2 vols, (Uppsala: the Scandinavian Institute of African Studies, 1973).

26. (CM/Res. 422 [XXV]). It further invited 'all Member-States to take individual and collective action with the Western Powers and Japan in order to persuade them to stop immediately the massive support they continue to grant the racist minority regimes of Southern Africa'.

27. CM/Res. 476 (XXVI).

28. Rhodesia is still referred to in all UN documents as 'Southern Rhodesia'. The OAU has described the territory as 'Zimbabwe' since 1970. Of recent books about Rhodesia and UDI, see particularly P. O'Meara, *Rhodesia: Racial Conflict or Co-existence?* (New York: Cornell University Press. 1975); D. Mutasa, *Rhodesian Black Behind the Bars* (London: Mowbrays, 1974); L. Vambe, *From Rhodesia to Zimbabwe* (London: Heinemann, 1976); D. Keyworth Davies, *Race Relations in Rhodesia 1972-73* (London: Rex Collings, 1975); M. Loney, *Rhodesia, White Racism & Imperial Response* (London: Penguin African Library, 1975): Larry W. Bowman, *Politics in Rhodesia: White power in African State* (Cambridge, Mass.: Harvard University Press, 1973); Robert C. Good, *The International Politics of the Rhodesian Rebellion* (London: Faber and Faber, 1973); G. M. Daniels (ed.), *Drums of War: The Continuing Crisis in Rhodesia* (New York: The Third Press, 1975) and E. Windrich, *The Rhodesian Problem: A Documentary Record 1923-1973* (London: Routledge and Kegan Paul, 1975). For an African point of view, see B. V. Mtshali, *Rhodesia: Background to the Conflict* (New York: Hawthorn Books, 1967), and E. Mlambo, *Rhodesia: the Struggle for a Birthright* (London: Hurst, 1972). For a white Rhodesian point of view see M. I. Hirsch, *A decade of crisis* (Salisbury: P. Dearlove, 1973).

29. *Resolution on Southern Rhodesia*, CM/Res. 14 (II).

30. CM/Res. 33 (III).

31. CM/Res. 50 (IV).

32. *Special Resolution on Southern Rhodesia* (ECM/Res. 11 [VII]), which expressed its grave concern over the split between ZAPU and ZANU; and *General resolution on Southern Rhodesia* (ECM/Res. II [V]), which is largely addressed to Great Britain asking it to meet its responsibilities in Rhodesia.

33. CM/Res. 62 (V).

34. AHG/Res. 8 (I)

35. AHG/Res. 25. Rev. II.

36. At the OAU Summit in Accra held only 2 weeks before UDI, the Rhodesian crisis received an absolute priority in all speeches of the African leaders as well as in their private consultations.

37. The following were the other measures decided upon by the Council:

— that all economic relations with Southern Rhodesia (including trade and payment transactions) should be stopped forthwith, and especially that the country should be denied sterling area facilities in respect of Commonwealth trade.

— that all accounts of Southern Rhodesia in Africa's banks should be blocked;

— that all travel documents issued or renewed by that illegal government should be treated as invalid.

— that all means of transportation, including aircraft, to or from Southern Rhodesia, should be denied all servicing and other facilities including the rights to overfly.

— that all OAU Member-States should cut off all communication channels, including telegraph, telephone, teleprinter or radio-telephone, with Southern

Rhodesia. (ECM/Res [IV])

38. For an excellent analysis of the pros and cons regarding the use of force in Rhodesia see Douglas G. Anglin, 'Britain and the Use of Force in Rhodesia', in Michael G. Fry (ed.), *Freedom and Change: Essays in Honour of Lester B. Pearson* (Toronto: McClelland and Stewart, 1975), pp. 43-75.

39. CM/Res. 75 (VI)

40. Security Council Resolution 216 (1965).

41. Security Council Resolution 217 (1965). The Resolution also requested all States not to recognize UDI and refrain from establishing diplomatic or any other relations with the Salisbury regime. All States were also asked to refrain from any action which would assist or encourage the illegal regime, to break all economic relations with Rhodesia (including an embargo on oil), and to stop providing it with arms.

42. In the 'Resolution on Rhodesia' (from then on calling it 'Zimbabwe') adopted by the OAU Summit in Rabat in 1970. CM/Res. 207 (XIV).

43. Quoted by *The Times* (London) of 1 December 1973, in an article entitled 'Britain criticizes UN assembly for its pointless resolutions'. The British objections to intervention into 'Rhodesian internal affairs' had been made clear eleven years earlier, in 1962. On 25 October of that year, the British delegate in the Fourth Committee, Godberg, rejected the UN decision to include Southern Rhodesia in the category of 'non-self-governing territories' and described the white minority regime as follows: 'Since 1923 Southern Rhodesia has had its own Government, legislature and administration as well as an army and police and has enjoyed the rights and privileges under both the 1923 and the 1961 Constitutions to an extent unparalleled in other British non-self-governing territories.'

44. *Resolution on sanctions against Rhodesia* (CM/Res. 348 [XXIII]), 11 June 1974.

45. CM/Res. 349 (XXIII). A third resolution adopted at Mogadishu concerned the oil embargo which the oil-producing countries were requested to impose on the white minority regimes of Southern Africa (CM/Res. 350 [XXIII]).

46. *Resolution on sanctions against the white minority regimes in Southern Africa*, CM/Res. 422 (XXIV).

47. For an account of the 'détente' negotiations, see Colin Legum, *Vorster's Gamble for Africa: How the Search for Peace Failed* (London: Rex Collings, 1976). The Zambian role is examined by Douglas G. Anglis in 'Zambia and Southern Africa détente', *International Journal* (Toronto), No. 3, 1975.

48. 'Some Aspects of Liberation', a speech by President Nyerere at Oxford University on 19 November 1975, published by Government Printer, Dar-es-Salaam.

49. On 9 December 1974, Abel Muzorewa (President of ANC), Ndabaningi Sithole (President of ZANU), Joshua Nkomo (President of ZAPU) and James Chikerema (President of FROLIZI) agreed to unite in the ANC, which they recognized as 'the unifying force of the people of Zimbabwe'. After agreeing on the structure of the enlarged ANC, the leaders of all movements recognized 'the inevitability of continued armed struggle and all other forms of struggle until the total liberation of Zimbabwe'. The full text of the agreement was published in the Dar-es-Salaam *Daily News*, 10 December 1974.

50. The full text of the speech was published in the Dar-es-Salaam *Daily News*, 9 April 1975.

51. The text of Minister's Mwaanga's speech was published in full in the Dar-es-Salaam *Daily News*, 9 April 1975. The speech also sums up the concessions agreed to by the white minority regime of Rhodesia with South Africa's

assistance, which included Smith's acceptance of the necessity to negotiate with the ANC leadership; the lifting of the ban on ZANU and ZAPU; the release of political prisoners and detainees; a general amnesty to African political activists abroad, and 'the creation of conditions conducive to free political activity and expression in Rhodesia'. The speech of the Ivory Coast Foreign Minister was quoted by Colin Legum in *Vorster's Gamble for Africa*, op.cit., p. 21.

52. The Resolution appeals to all Member-States 'to instruct their Ambassadors accredited in West European Countries to spare no effort in opposing the Pretoria regime's manoeuvres aimed at white-washing the apartheid regime'. It also asks them to 'render maximum support to the people of South Africa for the intensification of the armed struggle'. CM/Res. 428 (XXV).

53. President Nyerere in an interview with *The Observer*, on 7 March, disclosed that Zimbabwe guerrillas numbering 16,000 men had established in camps in Mozambique their 'own united military leadership'. They were referred to by President Nyerere as a 'third force' which would have a final say on whatever agreement might be reached on the settlement of the Rhodesian crisis.

54. *Resolution on Southern Africa*, CM/Res. 455 (XXVI).

55. The United States policy on Southern Africa had until late 1974 been guided by a National Security Study Memorandum 39, prepared in 1969 under the auspices of Kissinger. Its view of the situation in the area, fully shared by Kissinger himself, was stated as follows: 'The whites are here to stay and the only way that constructive change can come about is through them. There is no hope for the blacks to gain the political rights they seek through violence, which will only lead to chaos and increased opportunites for the Communists. We can by selective relaxation of our stance towards the white regimes, encourage some modification of their current racial and colonial policies, and through more substantial economic assistance to the black States help to draw the two groups together and exert some influence on both for peaceful change.' For an excellent study of the Memorandum, see El-Khawas-B. Cohen (ed.), *The Kissinger Study of Southern Africa* (Westport, Conn.: Lawrence Hill, 1976).

Despite Mozambique's independence, and the victory of MPLA in Angola over the West-sponsored and South-Africa-backed UNITA and FNLA, the US strategy changed only slightly. While the progressive governments of Mozambique and Angola were grudgingly acknowledged, the US administration still believed that this could never happen in Rhodesia, let alone in South Africa. It was largely from a wish to prevent a repetition of the Soviet triumph in Angola, which had reduced the sphere of Western influence to Rhodesia, South Africa and Namibia, that the United States intervened in the negotiations over Rhodesia. Closely connected with this, of course, are the huge US financial and economic interests in southern Africa, which a socialist-oriented government in Rhodesia would put into serious jeopardy.

56. There was a detailed account of Kissinger's mission and his talks with Ian Smith in *The Observer* of 26 September 1976, under the title: 'Rhodesia: Why the game is up'. Kissinger's peace plan provided for a supreme council of state made up equally of blacks and whites, with a white chairman. The council of state was to appoint a council of ministers with a majority of Africans and an African Prime Minister. It was supposed to draw up a constitution based on majority rule within two years. Ian Smith told the Rhodesians that he had received categorical assurances from Dr Kissinger that as soon as the necessary preliminaries had been completed economic sanctions would be lifted and the guerrilla war would end: with the lifting of sanctions there would be an injection of development capital that would provide an immediate stimulus to the economy. This interpretation of

Kissinger's plan for settlement was described by the five African front-line Presidents who met on 25 September 1976 at Lusaka 'as tantamount to legalizing the colonialist and racist structures of power'. They called on Britain to convene a conference outside Rhodesia to work out the structure and functions of the transitional government in Rhodesia. It is not without interest that ZIPA reacted sharply against the idea; on 29 September 1976 its spokesman, Dzinashe Machingura, said at Maputo that 'Britain had no right to convene a conference to decide the future of Rhodesia because the British Government was a colonial power and what we are fighting against is British colonialism.'

57. The full text of Ian Smith's speech was published in *The Times* (London), 24 September 1976.

58. *Resolution on Zimbabwe,* CM/Res. 457 (XXVI).

59. The Geneva conference was chaired by Sir Ivor Richard, British Ambassador to the United Nations, and attended by all factions of the ANC. At the time of the conference, the ANC presented itself as the 'Patriotic Front', made up of a group represented by Robert Mugabe of ZANU and Joshua Nkomo of ZAPU. Throughout the conference there was mounting pressure on the British Government to play a more 'positive' role in Rhodesia, largely by sending out British troops to be the guardians of the peaceful transfer of power to the black majority. A typical sample of this campaign was Bridget Bloom's article 'Britain's urgent dilemma over Rhodesia', published in *The Financial Times* (London), 23 November 1976.

60. For guidance on the recent literature on Portuguese African colonies, see Michel Flores, 'A Bibliographic contribution to the study of Portuguese Africa 1965-1972', in *A Current Bibliography on African Affairs* (Washington: African Biographical Center, Spring 1974), Volume 7, No 2.

61. The General Assembly rejected this argument, and on 15 December 1960 ruled that the Portuguese territories were non-self-governing and fell under the competence of the United Nations Charter provision concerning non-self-governing territories. (Chapters XI and XII of the UN Charter).

62. In 1970 the GDP of Portugal was £246 million, compared with £1,300 million for Nigeria and £511 million for Uganda.

63. See an excellent study published by the Dutch 'Angola Comite', Klarenburg, Amsterdam (S. S. Bosgra and C. H. van Krimpen, 'Portugal and NATO'). For a more recent study, see A. Humbaraci and N. Muchnik, *Portugal's African Wars* (London: Macmillan, 1974).

64. *Resolution on decolonization,* CM/Res 234 (V).

65. Those that abstained from voting on the Resolution were Chad, Zaire, Dahomey (Benin), Gabon, Ivory Coast, Lesotho, Malagasy, Malawi, Niger, Senegal, Swaziland, Togo, Tunisia, Upper Volta, Morocco, Cameroon, and Central African Republic — a significant dissent in the light of Article X (2) of the OAU Charter, which provides that 'all resolutions shall be determined by a two-thirds majority', which in this case was not secured.

66. The Cabora Bassa hydro-electric scheme involved the construction of the largest hydro-electric complex in southern Africa, with a total power capacity of 3,600mw. Its purpose was to transform the economy of Mozambique by settling one million white immigrants from Portugal, linking it more closely with South Africa by a huge injection of capital from the European and American companies operating in southern Africa. The 1970 OAU Summit in Addis Ababa adopted a declaration on the Dabora Bassa Hydro-Electric Dam (CM/St. 3 (XIV), in which the purpose of the project was defined as follows: 'The Cabora Bassa Dam is aimed at oppressing the people of Mozambique, the people of the rest of southern Africa and ultimately the entire people of Africa. This project is not only going

against the interests of the people of Africa and the Resolutions of the Organization of African Unity, but also the United Nations' many resolutions, with particular reference to economic and other interests impeding the implementation of the United Nations Declaration on the granting of independence to colonial countries and peoples. The dam will further increase the threat to international peace and security by strengthening the arm of those who are already committing crimes against humanity.' The Declaration condemned the countries participating in the project, namely West Germany, France, Italy, the United States and Britain. Following a campaign to dissuade Western countries from participating in the project, only the Swedish and Italian firms withdrew. They were commended in a resolution on decolonization adopted the same year (CM/Res. 234 (XV). See also K. Middlemans, *Cabora Bassa: Engineering and Politics in Southern Africa* (London: Weidenfeld & Nicholson, 1975).

67. For a detailed account of the event, see *Africa Contemporary Record 1970-71* (Rex Collings: London 1972), pp. B365-B371.

68. Resolutions ECM/Res. 17 (VII) and ECM/18 (VII), adopted at Lagos, 12 December 1970.

69. Security Council Resolution SC/290, 8 December 1970.

70. For the text of the report by Father Hastings and excerpts from the statements made at the Special Session of the Decolonization Committee, see *Objective: Justice,* a quarterly publication covering UN activity against apartheid, racial discrimination and colonialism, published by the UN Secretariat, New York, September 1973.

71. Quoted in *Africa Contemporary Record 1970-71*, p. C46.

72. There was a contradiction between Sweden's policy of providing humanitarian aid to PAIGC and of withholding recognition from Guinea-Bissau. This was partly due to British diplomatic pressure and partly, if not almost entirely, due to the Swedish economic interest in Portugal, which from the late 1960's was one of the main sources of cheap labour employed by Swedish companies in Portugal, for example in the textile and shoe industries.

73. GA Resolution 3031 of 2 November 1973.

74. OAU praise of Portuguese policy was also prompted by the address of Portuguese Foreign Minister Mario Soares to the 29th UN General Assembly, 23 September 1974. For its text see *Objective: Justice* (New York, 1974), Vol. 6, No. 4.

75. The transitional government was to be directed by a presidential council (composed of one representative each from the three liberation movements, working closely with a Portuguese-appointed High Commissioner) and by a twelve-member council of ministers. The agreement stipulated that machinery should be established to integrate the armed forces of the liberation movements — the thorniest problem of all. The agreement also gave to the transitional government the responsibility of establishing a commission to draft an electoral law, organizing electoral lists and registering lists of candidates (from the MPLA, UNITA and the FNLA only) for elections to be held not later than October 1975.

76. The text of the Nakuru agreement was published in *Africa*, No. 47 (London, July 1975).

77. Resolution CM/424 (XXV) on the Situation in Angola.

78. AHG Res. 72 (XII).

79. In his letter to *The Times* (London) of 6 January 1976, Michael Nicholson offered the following evidence of communist arms supplies to Angola: 'In April 1975 the Yugoslav freighter *Postoyna* docked in Luanda with a cargo of Russian military equipment. It was able to offload only trucks and crated S-A7 missiles before the Portuguese High Commissioner ordered its departure. The remainder of that cargo was offloaded at Pointe Noire, in Congo Brazzaville. A week later

two more Yugoslav freighters, the *Jaldo* and the *Mila Gojsalic,* successfully offloaded four hundred tons of Russian military supplies in Luanda. In the middle of May the East German freighter *Elbe* offloaded an unspecified tonnage of Russian arms in Luanda. In May and June eight Soviet cargo ships, including the *Josif Dubrovinsky,* docked at Pointe Noire offloading Russian arms, ammunition and armoured vehicles. And during March, April and May, 27 Soviet transport aircraft (AN12s, AN24s, IL18s) landed in Congo Brazzaville with military supplies for onward routing to the MPLA in Luanda and Cela.'

80. Both the Congo and Zaire governments expressed public support for the Cabindan people's 'right to self-determination'. The Congolese Prime Minister, Henri Lopes, stated in Paris on April 29 that 'Cabinda is historically and geographically different from Angola', and that the Cabindan people must have the right to determine their future relations with Angola. Mobutu supported a referendum in Cabinda in a speech on May 7, stating that Cabinda was not an integral part of Angola. (The two rival factions of FLEC have offices and bases in Congo and Zaire). See *Africa,* No. 47 (London, July 1975), p. 37. The Nigerian monthly, *Afriscope,* of January 1976, quoted evidence supplied by the Prime Minister of the MPLA Government, Lopodo Nascimiento, that maps captured from the FNLA leadership showed Angola without its northern part and without Cabinda.

81. For an interesting insight into Washington policy on Angola and its relevance to the Sino-Soviet dispute, see Colin Legum, 'A letter on Angola to American liberals', *The New Republic* (Washington), 31 January 1976.

82. For a survey of post-conference statements see *Africa Research Bulletin,* Vol. 13, No. 1 (February 1976), pp. 3884-3887. For a broader assessment of the war in Angola and postwar development, see Colin Legum, *After Angola: The War over Southern Africa — The Role of the Big Powers* (London: Rex Collings, 1976).

83. See for example Solomon Slonin, *South-West Africa and the United Nations: an International Mandate in Dispute* (Baltimore: John Hopkins University Press, 1973), which includes a detailed bibliography. For an African point of view, see A. U. Obozuwa, *The Namibian Question: Legal and Political Aspects* (Benin City, Nigeria: Ethiope Publishing Corporation, 1973),and I. Sagay, *The Legal Aspects of the Namibian Dispute* (University of Ife Press, Nigeria, 1975). For a South African point of view, see John Dugard, *The South-West Africa Namibia Dispute* (Los Angeles: University of California Press, 1973).

84. The Mandate system arose out of the international situation following the First World War. It was clearly necessary to modify the arbitrary forms of colonial rule, to respond to the aspirations of national liberation movements in colonial territories and to give hope to the colonial peoples that they would be able to achieve their freedom by peaceful means. The mandate was a new institution of international law entirely different from the agency or trusteeship as known in national law. It differed also from the protectorate, although some of the International Court of Justice in the 'advisory opinion' concerning the status of South-West Africa of 11 July 1950, considered 'the mandate was created in the interest of the inhabitants of the territory, and of humanity in general as an international institution with an international object — a sacred trust of civilisation'.

85. General Assembly Resolution 65(I) of 4 December 1946.

86. South-West Africa came before the International Court of Justice for the first time in 1949 when the General Assembly, by its Resolution 338 (IV) of 14 December 1949, asked the Court for an advisory opinion on the legal status of the territory. The Court confirmed that South Africa remained subject to the

international obligations set forth in Article 22 of the Covenant of the League of Nations and the Mandate, and was under an obligation to submit to the supervision and control of the General Assembly of the UN with regard to the exercise of the Mandate. The second occasion was in 1954, when the General Assembly, by its Resolution 904(IX) of 23 November, requested the Court to give a further advisory opinion as to whether 'Decisions of the General Assembly on questions relating to reports and petitions concerning the territory of South West Africa shall be regarded as important questions within the meaning of Article 18, par. 2 of the Charter of the United Nations'. The question was answered by the International Court of Justice, in its advisory opinion of 7 June, 1955, in the affirmative.

On the initiative of the Committee on South-West Africa, the General Assembly, by its resolutions of 5 December 1955, asked the International Court of Justice for yet another advisory opinion on South-West Africa, this time to ascertain whether the Committee was competent to interview the petitioners and whether such activity was in accordance with the advisory opinion of 11 July 1950. In its opinion on this point, delivered on 1 June 1956, the Court confirmed the competence of the Committee to grant oral hearings to petitioners.

87. International Court of Justice (ICJ) *Reports,* 1966, p. 323.

88. The 'Resolution on South-West Africa' (CM/Res.87), also pledged 'wholehearted co-operation with the United Nations in discharging its responsibilities with respect to South-West Africa'.

89. Advisory opinion of 21 June 1971 on 'Legal consequences for States of the continued presence of South Africa in Namibia (South-West Africa) notwithstanding Security Council Resolution 276 (1970)'. *ICJ Reports,* 1971.

80. Security Council Resolution 309 (1972) of 4 February 1972.

91. Resolution on Namibia, CM/Res. 300 (XXI).

92. Quoted in *Africa,* No. 22 (London, June 1973).

93. For the involvement of the Western countries in Namibia, see the study by R. Murry, J. Morris, J. Dugard and N. Rubin, 'The Role of Foreign Firms in Namibia', published by the Study Project on External Investment in South Africa and Namibia, *Africa Publication Trust,* (London 1974).

94. Security Council Resolution 366 (1974).

95. The following are the main points of the SWAPO document:
— South Africa must recognize the right of the Namibian people to independence and national sovereignty and Namibian terrtitorial integrity;
— South Africa must accept that SWAPO of Namibia is the sole authentic representative of the Namibian People;
— All political prisoners must be released and the banning order on SWAPO acting-President Immanuel Gottlieb Nathanael Nacuilili, must be set aside;
— the so-called R17 Emergency Regulations still operating in Northern Namibia must be recalled;
— all Namibians, of whatever political organization, now in exile, must be able to return freely to their country, without fear of arrest and any other form of victimization;
— South Africa must commit herself to the withdrawal of all her troops and police from Namibian territory.
Published in *Namibia Bulletin* (New York: United Nations), No. 1 (1975).

96. *Rand Daily Mail,* Johannesburg, 21 May 1975.

97. The text of the Declaration was as follows:
1. WE, the true and authentic Representatives of the inhabitants of South West Africa hereby solemnly DECLARE:
2. THAT in the exercise of our right to selfdetermination and independence we

are voluntarily gathered in this Conference in order to discuss the Constitutional future of South West Africa;

3. THAT we most strongly condemn and reject the use of force or any improper interference in order to overthrow the existing order or to enforce a new dispensation;

4. THAT we are firmly resolved to determine our future ourselves by peaceful negotiations and co-operation;

5. THAT mindful of the particular circumstances of each of the population groups it is our firm resolve, in the execution of our task, to serve and respect their wishes and interests;

6. THAT mindful of the interdependence of the various population groups and the interests of South West Africa in its entirety we resolve to create a form of government which will guarantee to every population group the greatest possible say in its own and national affairs which will fully protect the rights of minorities and which will do right and justice to all.

AND FURTHER WE DECLARE:

THAT we are resolved to devote continuous attention to social and economic conditions which will best promote the welfare, interests and peaceful co-existence of all the inhabitants of South West Africa and their posterity:

THAT we are resolved to exert ourselves towards the promotion of and deference towards human rights and fundamental freedoms of all without discrimination merely on the basis of race, colour, or creed.

WE THEREFORE RESOLVE:

(a) to draft a Constitution for South West Africa as soon as appropriate and if possible within a period of three years;

(b) to devote continuous attention to measures implementing all the aims specified in this declaration.

98. The National Convention consists of the following organizations opposed to South African rule of Namibia: the National Unity Democratic Organization (NUDO), the South-West African National Union (SWANU), the Basters Volks Party, the Voice of the People (representing the Namas and Damaras) and SWAPO.

99. The documents of the Turnhalle conference were published under the title 'Constitutional Conference of South West Africa' (Staatkundige Beraad, SWA, 1975). For the SWAPO attitue towards the conference and its reasons for rejecting the agreement, see an interview with Theo-Ben Gurirab, Secretary for Policy Matters of SWAPO, in *Africa*, No. 61 (London, September 1976), pp 32-33.

100. For a detailed analysis of the United States' 'covert operations against Namibia' see a confidential UN Memorandum published in *Counter Spy* (Washington, 1976), vol. 3, no. 2.

101. For the full text of Samora Machel's speech, see *The Daily News*, Dar-es-Salaam, 19 May 1977.

102. For the special West German interests in Namibian uranium see B. Rogers and Z. Cervenka, *The Nuclear Axis* (London: J. Friedmann, 1977).

## Chapter Nine

1. *Resolution on the continued occupation by Israel of part of the territory of the Arab Republic of Egypt,* AHG/Res. 70 (X).

2. Theodor Herzl in his programmatic novel *Altneuland,* published in 1902.

3. For a detailed analysis of Israeli development aid see Z. Y. Herschlag (ed.),

*Israel-Africa Co-operation* (Research Project of the Department of Developing Countries, Tel-Aviv University, 1970).

4. The Builders' Brigade was formed by the Ghana Government in 1957 and after 1960 reorganized into the 'Agricultural Army'. Its purpose was, briefly, to offer the youth of Ghana, particularly middle-school leavers, vocational training and 'preparation for mature citizenship'; it was also to maintain and operate large agricultural settlements and other sound public works, and to assist in establishing border settlements devoted to co-operative farming. By 31 December 1959, 12,000 young people had already been enrolled.

5. Quoted in Doudou Thima, *The Foreign Policy of African States* (London: Phoenix House, 1965), p. 66.

6. The full text of the resolution was reproduced in Colin Legum, *Pan-Africanism* (New York: Praeger, 1968), p. 188.

7. AHG/St. 2 (IV).

8. Two resolutions were adopted by the OAU in 1968. The first, entitled 'Resolution on the aggression against the United Arab Republic', was adopted by the Council of Ministers at its 10th Session in Addis Ababa in February (CM/Res. 134 [X]). It was subsequently endorsed by the Algiers Summit in September, where the resolution referred to in the text was also adopted (AHG/Res. 53 [V]).

9. AHG/Res. 56 (VI).

10. The following are the operative paragraphs of the UN Security Council Resolution 242 of 22 November 1967:
— withdrawal of Israeli armed forces from territories of recent conflict.
— termination of all claims and hostilities and the respect of the sovereignty, territorial integrity and political independence of every State in the area and their right to live in peace with secure and recognized boundaries free from threats or acts of force;
— the guarantee of freedom of navigation through international waterways in the area;
— just settlement of the refugee problem;
— the guarantee of the territorial inviolability and political independence of every State in the area through measures including the establishment of demilitarized zones.

11. AHG/Res. 62 (VII), 1970.

12. AHG/Res. 66 (VIII), 1971.

13. See Yassin El-Ayouty, 'The OAU and the Arab-Israeli Conflict: A Case of Mediation that Failed', in Y. El-Ayouty (ed.), *The Organization of African Unity After Ten Years* (New York, 1975). For an Israeli point of view, see Susan A. Gitelson, 'The OAU Mission and the Middle East Conflict', *International Organisation* (Boston, 1973), Vol. XXVII, No. 3.

14. The resolution on the Middle East adopted by the Council of Ministers at its 8th Extraordinary Session in Addis Ababa in November 1973 'draws the attention of world public opinion to the dangerous concept of preventive war applied by Israel and the minority racist regimes in Southern Africa'.

15. The lack of agreement among the members of the Committee of Ten about the OAU peace plan (which had been based on the report of the sub-committee) was shown by the split among the African delegations on the voting on the Middle East problem at the UN in December 1971. Cameroon, Nigeria and Senegal joined Ethiopia, Mauritania and Tanzania in sponsoring a twenty-one-country Afro–Asian resolution, incorporating amendments by six West European delegations, which reaffirmed that 'the acquisition of territory by force is inadmissible and that 'territories thus occupied must be restored'. It then simply called for the 'withdrawal of Israeli armed forces from territories occupied

in the recent conflict' and for the 'termination of all claims and of the state of belligerency, and for respect for and acknowledgement of the sovereignty, territorial integrity and political independence of every State in the area and its right to live in peace within secure and recognized boundaries free from threats or acts of force'. The Resolution was passed with a vote of 79 for, 7 against, and 36 abstentions.

16. AHG/Res. 67 (IX).

17. On the relationship of Israel with South Africa, see for example G. J. Tomeh, *Israel and South Africa* (New York: New World Press, 1973); S. Smith, *South Africa and Israel* (Research Report by Madison Area Committee on South Africa, 1971); and Samih Farsoun, 'South Africa and Israel: A Special Relationship' — a paper submitted to the Conference on the Socio-Economic Trends and Policies in Southern Africa (Dar-es-Salaam, 29 November — 7 December 1975), organized by the UN African Institute for Economic Development and Planning, Dakar. See also a well-documented publication of the German-African-Arab Bureau at Bonn, *Israel-Südafrika: Kooperation imperialistischer Vorposten* (Bonn, PDW, June 1976). In its editorial of 3 June 1973, *The Sunday Times of Zambia* wrote that: 'It would be highly dangerous to regard the mood of the Africans at the Summit as a "temporary aberration"caused by the unexpected eloquence of the African Arabs. This time, more than ever before, the State of Israel is being treated as a definite threat to the independence of all African countries, Arab and non-Arab. The Summit, then, was a victory for the Arabs, but it was a victory for Africa on a larger scale because the arrogance of the Israelis is not confined to the Arabs alone. It may be that to-day, but tomorrow it could easily be transferred to Black Africa. There are still Africans in this region, for instance, who are helping both the Rhodesians and South Africa in their struggle against the freedom fighters.'

18. The basis of this new understanding between the Arab and African States was evident in a communiqué issued by the Cabinet of King Faisal of Saudi Arabia prior to his visit to five African States (Chad, Mauritania, Niger, Senegal and Uganda) in November 1972. (Statement of the Royal Cabinet, Riyadh, published in *Replica*, Saudi Publishing House, No. 1910, 11 November 1972.) It expressed hope 'that the Arab countries and the entire continent of Africa would work together after the total liberation of Palestine for freeing the occupied African territories one after another, including Rhodesia'. The Saudi Arabian loan of 43 million shillings to Uganda accompanies the argument.

19. President Sadat, who had agreed at the last moment to attend the Summit, dissociated himself openly from Gaddafi's tactics but took the opportunity to warn the Emperor of the importance of loosening his ties with Israel. President Boumedienne went even further. In confidential discussions with Ethiopian leaders during the Addis Ababa Summit he offered to use his influence in Arab circles to halt support for the Eritrean Liberation Front (which at that time came mainly from Libya, Syria, Iraq and South Yemen) provided the Emperor renounced his ties with Israel. His offer was communicated to the Ethiopian Cabinet and seriously discussed in May 1973, but although the Ethiopian Minister was persuaded, the Emperor was not. Colin Legum, 'Africa, the Arabs and the Middle East', *Africa Contemporary Record (London, Rex Collings, 1974) p. A5.*

20. 'This regime is playing two roles', said the Libyan Information Minister. 'The first is enabling American monopolist imperialism through its military base (the Kagnew communication base in Eritrea), to threaten the sovereignty and safety of the continent. The second is occupying Eritrea, displacing its people and persecuting them . . . In this way Haile Selassie is doing as the saying goes: he has given something he does not possess to someone who is not entitled to it.' Quoted

in *The Times* (London), 28 May 1973.

21. AHG/Res. 71 (X), adopted on 28 May 1973.

22. ECM/St. 14 (VIII), of 21 November 1973.

23. ECM/Res. 20 (VIII).

24. All these resolutions were passed unanimously, but Lesotho, Swaziland and Botswana (which had not broken off their relations with Israel) all made reservations on the application of the oil embargo, since they are wholly dependent for their sources of supply on the Republic. (Malawi, the fourth country still retaining its ties with Israel, did not attend the meeting.'

25. *Le Monde*, Paris, 29 November 1973.

26. The original idea was to give 1 per cent loans, but the Africans wanted funds to be deposited with the African Development Bank to be allocated by the OAU. The Arabs agreed, and in 1975 the OAU allocated the first fund as follows: Tanzania ($14 Million), Ethiopia ($14 million), Zambia ($13 million), Zaire, Morocco and Uganda ($12 million each) and Sudan ($1 million).

27. Sudan has become the largest recipient of the Arab aid to Africa. In addition to $400 million credit received by Sudan in 1977 from Saudi Arabia, the Arab Authority for Development and Agricultural Investment (AADAI) established in 1976 has decided to invest $6 billion into Sudan over the next 25 years.

28. 'Africa's Oil Resources', *Africa* (London, September 1975).

29. *Jeune Afrique*, Paris, 2 February 1974, pp. 16-17.

30. Colin Legum 'Africa, Arabs and Oil', *Africa Contemporary Record 1974-5* (London: Rex Collings, 1975), p. A105.

31. *Resolution on the Middle East and Occupied Arab Territories*, CM/Res. 425 (XXV).

32. AHG/Res. 76 (XII).

33. AHG/Res. 77 (XII).

34. For a comprehensive account of Israeli–South African co-operation, see 'Israel — South Africa (Co-operation of Imperialist Outposts)', published by Progress Dritte Welt (Bonn, 1976).

35. For a detailed recent review of Afro-Arab political and economic co-operation, see *Revue francaise d'études politiques africaines* (Paris, December 1976), No 132. It contains useful essays by Albert Bourgi, Pierre Pean and Paul Balta.

36. Quoted by Colin Legum in 'Africa, Arabs and Oil', op.cit., p. A107. See also E. C. Chibwe, *Arab Dollars for Africa* (London: Croom Helm, 1976).

37. *The Times* (London, 4 March 1974), reporting on a conference of the western bankers, stated that the Arab countries will follow past practices and deposit their money in Beirut, London and Zurich where it will become a part of 'Eurocurrency market'. 'The orginal Arab depositor', wrote *The Times,* 'neither knows nor cares at this stage who is the ultimate borrower as long as he gets the agreed interest on his deposit.' According to the estimates by R. Marbro and E. Monroe in *International Affairs,* January 1974, the combined surplus of Saudi Arabia, Kuwait, Abu Dhabi and Libya will reach £35-50 billion by 1980.

## Chapter Ten

1. The EAC was established in a treaty signed by Kenya, Tanzania and Uganda on 6 June 1967. It came into force on 1 December 1967. Its objectives were, *inter alia*, to strengthen and regulate industrial, commercial and other relations of the partner-States; to establish common customs and excise tariffs and abolish

restrictions in inter-partner-State trade; to introduce a long-term agricultural policy, establish an East African Development Bank, harmonize monetary policies and co-ordinate economic planning and transport policies. The text of the Treaty was published by the East African Common Services Organization and was reproduced for example in *Basic Documents on African Affairs*, Ian Brownlie (ed.), (London: Oxford University Press, 1971). For documentation of the attempts at integration in East Africa, see Donald Rothchild, *Politics of Integration*, (Nairobi: East African Publishing House, 1968). For general information see *A handbook of the EAC*, published by the Information Division of the EAC in Nairobi in 1972.

2. The Economic Commission for Africa was established by Resolution 671A (XXV) of the Economic and Social Council of the UN (29 April 1958) which also defines its terms of reference. These were subsequently amended by Resolution 974D (XXVI) of 5 July 1963 and by Resolution 1343 (XLV) of 18 July 1968. The tasks of the ECA, 'acting within the framework of the policies of the United Nations and subject to the general supervision of the economic and Social Council', were stated to be to:

— initiate and participate in measures for facilitating concerted action for the economic development of Africa, including its social aspects, with a view to raising the level of economic activity and levels of living in Africa, and for maintaining and strengthening the economic relations of countries and territories of Africa, both among themselves and with other countries of the world;

— make or sponsor such investigations and studies of economic and technological problems and developments within the territories of Africa;

— undertake or sponsor the collection, evaluation and dissemination of such economic, technological and statistical information;

— perform such advisory services as the countries and territories of the region may desire;

— assist the Economic and Social Council of the United Nations in discharging its functions within Africa in connexion with economic problems, and problems of technical assistance;

— assist in the formulation and development of co-ordinated policies as a basis for practical action in promoting economic and technological development in Africa.

The work of ECA was described, or rather dismissed, by James S. Maggee in 'ECA and the Paradox of African Co-operation', *International Conciliation*, November 1970, New York. It touches also on the relationship between the ECA and the OAU.

3. For an insight into the economic situation in Africa at the time of the establishment of the OAU, see 'A Survey of Economic Conditions in Africa 1960-1964' E/CN 14/397 of 9 May 1967. For the recent facts and figures see *Economic Bulletin for Africa* (New York: United Nations, 1974).

4. E/CN 14/L170 of 1 March 1963: 'Draft Report of the Fifth Session to the Economic and Social Council'.

5. The inaugural meeting of the Board of Governors of the African Development Bank was held in Lagos from 3 to 7 November 1964.

6. ECA adopted a Resolution at its 96th Plenary Meeting on 28 February 1963 on 'Conference of Heads of State in Addis Ababa' (E/CN 14/Res. 75(V)1963), commending the initiative for convening such a conference to meet the urgent need for unity and a strengthening of African solidarity.

7. This paper was subsequently developed by Dr Chukaka Okonjo of Ibadan University (ECA's Regional Planning Advisor) into a study entitled 'Economic

Unity through Co-ordinated Development in Africa'; a revised version was published as an ECA Document, E/CN 14/239 Part B, on 13 January 1964.

8. CM/Res. 26(II) and CM/Res.43(III) on 'UN World Trade Conference', adopted in Lagos 1964 and in Cairo 1964, respectively; and the *Resolution on Economic Problems* (CM/Res. 98 VIII), adopted in Addis Ababa in 1967, which was the first acknowledgement of the OAU Secretariat's efforts at getting the OAU involved in African economics.

9. UN Document A/6174 of 16 December 1965.

10. Resolution on the relationship between the ECA and the OAU, CM/Res. 72(V).

11. Resolution CM/Res. 98 (VIII), adopted on 4 March 1967 at the 8th Ordinary Session of the Council at Addis Ababa, endorsed Diallo Telli's report on African Economic Co-operation (Doc. CM/148).

12. CM/Res. 123(IX).

13. This is how the postponement of action on an African common market was justified by an ECA resolution adopted in 1963 (E/CN.14/RES/86 [V] ).

14. The Declaration contains the recommendations of the African countries on the various questions on the agenda of UNCTAD II. It subsequently became the basis of the joint OAU/ECA 'Africa's Strategy for Development in the 1970s'. The text of the 'African Declaration of Algiers' was published by the ECA (Doc.E/CN.14/UNCTAD II/PM.2/Rev.2).

15. Resolution on 'Africa and UNCTAD III', CM/Res.158(XI).

16. E/CN.14/RES/190(IX), of 11 February 1969.

17. CM/330, Part II.

18. CM/Res. 219(XV). The memorandum attached to the resolution set forth the economic and social priorities of the OAU in the following order:
— intensification of regional co-operation with a view to defining and carrying out projects of concern to the markets of several countries;
— mobilization of domestic financial resources in order to establish African funds in the service of development;
— acceleration of the process of industrial development on the continent, with particular emphasis on multinational projects;
— increased inter-African trade through improved knowledge of the economic resources and production of each country;
— harmonization and co-ordination of legislation and customs procedures;
— intensification of monetary co-operation and the instituting of payments agreements between African states;
— promotion of the construction of an all-African road network;
— co-operation between African air transport companies with a view to increasing trade and promoting tourism.
— provision of an All-African telecommunications system (Addis Ababa Plan);
— joint utilization of higher educational systems and systems for the training of supervisory staff in the fields of economic and social development;
— harmonization of social and labour legislation;
— setting up of a system of inter-African technical assistance (exchanges of trained staff and manpower);
— assistance to African non-governmental organizations, to help them achieve unity and to associate them with the work of the OAU.

19. The Conference of Ministers was a new body of the ECA, set up after its reorganization in 1969; it met biannually, whereas the earlier conferences of the ECA had been annual.

20. E/CN 14/Res.218(X) and E/CN 14/Res.238(XI), published in Addis Ababa in November 1973 as an ECA publication entitled 'Africa's Strategy for

Development in the 1970s'.

21. This is how the requirements were defined by the ECA's Executive Secretary, Dr. Robert Gardiner, in his address to the Dag Hammarskjöld seminar on a Strategy of Development for Africa, held in August 1971 at Uppsala.

22. See *Directory of Intergovernmental Co-operation Organizations in Africa,* published by ECA in 1972 (E/CN/14/CEC/Rev.1.6 June 1972).

23. General Assembly Resolutions 3201(S-VI) and 3202(S-VI) 1974.

24. General Assembly Resolution 3281(XXIX) of 12 December 1974.

25. General Assembly Resolution 1897 (XVIII) of 11 November 1963.

26. Document NAC/ALG/CONF.4/M/L.18.

27. The Organization of the Petroleum Exporting Countries (OPEC) was established in 1960 'to unify and co-ordinate members' petroleum policies and to safeguard their interests generally'. Its members are Algeria, Ecuador, Indonesia, Iran, Iraq, Kuwait, Libya, Nigeria, Qatar, Saudi Arabia, Unted Arab Emirates, Venezuala and Gabon (associate member).

28. Res.3362(S-VII) on 'Development and international economic co-operation' (16 September 1975).

29. Raw materials were the main topic of the Dakar Conference, the aim of which was to discuss a common strategy (outlined in the Dakar Declaration) of developing countries for the UNCTAD meeting at Geneva which was held a week later.

30. For the proceedings of the Lima Conference (and for the full text of all resolutions), see *Review of International Affairs,* Belgrade, No. 611 and 612 (21 September and 5 October 1975).

31. The Lima Declaration and Plan of Action on Industrial Development Co-operation was published as a UN Document A/10217.

32. Res. 256 (XII).

33. CM/Res.437(XXV) 'Resolution on the New International Economic Order and the Forthcoming Special Session of the General Assembly.

34. The key note of the Commonwealth approach was the British Prime Minister Harold Wilson's opening statement that 'the British Government fully accepts that the relationship, the balance, between rich and poor countries is wrong and must be remedied ... that the wealth of the world must be redistributed in favour of the poverty-stricken and of the starving'. The six commitments agreed upon by the conference were as follows:

— the desirability should be recognized of conducting trade in food and raw materials in accordance with equitable arrangmeents worked out in agreement between producers and consumers;

— producer countries should undertake to maintain adequate and secure supplies to consumer countries.

— consumer countries should undertake to improve access to markets for primary products of interest to producers in developing countries;

— as an established principle, commodity prices should be equitable to consumers and remunerative to efficient producers;

— in particular, the need to expand total production of essential foodstuffs should be recognized;

— the aim should be to encourage the efficient development, production and marketing of commodities both mineral and agricultural, including forest products, and efficient processing of those commodities in developing countries.

35. The convention covers all of independent black Africa, most of the Caribbean and three Commonwealth Pacific islands — Fiji, Samoa and Tonga. The agreement provides the developing countries with privileged access to the EEC for

all their exports, with a stabilization fund to compensate the developing countries for any fall in market prices of a number of basic products, financial aid amounting to $4,068 million over five years, and better distribution of labour in favour of developing countries through industrial co-operation.

36. For a selection of the main points of the speeches of ten African delegates, see *Africa* (London: December, 1975), No. 52.

37. For a most comprehensive document on Algerian policy on the New International Economic Order, see 'Petroleum, raw materials and development', a memorandum submitted by Algeria to the 6th special session of the UN General Assembly, and published on 10 April 1974 by Sontrach, Algiers.

38. The developing countries within their Group of 77, selected the following participants: Brazil, Argentina, Peru, Mexico, Jamaica, Venezuala, Algeria, Zaire, Egypt, Nigeria, Zambia, Cameroon, India, Iran, Iraq, Indonesia, Pakistan, Saudi Arabia and Yugoslavia. They also proposed that the conference be expanded with the participation of Malaysia, the Ivory Coast, and Columbia. The industrially developed Western countries in the OECD selected Japan, the USA, the EEC. Canada, Sweden, Switzerland, Spain and Australia.

39. For example, in his address to the fourth Assembly of the Association of African Central Banks (AACB) held in August 1975 in Kinshasa, President Mobutu called for an African Summit conference to be devoted entirely to the economic problems. He criticized the OAU for still concentrating on divisive political issues exclusively at a time of world economic crisis.

40. The text of Mobutu's speech was reproduced in the BBC Summary of World Broadcasts, ME/5384, 8 December 1975.

41. For an earlier OAU policy on regional groupings, see Z. Červenka, *The Organization of African Unity and its Charter* (New York: Praeger, 1969), Chapter 7.

42. The UNCTAD Common Fund Conference was held in March 1977 in Geneva. It discussed the setting up of a $6 billion fund to stabilize commodity prices. It ended on 1 April 1977 without any agreement reached except for the consensus on re-convening the Conference sometime in late 1977.

43. The central demand of the developing countries at the Paris Conference on International Economic Co-operation known as the North-South Dialogue, was a moratorium on all repayment of their debts which were estimated to have reached $180,000 million in 1977 (excluding the debts of the oil-producing countries). The EEC and the United States' offer of a $1,000 million fund to provide short-term financial relief to the world's poorest countries fell short of the expectations of the 'South', and the closing session of the conference on 30 May — 2 June 1977 at the ministerial level was viewed by many observers as the funeral of the New International Economic Order.

Appendix 1

# THE MEMBERS OF THE ORGANIZATION OF AFRICAN UNITY IN 1977

| State | Capital | Area in $km^2$ | Population (estimated) | Date of independence |
|---|---|---|---|---|
| Algeria | Algiers | 2,381,741 | 16,731,000 | 5 July 1962 |
| Angola | Luanda | 1,246,700 | 6,100,000 | 11 November 1975 |
| Benin | Porto Novo | 113,048 | 3,128,000 | 1 August 1960 |
| Botswana | Gaborones | 600,372 | 706,000 | 30 September 1966 |
| Burundi | Bujumbura | 27,834 | 3,500,500 | 1 July 1962 |
| Cameroun | Yaoundé | 475,442 | 6,336,000 | 1 January 1960 |
| Cape Verde | Praia | 3,929 | 330,000 | 5 July 1975 |
| Central African Republic | Bangui | 622,984 | 1,735,000 | 13 August 1960 |
| Chad | Ndjamena | 1,284,000 | 4,018,000 | 11 August 1960 |
| Comoro Islands | Moroni | 2,236 | 312,574 | 6 July 1975 |
| Congo | Brazzaville | 342,000 | 1,254,000 | 15 August 1960 |
| Djibouti | Djibouti | 23,000 | 210,000 | 27 June 1977 |
| Egypt | Cairo | 1,001,449 | 37,746,000 | 28 February 1922 |
| Equatorial Guinea | Malabo | 28,051 | 337,500 | 12 October 1968 |
| Ethiopia | Addis Ababa | 1,221,900 | 27,878,000 | Independent throughout |
| Gabon | Libreville | 267,667 | 1,092,500 | 17 August 1960 |
| Gambia | Banjul | 11,295 | 580,000 | 18 February 1965 |
| Ghana | Accra | 238,537 | 9,742,000 | 6 March 1957 |
| Guinea | Conakry | 245,857 | 5,477,000 | 28 September 1958 |
| Guinea Bissau | Bissau | 36,125 | 549,000 | 24 September 1973 |
| Ivory Coast | Abidjan | 322,463 | 4,852,000 | 7 August 1960 |

| Country | Capital | | | |
|---|---|---|---|---|
| Kenya | Nairobi | 13,378,000 | 582,646 | 12 December 1963 |
| Lesotho | Maseru | 1,055,000 | 30,355 | 4 October 1966 |
| Liberia | Monrovia | 1,601,000 | 111,500 | 26 July 1947 |
| Libya | Tripoli | 2,422,000 | 1,759,540 | 24 December 1951 |
| Malagasy Republic | Tananarive | 8,421,000 | 587,041 | 26 June 1960 |
| Malawi | Zomba | 4,980,000 | 118,484 | 6 July 1964 |
| Mali | Bamako | 5,652,000 | 1,240,000 | 22 September 1960 |
| Mauritania | Nouakchott | 1,376,000 | 1,030,700 | 28 November 1960 |
| Mauritius | Port Louis | 888,000 | 2,045 | 12 March 1968 |
| Morocco | Rabat | 16,898,000 | 446,550 | 2 March 1956 |
| Mozambique | Lourenço Marques | 9,394,000 | 786,763 | 25 June 1975 |
| Niger | Niamey | 4,566,000 | 1,267,000 | 3 August 1960 |
| Nigeria | Lagos | 81,753,000 | 923,768 | 1 October 1960 |
| Rwanda | Kigali | 4,136,000 | 26,338 | 1 July 1962 |
| Sao Tomé & Principé | Sao Tomé | 79,000 | 964 | 12 July 1975 |
| Senegal | Dakar | 4,313,000 | 196,192 | 25 August 1960 |
| Seychelles | Victoria | 65,000 | 277 | 28 June 1976 |
| Sierra Leone | Freetown | 2,777,000 | 71,740 | 27 April 1961 |
| Somali Republic | Mogadishu | 3,184,000 | 63,657 | 1 July 1960 |
| Sudan | Khartoum | 16,166,000 | 2,505,813 | 1 January 1956 |
| Swaziland | Mbabone | 467,000 | 17,363 | 6 September 1968 |
| Tanzania | Dar es Salaam | 15,095,000 | 839,701 | 9 December 1961 |
| Togo | Lome | 2,219,000 | 56,000 | 27 April 1960 |
| Tunisia | Tunis | 5,718,000 | 164,150 | 20 March 1956 |
| Uganda | Kampala | 10,957,000 | 236,860 | 9 October 1962 |
| Upper Volta | Ouagadougou | 5,878,000 | 274,122 | 5 August 1960 |
| Zaire | Kinshasa | 24,344,000 | 2,344,885 | 30 June 1960 |
| Zambia | Lusaka | 4,909,000 | 752,614 | 24 October 1964 |

# Appendix 2

# CHARTER OF THE ORGANIZATION OF AFRICAN UNITY

We, the Heads of African States and Governments assembled in the City of Addis Ababa, Ethiopia;

CONVINCED that it is the inalienable right of all people to control their own destiny;

CONSCIOUS of the fact that freedom, equality, justice and dignity are essential objectives for the achievement of the legitimate aspirations of the African peoples;

CONSCIOUS of our responsibility to harness the natural and human resources of our continent for the total advancement of our peoples in spheres of human endeavour;

INSPIRED by a common determination to promote under-standing among our peoples and co-operation among our States in response to the aspirations of our people for brotherhood and solidarity, in a larger unity transcending ethnic and national differences;

CONVINCED that, in order to translate this determination into a dynamic force in the cause of human progress, conditions for peace and security must be established and maintained;

DETERMINED to safeguard and consolidate the hard-won independence as well as the sovereignty and territorial integrity of our States, and to fight against neo-colonialism in all its forms;

DEDICATED to the general progress of Africa;

PERSUADED that the Charter of the United Nations and the Universal Declaration of Human Rights, to the principles of which we reaffirm our adherence, provide a solid foundation for peaceful and positive co-operation among States;

DESIROUS that all African States should henceforth unite so that the welfare and well-being of their peoples can be assured;

RESOLVED to reinforce the links between our states by establishing and strengthening common institutions;

HAVE agreed to the present Charter.

## ESTABLISHMENT

### Article I

1.  The High Contracting Parties do by the present Charter establish

228

an Organization to be known as the ORGANIZATION OF AFRICAN UNITY.

2.  The Organization shall include the Continental African States, Madagascar and other Islands surrounding Africa.

## PURPOSES

*Article II*

1.  The Organization shall have the following purposes:
    (a)  to promote the unity and solidarity of the African States;
    (b)  to co-ordinate and intensify their co-operation and efforts to achieve a better life for the peoples of Africa;
    (c)  to defend their sovereignty, their territorial integrity and independence;
    (d)  to eradicate all forms of colonialism from Africa; and
    (e)  to promote international co-operation, having due regard to the Charter of the United Nations and the Universal Declaration of Human Rights.

2.  To these ends, the Member-States shall co-ordinate and harmonize their general policies, especially in the following fields:
    (a)  political and diplomatic co-operation;
    (b)  economic co-operation, including transport and communications;
    (c)  educational and cultural co-operation;
    (d)  health, sanitation, and nutritional co-operation;
    (e)  scientific and technical co-operation; and
    (f)  co-operation for defence and security.

## PRINCIPLES

*Article III*

The Member-States, in pursuit of the purposes stated in Article II, solemnly affirm and declare their adherence to the following principles:

1.  the sovereign equality of all Member-States;
2.  non-interference in the internal affairs of States;
3.  respect for the sovereignty and territorial integrity of each State and for its inalienable right to independent existence;
4.  peaceful settlement of disputes by negotiation, mediation, conciliation or arbitration;
5.  unreserved condemnation, in all its forms, of political assassination as well as of subversive activities on the part of neighbouring States or any other State;
6.  absolute dedication to the total emancipation of the

229

African territories which are still dependent;

7. affirmation of a policy of non-alignment with regard to all blocs.

## MEMBERSHIP

### Article IV

Each independent sovereign African State shall be entitled to become a Member of the Organization.

## RIGHTS AND DUTIES OF MEMBER STATES

### Article V

All Member-States shall enjoy equal rights and have equal duties.

### Article VI

The Member-States pledge themselves to observe scrupulously the principles enumerated in Article III of the present Charter.

## INSTITUTIONS

### Article VII

The Organization shall accomplish its purposes through the following principal institutions:

1. the Assembly of Heads of State and Government;
2. the Council of Ministers;
3. the General Secretariat;
4. the Commission of Mediation, Conciliation and Arbitration.

## THE ASSEMBLY OF HEADS OF STATE AND GOVERNMENT

### Article VIII

The Assembly of Heads of State and Government shall be the supreme organ of the Organization. It shall, subject to the provisions of this Charter, discuss matters of common concern to Africa with a view to co-ordinating and harmonizing the general policy of the Organization. It may in addition review the structure, functions and acts of all the organs and any specialized agencies which may be created in accordance with the present Charter.

## Article IX

The Assembly shall be composed of the Heads of State and Government or their duly accredited representatives and it shall meet at least once a year. At the request of any Member-State and on approval by a two-thirds majority of the Member-States, the Assembly shall meet in extraordinary session.

## Article X

1. Each Member-State shall have one vote.
2. All resolutions shall be determined by a two-thirds majority of the Members of the Organization.
3. Questions of procedure shall require a simple majority. Whether or not a question is one of procedure shall be determined by a simple majority of all Member-States of the Organization.
4. Two-thirds of the total membership of the Organization shall form a quorum at any meeting of the Assembly.

## Article XI

The Assembly shall have the power to determine its own rules of procedure.

## THE COUNCIL OF MINISTERS
### Article XII

1. The Council of Ministers shall consist of Foreign Ministers or such other Ministers as are designated by the Governments of Member-States.
2. The Council of Ministers shall meet at least twice a year. When requested by any Member-State and approved by two-thirds of all Member-States, it shall meet in extraordinary session.

## Article XIII

3. The Council of Ministers shall be responsible to the Assembly of Heads of State and Government. It shall be entrusted with the responsibility of preparing conferences of the Assembly.
4. It shall take cognisance of any matter referred to it by the Assembly. It shall be entrusted with the implementation of the decision of the Assembly of Heads of State and Government. It shall co-ordinate inter-African co-operation in accordance with

231

instructions of the Assembly and in conformity with Article II (2) of the present Charter.

## Article XIV

1. Each Member-State shall have one vote.
2. All resolutions shall be determined by a simple majority of the members of the Council of Ministers.
3. Two-thirds of the total membership of the Council of Ministers shall form a quorum for any meeting of the Council.

## Article XV

The Council shall have the power to determine its own rules of procedure.

## GENERAL SECRETARIAT

### Article XVI

There shall be an Administrative Secretary-General of the Organization, who shall be appointed by the Assembly of Heads of State and Government. The Administrative Secretary-General shall direct the affairs of the Secretariat.

### Article XVII

There shall be one or more Assistant Secretaries-General of the Organization, who shall be appointed by the Assembly of Heads of State and Government.

### Article XVIII

The functions and conditions of services of the Secretary-General, of the Assistant Secretaries-General and other employees of the Secretariat shall be governed by the provisions of this Charter and the regulations approved by the Assembly of Heads of State and Government.

1. In the performance of their duties the Administrative Secretary-General and the staff shall not seek or receive instructions from any government of from any other authority external to the Organization. They shall refrain from any action which might reflect on their position as international officials responsible only to the Organization.
2. Each member of the Organization undertakes to respect the

exclusive character of the responsibilities of the Administrative Secretary-General and the staff and not to seek to influence them in the discharge of their responsibilities.

3. The original instrument, done, if possible in African languages, in English and French, all texts being equally authentic, shall be deposited with the Government of Ethiopia which shall transmit certified copies thereof to all independent sovereign African States.

4. Instruments of ratification shall be deposited with the Government of Ethiopia, which shall notify all signatories of each such deposit.

## ENTRY INTO FORCE

### Article XXV

This Charter shall enter into force immediately upon receipt by the Government of Ethiopia of the instruments of ratification from two thirds of the signatory States.

## REGISTRATION OF THE CHARTER

### Article XXVI

This Charter shall, after due ratification, be registered with the Secretariat of the United Nations through the Government of Ethiopia in conformity with Article 102 of the Charter of the United Nations.

## INTERPRETATION OF THE CHARTER

### Article XXVII

Any question which may arise concerning the interpretation of this Charter shall be decided by a vote of two-thirds of the Assembly of Heads of State and Government of the Organization.

## ADHESION AND ACCESSION

### Article XXVIII

1. Any independent sovereign African State may at any time notify the Adminstrative Secretary-General of its intention to adhere or accede to this Charter.

2. The Administrative Secretary-General shall, on receipt of such notification, communicate a copy of it to all the Member-States. Admission shall be decided by a simple majority of the Member-States. The decision of each Member-State shall be

transmitted to the Administrative Secretary-General, who shall, upon receipt of the required number of votes, communicate the decision to the State concerned.

## MISCELLANEOUS

### Article XXIX

The working languages of the Organization and all its institutions shall be if possible African languages, English and French.

### Article XXX

The Administrative Secretary-General may accept on behalf of the Organization gifts, bequests and other donations made to the Organization, provided that this is approved by the Council of Ministers.

### Article XXXI

The Council of Ministers shall decide on the privileges and immunities to be accorded to the personnel of the Secretariat in the respective territories of the Member-States.

## CESSATION OF MEMBERSHIP

### Article XXXII

Any State which desires to renounce its membership shall forward a written notification to the Administrative Secretary-General. At the end of one year from the date of such notification, if not withdrawn, the Charter shall cease to apply with respect to the renouncing State, which shall thereby cease to belong to the Organization.

## AMENDMENT OF THE CHARTER

### Article XXXIII

This Charter may be amended or revised if any Member-State makes a written request to the Administrative Secretary-General to that effect; provided, however, that the proposed amendment is not submitted to the Assembly for consideration until all the Member-States have been duly notified of it and a period of one year has elapsed. Such an amendment shall not be effective unless approved by at least two-thirds of all the Member-States.

IN FAITH WHEREOF, We, the Heads of African State and Government have signed this Charter.

*Done in the City of Addis Ababa, Ethiopia this 25th day of May, 1963.*

| | |
|---|---|
| *Algeria* | President Ben Bella |
| *Burundi* | King Mwambutsa |
| *Cameroon* | President Ahmadou Ahidjo |
| *Central African Republic* | President David Dacko |
| *Chad* | President François Tombalbaye |
| *Congo (Brazzaville)* | President Fulbert Youlou |
| *Congo (Kinshasa)* | President Joseph Kasavubu |
| *Dahomey* | President Hubert Maga |
| *Ethiopia* | Emperor Haile Selassie |
| *Gabon* | President Leon M'ba |
| *Ghana* | President Kwame Nkrumah |
| *Guinea* | President Sékou Touré |
| *Ivory Coast* | President Félix Houphouet-Boigny |
| *Liberia* | President William V. S. Tubman |
| *Libya* | King Idris I |
| *Malagasy Republic* | President Philibert Tsiranana |
| *Mali* | President Modibo Keita |
| *Mauritania* | President Makhtar Ould Daddah |
| *Niger* | President Hamani Diori |
| *Nigeria* | Prime Minister Alhaji Sir Abubakar Tafawa Balewa |
| *Rwanda* | Foreign Minister Callixte Habamenshi |
| *Senegal* | President Léopold Sédar Senghor |
| *Sierra Leone* | Prime Minister Sir Milton Margai |
| *Somalia* | President Abdullah Osman |
| *Sudan* | President Ibrahim Abboud |
| *Tanganyika* | President Julius Nyerere |
| *Tunisia* | President Habib Bourguiba |
| *Uganda* | Prime Minister Milton Obote |
| *United Arab Republic* | President Gamal Abdul Nasser |
| *Upper Volta* | President Maurice Yameogo |

# INDEX

Abako, 84
ADB *see* African Development Bank
ANC, 62, 129, 133, 134, 162, 199,
   201, 210, 212, 213
APL, 85, 89, 90
APLI, 49
Abboud, President Ibrahim, 235
Abdulaye, Diallo, 78
Abidjan, 93, 182, 192
Abidjo, President, 32, 33, 34, 67, 68,
   98, 105, 116, 159, 235
Aburi, 99
Accra, 4, 38, 187; Conference of
   Independent African States (1958)
   10, 12, 14, 194
Accra Declaration on the new
   strategy for the Liberation of
   Africa (1973), 55, 58–9, 60
Addis Ababa, 26, 29, 30, 31, 32, 33,
   35, 37, 40, 41, 43, 48, 51, 54,
   55, 59, 63, 67, 72, 78, 80, 81,
   86, 181, 228; Nigerian Peace
   Talks in, 102–103, 105–6
Adedeji, Dr. Adebayo, 189
Adetoro, Chief J.E., 175
Adoula, Prime Minister Cyrille, 84,
   85, 86, 204
Afghanistan, 192
*Africa*, 172, 210, 215, 216, 217,
   221, 225
*Africa Contemporary Record*, 201,
   210, 215, 221
*Africa Research Bulletin*, 199, 200,
   202, 203, 206, 216
African Charter of Casablanca (1961),
   191
African Civil Aviation, 35
African Data Bank, 188
African Declaration of Algiers
   (1968), 180, 183
African Declaration on Co-operation,
   Development and Economic
   Independence (OAU 1973), 38
African Development Bank, 35, 168,
   171, 174, 177, 182, 184, 221,
   222
African Energy Commission, 188
African High Command, 38–9, 40,
   42, 43, 157, 198

African Institute for Economic
   Development and Planning, 177,
   184
African Ministerial Conferences, 37
African National Congress of South
   Africa, 162, 200
African National Council (of
   Rhodesia), 129, 132
African Payment Union, 188
African People's League for
   Independence, *see* APLI
African Plan for the Implementation
   of the Programme of Action on
   the Establishment of a New
   International Economic Order
   (ECA 1975), 184
African Scouts Union, 194
African Trade Union, 194
African Youth Organization, 194
*Afrique Express*, 206
Afro-Arab Relations, 30, 32, 34, 63,
   174–5, 220–1; Afro-Arab
   Alliance, 156, 162–170;
   committee on, 172–3; Summit
   on (Cairo 1977), 172–4, 220
Ahmed, Sheik Sabah Al, 173
Air France, 83, 171
Akinyemi, Dr. Bolaji, 96, 175
Albertville, 85
Algeria, 3, 41, 44, 48, 49, 52, 53, 55,
   58, 66, 67, 73, 77, 79, 84, 86,
   92, 118, 129, 142, 145, 183, 185,
   191, 225, 226; independence, 1;
   and Morocco, 69, 202; and Spain,
   69; and Tunisia, 69; and Rhodesia,
   124; and Middle East, 164
Algiers, 37, 180; Non-alignment
   Conference (1973), 15, 183; OAU
   Assembly of Heads of State in,
   103–4, 108
All-African Cinema Union, 35
All-African Trade Organization, 35
Allende, President, 15
Alver, 141
Amin, President Idi, 44, 66, 69, 120,
   141, 142, 143, 145, 146, 171,
   172, 174; and overthrow of
   Milton Obote, 80–2
Amonoo, Harry, 30, 197

227

Sithole, Ndabaningi, 123, 132, 134, 212

Six Day War, 160

Smith, Ian, 41, 122, 123, 124, 125, 126, 127, 128, 131, 132, 133, 134, 213, 214

Smuts, General, 149

Soares, Mario, 139, 215

Somalia, 34, 49, 52, 79, 80, 87, 115, 118, 142, 145, 158, 163, 167, 173, 191, 196, 227; and Ethiopia, 8–9, 26, 32, 67, 69, 83; President Osman, 8; and Kenya, 26, 67, 69

Soumailot, Gaston, 85, 92, 94

South Africa, 7, 8, 13, 16, 22, 23, 33, 38, 39, 40, 43, 47, 59, 63, 66, 68, 82, 136, 162, 163, 193; OAU strategy on, 26, 83, 110–22; 'dialogue with', 18–19, 46, 56, 116–20, 196, 210; intervention in Angola, 58, 66, 143–8; supply of arms to, 61, 111, 112, 113, 114, 120; and mercenaries, 85; aid to Biafra, 108; sanctions against, 111, 112, 113, 114, 120, 207–8; and Rhodesia, 125, 127, 128, 132; policy of detente with, 127–34; and Namibia, 149–55, 216, 217; Atomic Energy Act, 154; Oil Embargo of by Arab States, 165–6; and Israel, 171, 172, 220; books on, 209, 210; Legal and political status of, 210

South-West Africa, see Namibia

Southern Africa, liberation of, 7, 8, 13; see also decolonization, liberation struggle

sovereignty, 7, 9, 12, 13, 64, 195, 229

Soweto, massacre in, 121

Spaak, Paul-Henri, 91

Spain, 85, 94, 137; and Spanish Sahara, 69

Spanish Sahara, 69, 71

*The Spark* (Ghana), 10, 53, 200

Spinola, General Antonio de, 136, 137, 138

Sri Lanka, 191, 192

Stanleyville, Peoples Republic of the Congo in, 85, 86, 87; 'Stanleyville drop', 89–94; European hostages in, 89;

massacre of civilian population (1964), 91

Stockholm International Peace Research Institute (SIPRI), 199

Strait of Tiran, 161

subversion, 5, 14, 22, 69, 74–6; and refugees, 72, 73

Sudan, 2, 23, 33, 41, 78, 83, 86, 92, 96, 115, 124, 145, 173, 174, 175, 191, 192, 227; and Ethiopia, 43; refugees in, 72

Suez Canal, 157, 161, 164, 209

*Sunday Times of Zambia*, 220

Swaziland, 145, 164, 167, 227; and South Africa, 117, 122

Sweden, 60, 61; and Biafra, 106; and Portugese colonies, 215

Swedish International Development Agency (SIDA), 60

Switzerland, 171; and Biafra, 106; and Rhodesia, 126

Syria, 173, 192; and Israel, 156

TANU, 52

Tanaka, Judge, 150

Tanganyika, *see* Tanzania

Tanganyika African National Union, *see* TANU

Tanzania, 3, 26, 30, 33, 42, 44, 45, 51, 52, 53, 62, 67, 78, 79, 115, 140, 145, 159, 163, 167, 173, 227; and Uganda, 32, 81–2, 174, 203; and Burundi, 32; and Malawi, 69; refugees in, 72; and Biafra, 98, 105, 108; and Southern Africa, 118, 124, 127, 129, 132; and Kenya, 182

Telli, Diallo, 29, 30, 31, 32, 41, 80, 88, 105, 112, 160, 178, 179, 180, 194, 223

territorial integrity, 12, 13; *see also* sovereignty

Territory of the Afars and Issas; *see* Djibouti

Tete, 136, 137

Thailand, 192

Third World, the, 32, 160, 167, 175, 183, 185, 189; need of for Arab aid, 168

*Time*, 5, 192; on the Congo Crisis, 90–1

*Times, The* (London), 137, 189, 212, 214, 215, 221

Usher, Arsene Assouane, 130

Van Zijl, Eben, 153
Vandewalle, Colonel, 90
Versailles Peace Treaty (1918), 149
Viet-Cong, 58
Vietnam, 15, 58, 78, 192
Vorster, John, 41, 119, 127, 128,
    129, 130, 131, 132, 153, 154,
    155, 171, 208, 209, 212, 213

WHO, *see* World Health
    Organization
Wachuku, Jaja, 5, 77, 92
Waiyaki, Dr., 129
Waldheim, Dr. Kurt, 66
Walvis Bay, 155
Warsaw Pact, 15, 40
Washington, D.C., 61, 88
*Weekly Review* (Kenya), 169, 202
West Africa, 2
*West Africa*, 206
Westlake, Melvyn, 189
Williams, Colonel Frank A., 90
Wilson, Harold, 224; and Rhodesia,
    122
Windhoek, 153
Wiriyamu, massacre, 137–8
World Health Organization (WHO),
    37
Worsley, Marcus, 126

Yameogo, President, 75, 235
Yaounde, Cameroon, and APSC, 35
Yemen, 192
Yifru, Ketema, 78, 107
Yoruba, the, 70
Youlou, President Fulbert, 235
Yugoslavia, 40, 60, 61; and Biafra,
    106

ZANU, 47, 62, 129, 134, 199, 201,
    212, 213
ZAPU, 47, 62, 129, 199, 201, 212,
    213
ZIPA, 63, 132
Zaire (Congo), 17, 30, 33, 47, 52,
    75, 83, 98, 140, 142, 144, 145,
    146, 157, 159, 169, 170, 173,
    187, 191, 192, 204, 216, 227;

and UN policy, 1, 36, 66;
    rebellion (1964), 26; Shaba,
    invastion of, 43, 66, 83, 95–6,
    148, 174; refugees in, 72; and
    South Africa, 115, 118, 121
Zambia, 23, 34, 48, 52, 62, 67, 80,
    81, 115, 122, 132, 140, 145, 148,
    160, 163, 168, 170, 174, 227;
    and Malawi, 69; refugees in, 72;
    and Biafra, 98, 105, 108; and
    Rhodesia, 124, 127, 129; and
    South Africa, 208–9
Zewalde, Girmay, 146
Zimbabwe, 41, 47, 62, 125, 126,
    128, 129, 130, 131, 132, 133,
    134, 146, 155, 211, 213
Zinsou, Dr., 30
Zionism, 156, 159, 164–5; as
    racism, 170